# Richard Kern's Far West Sketches

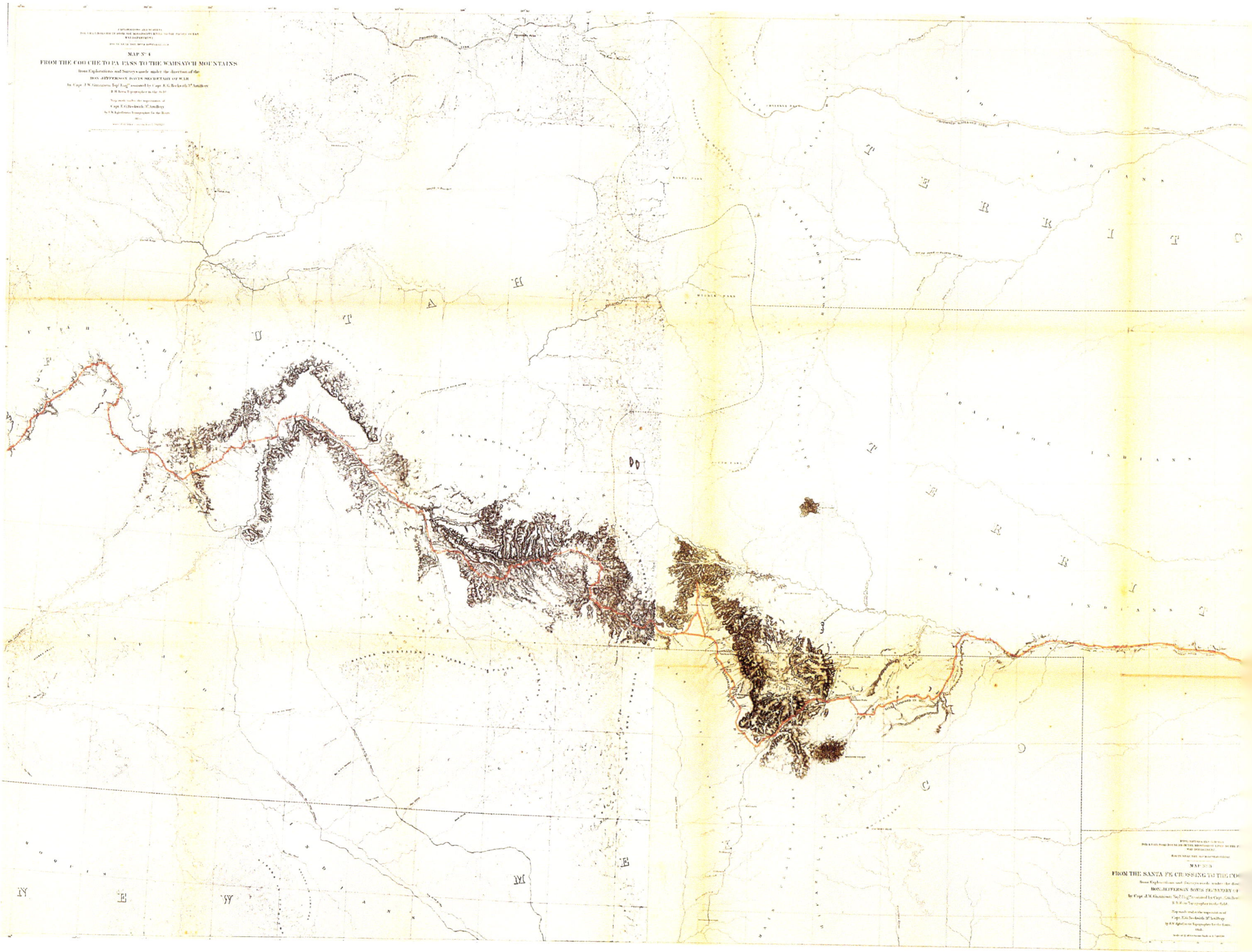
MAP Nº 4
FROM THE COO CHE TO PA PASS TO THE WAHSATCH MOUNTAINS
from Explorations and Surveys made under the direction of the
HON. JEFFERSON DAVIS SECRETARY OF WAR
MAP Nº 5
FROM THE SANTA FE CROSSING TO THE CO
HON. JEFFERSON DAVIS SECRETARY OF

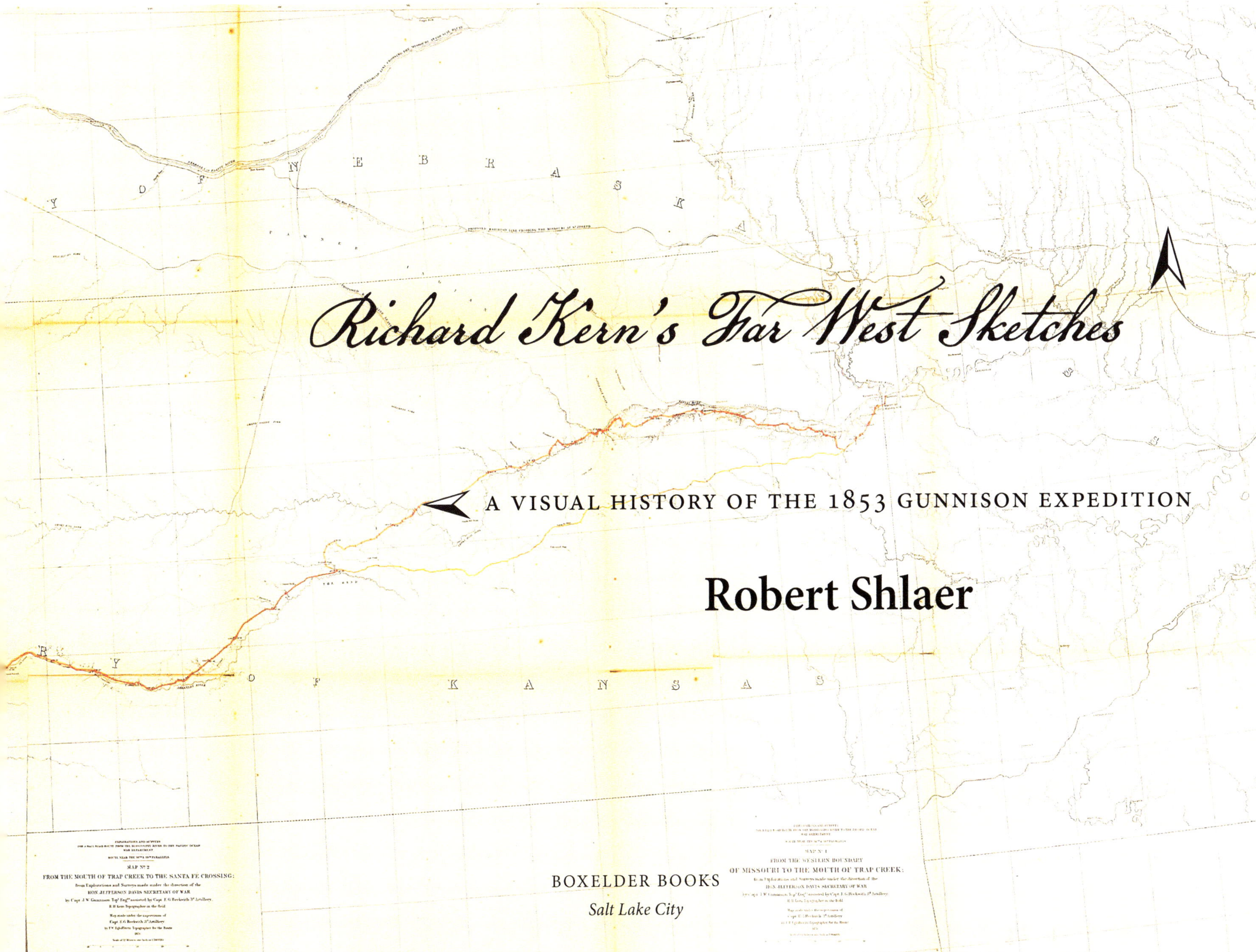


# *Richard Kern's Far West Sketches*

## A VISUAL HISTORY OF THE 1853 GUNNISON EXPEDITION

**Robert Shlaer**

BOXELDER BOOKS
*Salt Lake City*

BOXELDER BOOKS
An imprint of the University of Utah Press



*To study the high-resolution images, visit* **kernsketches.com**

LIBRARY OF CONGRESS CATALOGING-IN-PUBLICATION DATA

Names: Shlaer, Robert, author, photographer (expression)
Title: Richard Kern's Far West sketches : a visual history of the 1853Gunnison expedition / Robert Shlaer.
Description: Salt Lake City : University of Utah Press, [2021] | Includes bibliographical references.
Identifiers: LCCN 2020042505 (print) | LCCN 2020042504 (ebook) | ISBN 9781647690182 (ebook) | ISBN 9781647690199 (hardcover) | ISBN 9781647690175 (paperback)
Subjects: LCSH: Kern, Richard H., 1821-1853--Criticism and interpretation. | Gunnison, J. W. (John Williams), 1812-1853. | Beckwith, E. G. (Edward Griffin), 1818-1881. | Gunnison Expedition (1853) | Pacific railroads--Explorations and surveys--Pictorial works. | Gunnison Massacre, Utah, 1853. | Military topography--Utah Territory. | Utah Territory--Discovery and exploration--Pictorial works.
Classification: LCC NC139.K47 S55 2021 (ebook) | LCC NC139.K47 (print) | DDC 741.09792--dc23
LC record available at https://lccn.loc.gov/2020042505

ON THE COVER: **From the Coo-che-to-pa Pass to the Wahsatch Mountains**; from *Explorations and Surveys made under the direction of the Hon. Jefferson Davis Secretary of War* by Capt. J.W. Gunnison. Topl. Engrs. assisted by Capt. E.G. Beckwith 3d Artillery. R.H. Kern Topographer in the field. Map made under the supervision of Capt. E.G. Beckwith 3d Artillery by F.W. Egloffstein, Topographer for the Route. 1855. Explorations and surveys for a railroad route from the Mississippi River to the Pacific Ocean. War Department. Route near the 38th & 39th Parallels. Map No. 4. Engr. by Selmar Siebert. Digital image copyright ©2000 by Cartography Associates and shared under a Creative Commons license.

*In Memory of*

*Alice Dodge Wallace, 1920-2020*

HUERFANO BUTTE. SKETCH BY RICHARD HOVENDON KERN, AUGUST 8, 1853. 30 X 20 CM.

# Contents

# *Publisher's Note*

*High-resolution images of the maps, drawings, and photographs found in this book are available to be enlarged, compared, and studied in detail, providing an immersive experience of this important and ill-fated expedition.*

*To see these materials, visit kernsketches.com.*

# Prelude

*Views sketched in 1853 by an artist in the employ of the U.S. Army; the drawings taken by a band of Pahvant Indians after massacring their creator, along with seven of his companions; recovered by Indians and Mormon settlers, brought to Salt Lake City, returned to the remnant of the expedition from whence they originated, carried to Washington, D.C., and soon vanished again; now without provenance, came unnoticed into an immense collection of Americana belonging to Edward E. Ayer of Chicago that he donated to the Newberry Library in 1911; safe but still in hiding because of a cataloging error, and finally identified to be the twice-lost, now twice-recovered visual narrative of the Gunnison expedition as drawn by Richard Hovendon Kern.*

PLATE 1. Richard Hovendon Kern, from a daguerreotype, courtesy the Huntington Library.

IN 1994 I BEGAN WORK ON A VISUAL HISTORY of John Charles Frémont's fifth expedition of 1853-54, particularly on the daguerreotypes that Solomon Nunes Carvalho made during that spectacularly difficult winter journey (Shlaer, 2000). Along with Carvalho, Frémont employed a second artist, Baron Friedrich Wilhelm von Egloffstein, a recent German immigrant who also acted as topographer. Some of the woodcut illustrations in Frémont's later *Memoirs of My Life* (1886) might have originated with sketches by Egloffstein, and since very few of his original drawings are known to exist, I sent letters of inquiry to a number of likely archives and libraries to see if any of them possessed such material. I received a reply from Robert Karrow, curator of special collections at the Newberry Library in Chicago, that yes; the Newberry had a whole album of Egloffstein drawings!

The Newberry's title for it was simply "Ayer MS 794a," and since the staff had photographed its contents I was able to order a study set of 35mm transparencies. As soon as I received the slides I looked them over to see if any were the precursors to those Frémont had published, but it quickly became clear to me that the drawings, more than 100 of them, were not by Egloffstein. They were the work of Richard Hovendon Kern, who had been both topographer and artist to a government-sponsored railroad reconnaissance through the Rocky Mountains in 1853, one led by Captain John Williams Gunnison of the Army Corps of Topographical Engineers.

Although disappointed in my original expectations, I had before me an undiscovered treasure, a vast panorama of the West from 1853 that would provide material for another large-scale research project in visual history: finding the sites represented by Kern and documenting them photographically. Because I had repeatedly traveled over Frémont's path of 1853-54, and because Gunnison, in his search for a railroad route to the Pacific Ocean, took a path that was often close to or the same as Frémont's, I could make the case that I was peculiarly qualified to work on the Kern material. I then obtained permission to study and publish the contents of the album from Mary Wyly, then the acting director of the Newberry Library.

To visually represent the landscape, commanders of pre-Civil War western explorations generally employed the only method of the time that could be relied upon with certainty: drawings and paintings by an artist with the expedition. It is in this tradition, where the assured hand and the far-seeing eye of a skilled expeditionary artist were valued more highly than what was then the blurred, inconsistent, and merely mechanical product of the newly invented process of photography, that Richard Kern naturally finds his place of honor.

Though not the most prominent among the artists of the Old West, he is hardly an unknown, for in 1975 the Amon Carter Museum of Fort Worth, Texas, purchased a collection of twenty-one watercolors and four pencil sketches by Kern. To celebrate that acquisition the late historian David J. Weber wrote an extensive biography and appreciation of him (Weber, 1985). It includes virtually everything known about the artist at the time and reproduces many of his previously inaccessible drawings and paintings, but the sketches in the Newberry Library were not then properly identified, and Weber had been unaware of them. Weber's story of Kern's life is therefore an essential preamble to the present work, and I gratefully acknowledge that most of the historical and biographical information on Richard Kern incorporated here is derived directly from Weber. A second source of great value is a biography by Robert Hine (1981) of Richard's younger brother and close companion, Edward Meyer Kern. It rounds out the story of their family and of the influence Edward had on Richard's art and life.

Looking for a possible co-author, I brought reproductions of some of the drawings to Weber, and upon seeing them he exclaimed: "It's like looking at an old friend!" But he declined to work with me on them, saying that he had done the biography only as a favor to the Amon Carter Museum, and that he really was not at all an art historian. I did form a collaborative relationship with Bonnie Hardwick, at the time the curator of the Bancroft Collection at the Bancroft Library on the Berkeley campus of the University of California. She had been of the greatest assistance to me in my earlier project on Frémont's fifth expedition, and once again her efforts were of the utmost value. She contributed most of the archival and library research, found for me several of the scenes that Kern drew, and with her sharp eye and dispassionate judgment, frequently put my own opinions to the test.

While still heavily involved in the fieldwork on Frémont and Carvalho, I began to seek out Kern's views along Gunnison's route. Because the regions the two expeditions traversed were often the same, and their paths sometimes even identical, I thought it might be more efficient to work on both projects simultaneously. I was able to find a number of the more accessible of the Gunnison-Kern sites and document them for future reference with snapshots, but I soon discovered that dividing my attention this way was unsustainable, so I put work on Kern aside until I had finished with Frémont and Carvalho in 2000.

From my initial brief experience with the sketches and their subjects I learned three valuable things: First, while Kern's drawings seemed to be but tiny representations on small fragments of paper, that perception did not correspond to the breadth and grandeur of his subjects. A simple sketch on a sheet perhaps six inches wide could encompass a field of view of 120° or more in lateral extent, which meant that a single exposure with an ordinary camera, even one equipped with a short-focus lens that could cover an extremely wide angle, would fail to encompass the subject with adequate clarity.

Second, I learned that Kern always employed anamorphic distortion in his representations. To varying degrees he would stretch the vertical dimension of a scene in relation to the horizontal, or, what amounts to the same thing, compress the horizontal dimensions of the scene relative to the vertical, squeezing it together like an accordion, if you will. The result is to magnify the sense of grandeur by adding an imposing height to the verticality of a scene, while at the same time making space on the paper to represent its details with clarity. Looking at the same thing in a slightly different way, Kern compressed the horizontal dimension of a scene to encompass it within the limits of his paper while avoiding having to reduce its vertical dimension to seeming insignificance.

Third, the opacity of the atmosphere that I encountered frequently limited the visibility of distant objects, so that even if I could discern the far-off details that Kern saw and sketched, they were often so vague in appearance and so low in contrast as to be barely visible in a photograph. I imagine that atmospheric clarity in the West was far better in 1853 than it is today, but I have also observed that visibility has so declined since I began this project that were I to embark on it today (in 2021) it would be nearly impossible to carry out. Yet even if the air were clear, or if the subject were fairly close so that subtle details could readily be seen, the ability of my photographs to render those details intelligibly was far inferior to what Kern could do with a few strokes of his pencil. Even today that tool remains superior to the camera when it comes to separating the important from the irrelevant.

Lieutenant E. G. Beckwith, Gunnison's second in command on this railroad reconnaissance, commented on the degradation of the atmosphere that accompanied civilization, and on how the transparency of western air added to the certainty with which he could describe the character of far distant terrain:

> And after the most careful observation and study I have been able to bestow upon the various chains of mountains and water-courses upon the route, seen at least during parts of every day, in the clear atmosphere of the elevated mountain regions, with

> a distinctness of outline and clearness of detail at distances difficult to be realized by persons who are only familiar with the extent, beauty, and grandeur of landscape views in the comparatively moist and clouded atmosphere of the more civilized portions of our country, I hazard nothing in saying that no other line exists, in the immediate vicinity of this, worthy of any attention in connexion with the construction of a railroad from the Mississippi river to the Great Basin (Gunnison-Beckwith *Report*, 87).

In the spring of 2000 I turned my full attention to searching out and photographing the scenes that Kern depicted for Gunnison in 1853. It was not the broad outlines, nor was it the aesthetic grace of the views that I sought to capture photographically; rather it was the "stuff" of the scenes, the topographic details and geological formations, in order to compare them with those in the sketches. The beautiful, the dramatic, the picturesque, and the sublime character of the views I left to fend for themselves, though often with unexpectedly creditable results. At the time there were no adequate digital cameras, and those that promised even a modicum of quality cost a huge amount of money, so of necessity I worked in the now obsolescent medium of film. Had I begun today I would have chosen instead a digital camera, with its ability to immediately display the results. Not knowing what I would encounter and not wishing to judge on the spot the single most effective way to capture a particular scene, I endeavored to photograph each view on three different types of film: color negative, infrared black and white with a filter to block visible radiation, and panchromatic black and white. With panchromatic film I almost always employed a filter before the lens—red, yellow, or ultraviolet blocking—to prevent the shorter wavelengths of light scattered by the atmosphere from reaching the film and decreasing the photographic contrast. Occasionally I used a blue filter to increase the effects of scattering by the air and bring out planes of depth in a scene more clearly, by creating a photographically enhanced "atmospheric perspective." For infrared film the correct exposure is impossible to judge conventionally, and bracketing used up an immense amount of time and film, so I devised an exposure meter sensitive only to infrared light that I calibrated to my film.

The photographs were made with 35 mm reflex cameras and a set of interchangeable lenses that ranged from 19 mm wide-angle to 450 mm telephoto, although the extremes of this range were rarely put to use. When, as was often the case, conventional lenses could not render details with satisfactory sharpness and contrast in a single frame, the camera was mounted on a panoramic head, then carefully leveled so it neither tilted side to side nor looked upward or downward. I would choose a lens of a focal length such that the most elevated feature in the scene, or less commonly the lowest detail of interest, was just included within the vertical limits of the camera's frame. With calibration markings on the panoramic head as a guide I would make multiple exposures, rotating the head about its vertical axis between each one, so that adjacent frames overlapped by about 50 percent. After development the negatives were scanned at high resolution into a computer, and the multiple-exposure panoramas then stitched into a single whole by a program designed for the purpose, Panoramafactory™.

How well do my photographs match the scenes to which I have attached them? In the majority of cases I believe that I have correctly identified the subject of the sketch in question, and that in most of those I have chosen a vantage point close to the one Kern occupied and that allows a tolerably good representation of the scene as he saw and sketched it. Since his drawings are not precision "photographic" delineations, the exact point of view can only be approximated, and the final choice made in the face of competing inaccuracies, approximations, and confusions. Sometimes I had to make decisions with untoward rapidity because of changing conditions of illumination, weather, or oncoming (often living) physical hazards. The most effective cues to the correct point of view are the relations and alignments of near to distant landforms. The drawings vary immensely in quality of representation and specificity of detail, both among themselves and within a single sketch. In the best of them there is practically no question of the appropriate vantage point, for moving a few yards in any direction falsifies the overall correspondence. If the quality of a drawing is lower or less specific than the best, or if the labeling is a bit dubious, my choice of place and point of view would become increasingly suspect, and an overall impression, or *Gestalt*, of the scene might have to substitute for carefully studied and aligned details. In a good number of cases I admit that my imagination may have overwhelmed the limited factual material, and I leave to the reader or to my successors in the field the freedom to accept or reject any of my "identities." On more occasions than I care to admit, I invested time and energy photographing a scene only to realize later or, worse, have it pointed out to me by someone else, that I had incorrectly paired a drawing with the landscape. As I searched over mountains and through deserts, self-delusion was my constant companion, and it often took days of patient reflection or the comments of sharp-eyed, clear-thinking friends to separate me from it.

I finally had to face the reality of diminishing returns, to accept the remaining uncertainties and the outright failures, to give up my indulgence in the boundless pleasures of searching the wilds for Kern's scenes, and to write this book. I believed that I had finished on several occasions, only to be off again on a quest for more. The contradictory pressures involved are almost too much to resist: When I would discover a scene that I earlier could not, the euphoria of the event pushed me forward into thinking that one more trip would result in yet one more discovery. Some of those undiscovered sights are out there yet, beckoning to me with a Siren's call.

Most places where I worked are on public land, but when they are on private land I would try to locate the owner or manager to gain permission to enter; if I did not find someone with authority I consulted neighbors, who invariably reassured me that there would be no objection to what I wished to do. Failing that, I did not trespass on private land or cross a fence line that was posted; I did not drive off roads, but preferred to park by the edge and walk when necessary. In remote areas the fences often have no signs, in which case I would climb over or crawl under them; if I passed through a gate that was unlocked I was always careful to close it behind me. If I were discovered to be where perhaps I shouldn't, I wanted to be sure that I was guilty of nothing but simple trespass, not of vandalism, and I didn't want to leave any trace of having been there in the first place. Ranchers often suffer damage from intruders that might incline them away from welcoming strangers on their land, but for all that, I have never experienced an unpleasant incident; I have met ranchers all over Colorado and Utah, in a great variety of circumstances, and have always found them welcoming and hospitable. When I explain why I wish to enter their land, invariably their curiosity is aroused and the permission forthcoming, for they typically have a deep interest in the history of their portion of the earth. From them I have had things brought to my attention, puzzles resolved, questions asked, and places shown to me that otherwise would have entirely escaped my attention. Those who live among the beauties of the West acquire throughout their lives a wealth of ancestral and community lore, as well as a familiarity with and sensitivity to their environs that I, in my brief time visiting, can never approach.

In this work Kern's sketches are presented in chronological and therefore geographic order, from east to west, but that arrangement is far from the sequence in which I located and photographed his views. My examinations were conducted by passing back and forth over segments of the trail in an irregular manner, determined by the season, the weather, external necessities, newly acquired knowledge, or momentary predilection. In trying to illuminate a point about a drawing I may refer to fragments of knowledge about Kern's technique, style, preferences or activities that I gained from somewhere else, perhaps much farther on in the expedition's travels, and consequently out of their actual order. Although I was driven to this expedient more often than I would like, it rarely disturbs the continuity of the narrative.

The sketches frequently have some indication of place, date, or subject written on them, and although these appear for the most part to be appropriate, they must be approached with care; the inscriptions on many range from mildly to wildly misleading, even when clearly in Kern's own hand. The reasons for this are not always apparent; it would seem that as a topographer Kern should have taken particular care with identifications, yet he often did not, and it can sometimes be demonstrated through his errors that he added the title days or weeks after making a drawing.

A related difficulty occurs with proper names. Even today, as we live in the shadow of GPS satellites, the name of a geographical feature can easily multiply, simplify, broaden, abbreviate, mutate, migrate, transform, translate, transliterate, or simply disappear, often leaving books and maps to disagree with each other *sans* explanation. Wherever possible I name the major geographical features in the sketches using information from field observations, compass readings, topographic maps, nineteenth-century gazetteers, or sometimes after the fact by reference to Google Earth. Because it can be difficult to ascertain just what is in a view, readers should be alert to possible errors here. The names employed by members of the Gunnison expedition in their personal journals, in printed narratives, as notes on drawings, and as captions on illustrations, provide countless opportunities for confusion and misunderstanding. From 1853 to the present they prove to be so slippery and unstable that it is a source of astonishment and gratification when one of them remains recognizable, or perhaps even unchanged, over a century and a half. As a result I have tried to regularize my treatment of names as they occur. Wherever one is obscure or significantly different from that in use today I include its equivalent in parentheses.

The reasons for publishing reproductions of these sketches by Richard Kern are twofold. First, they will be available to scholars and the interested public in a way that will reduce the need to handle and examine the originals. For those whose interests may veer toward the scholarly I have included notes, dimensions, and observations about the drawings that sometimes go into too much detail to make pleasant reading. I hope that you will simply skip over such minutiae if you wish.

The second purpose is to try to understand Kern's artistic idiom and sensibilities, and to evaluate his skill and methods of representing the landscape—by locating the scenes Kern sketched and photographing them, for purposes of comparison.

In attempting to create a coherent, if expansive, narrative of the expedition and its illustrations, I make liberal use of quotes from the Gunnison-Beckwith *Report*. A reader who wishes to penetrate more deeply into the experiences of Gunnison, Beckwith, and Kern may prefer to go further, reading the full *Report* and following it in conjunction with the sketches and photographs presented here. The *Report* has been scanned by Google Books and is freely available to either read online or download as a facsimile in PDF format (Gunnison, John W., and E. G. Beckwith, 1855).

There are four other first-hand sources that are both useful and informative. The first is Lieutenant Beckwith's personal diary, now in the Huntington Library in San Marino, California. Beckwith created the *Report* by substantially transcribing his diaries, but did not do so completely; he occasionally left out information that usefully bears upon events, sometimes inserted his later reflections, and intermittently added material quoted from Captain Gunnison's writings, now lost, that came into his possession after the latter's demise.

Second is an account kept in German by the botanist Frederick Creutzfeldt, titled "Memorandum-book." A handwritten copy, along with an English translation, is in the Smithsonian Institution Archives. In it Creutzfeldt recorded his observations as well as his disgruntled complaints, and he often fills in details or offers a point of view quite different from that in the official *Report*. Because the pagination is inconsistent in the typescript translation of Creutzfeldt's journal, I will reference quotations from it by date.

Third is the book *The Land Between*, by Dr. James Schiel, another German scientist who went with Gunnison as both geologist and physician. He wrote it after he returned to Germany, and apparently had with him a copy of the Gunnison-Beckwith *Report* that he edited, condensed, and translated to present as his own account in German. That would seem to make it less useful than its source, but frequently Schiel includes both his own independent observations and excerpts from his notes. (Two satisfactory translations of Schiel's book are listed in the bibliography; I make page references to the version by Bachmann and Wallace, 1957.)

Finally there are letters in the Huntington Library written intermittently by Captain Gunnison. Though not in narrative form, they offer some insight into his thinking about the expedition and his reactions to events and experiences while leading it.

References may be found within the bibliography in their complete form, but for brevity they are often shortened in the text; for instance, the Gunnison-Beckwith *Report* is referenced so frequently that I have simplified it to just "G-B" followed by a page number.

## Acknowledgments

A PROJECT OF THIS MAGNITUDE, one that encompassed such a broad field of view while encountering so many imponderables, could never have been done without the assistance from individuals and institutions that are seemingly beyond number. So dependent have I been on the unselfish cooperation and participation of others that to completely detail all of their contributions would seriously overload this already ponderous account. A simple mention will often have to suffice, leaving it to the reader to imagine the contribution each has made to the completed work.

When I first thought to pursue the drawings Richard Kern made for Captain John W. Gunnison in 1853, I knew immediately that I would eventually carry the task to completion. What I could not then know was how quickly I could proceed, nor how well. The generosity and rapidity with which support and financing materialized gave me almost immediate answers to those questions: I was able to act as swiftly as I could manage, and demand from myself work of quality that strained the limits of my abilities. I never had to restrict the amount of time and effort I could devote to my searches, nor accept avoidable compromises in the quality of my photographic documents. My principal source of support, which was most generous and unstinting, came from the late Alice Dodge Wallace and the Avenir Foundation, Inc. of Colorado. The Utah Humanities Council (Cynthia Buckingham, Director), made a significant contribution out of a fund established with it by Robert Kent Fielding for the study of Gunnison and his expedition. Willie Anne Wright, of Richmond, Virginia, through her own initiative, presented a liberal contribution to the project. Two sponsoring organizations, Museum Development Associates (M. Susan Barger, Director), and Recursos de Santa Fe (Ellen Bradbury-Reid, Director) administered these grants for me. Bonnie Hardwick, who was at the time the Curator of the Bancroft Collection in Berkeley, California, and who received for the purpose a generous grant from the University of California

Research Grants for Librarians, performed the far-reaching archival research upon which I so much depended. She also located several of the scenes that were depicted by Kern in 1853, and contributed invaluable critiques of the ongoing work. The Jentel Foundation of Wyoming provided me with a month of quiet but stimulating seclusion in the most hospitable and appealing circumstances, during which time the first draft of this book took form.

The topographic sketches that are the subject of this endeavor were found in the Newberry Library of Chicago, Illinois. Robert Karrow Jr., the curator of maps and special collections, first brought the album of them to my attention; Mary Wyly, then acting director, granted me permission to work on its contents and to publish them; John Powell and Catherine Gass of the library's Digital Imaging Services provided me with the very high quality photographs of these objects that make up the core of this publication. The reproduction of the daguerreotype portrait of Richard Kern came through the kind offices of Jennifer Watts, Peter Blodgett, and Katrina Denman of the Huntington Library of San Marino, California. Eben Dennis, special collections librarian of the Maryland Historical Society in Baltimore, Maryland, located and provided me with the handwriting samples of the expedition's astronomer, Sheppard Homans.

The creation of this book and the organization of the material it contains would hardly have been possible without the help and support of Lyle York, who edited the text, and Matthew Wilson, who suggested improvements. Ellen Dornan and Craig Goldsmith made the presentation of the visual material possible by turning it into an electronic book with a keyed, scrolling presentation of the panoramic images. Ken Rockwell of the J. Willard Marriott Library provided astute comments and help with some of the locations. Thanks to John Alley, Jessica Booth, and Glenda Cotter at The University of Utah Press for their assistance in publication of the book under their Boxelder Books imprint.

Perhaps the most diffuse and difficult-to-define category includes those who by their friendship and supportive actions lent moral, intellectual, and physical strength to my endeavors. A detailed account of such contributions would be a chapter in itself. I salute the late Lynne Baur, Cynthia Buckingham, Ardis Burst, Allison Colborne, Anne and David Cole, Ilene Dunn, Tom Edmondson and Nancy Heugh, Jan and De Herman, Lidian King, Willard and Kay Lewis, Greg MacGregor and Jo Whaley, Margeaux, George Miles, David Miller, the late Ree Mobley, the late John Morton, Carolyn Mueller, Arthur Olivas, Charles and Susan Palmer, Patricia Joy Richmond, Gerri Rock, Kristin Rowley, the late John Rubel, the late Richard Rudisill, the late Leigh Shallenberger, the late Allen Shlaer, the late Bill Shlaer, Cynthia Shlaer, Joe Traugott and Laurel Wallace, the late David Weber, and Russell Young.

In the course of my travels I frequently met local residents, many of whom helped me make substantial advances and discoveries. They were often able to inform me of local history, identify the source of a drawing that had otherwise eluded me, name landmarks, grant me permission to enter private land, locate a trail, point me in the right direction, or alert me to the likelihood that I was following a false lead. I was not always able to obtain their names, but where possible I have identified them in the text and acknowledged their contributions.

Patience is truly an offering to such a time-consuming venture. My wife, M. Susan Barger, and my children, Leah and Ben Shlaer, along with my daughter-in-law, Marie Goeritz, deserve the highest accolades for exhibiting it in such large measure.

For those whom I have inadvertently or through my ignorance omitted, and to those whose contribution came too late for inclusion, I offer a sincere apology along with my profound gratitude.

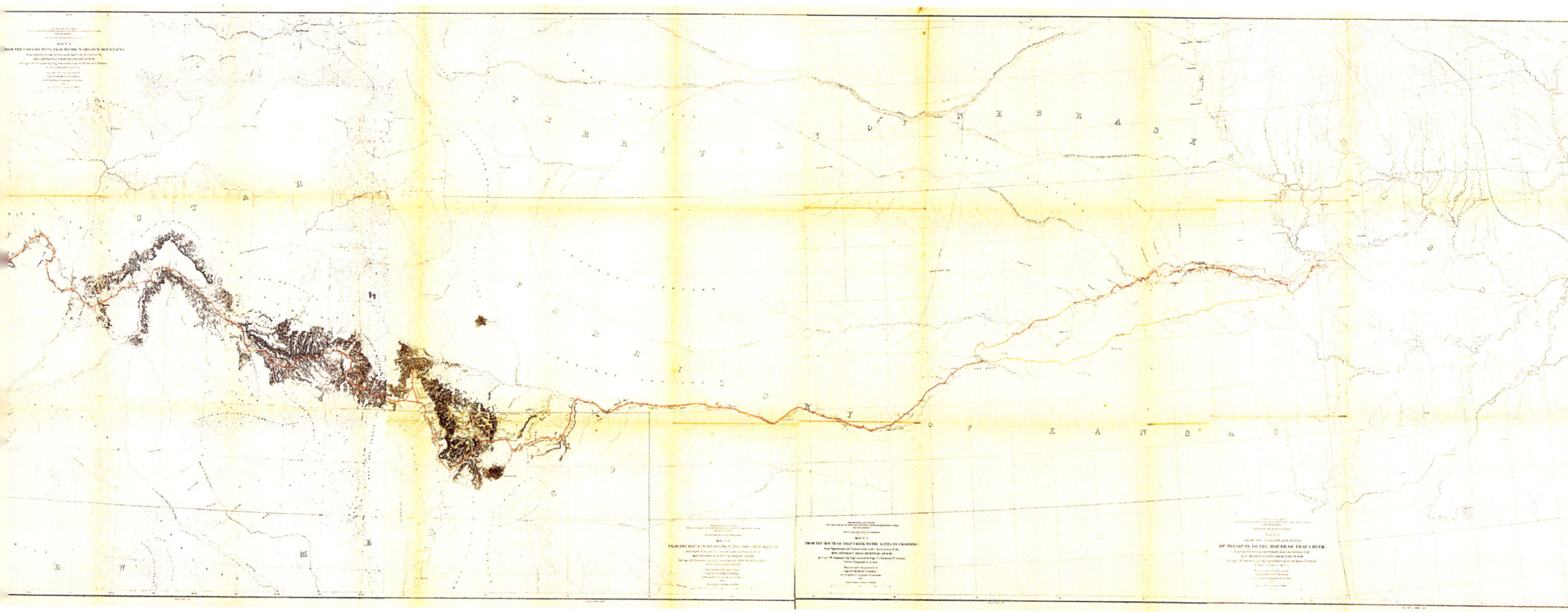

# Introduction

## THE "CENTRAL ROUTE TO THE PACIFIC"

*The Newberry Library of Chicago harbors a little album, "Ayer MS 794a," with a dark green cloth cover bearing an embossed design within a border of small gold dots and gilt edges. Open it, and glued to the inside of the front cover is its title page, one to fire the imagination with intimations of daring exploits in the company of three of the most courageous and significant explorers of the mid-nineteenth century.*

The bold calligraphic hand reads:

THE FAR WEST
Explorations of the country from the Missisippi river to the
Pacific Ocean
by
Gunnison, Frimont, Beckuith
in
1853-1854.
Executed (in water-colors and indian-ink) for the Congress
in 1854-1855
by Schumann.

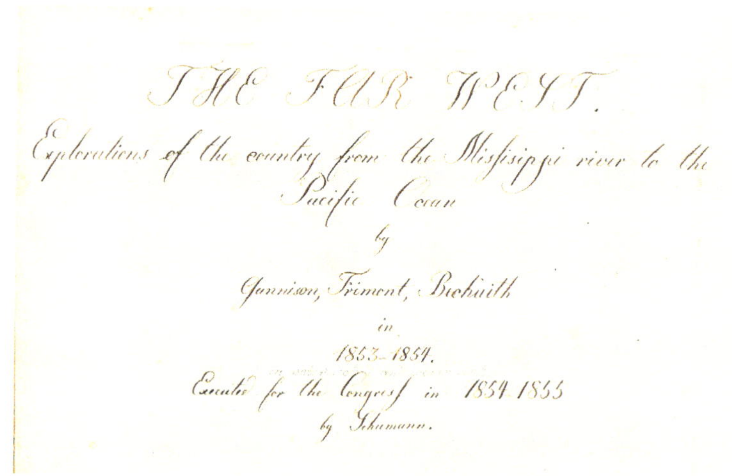

PLATE 2. Title page

Captain John Williams Gunnison, of the U.S. Army Corps of Topographical Engineers, accompanied Captain Howard Stansbury as second in command on an exploration across the Great Plains to the Valley of the Great Salt Lake in 1849 and 1850. In 1853 Gunnison was selected to lead a reconnaissance along the proposed "Central Route to the Pacific" from St. Louis to San Francisco that ran roughly along the thirty-eighth parallel, and to determine if it was suitable for a projected railroad from the Mississippi River to the Pacific Ocean. On October 26, 1853, at Sevier Lake in west-central Utah, the unfortunate Captain Gunnison, the topographic artist Richard Kern, the botanist Frederick Creutzfeldt, and five other members of the expedition, were killed in what is now known as the Gunnison Massacre.

Colonel John Charles Frémont led a pair of surveying expeditions for the Topographical Engineers along the Oregon Trail in 1842 and 1843-44, then one to California in 1845-46. His extensive (and with the help of his wife, Jessie Benton Frémont, elegant) writings on the subject made him the most romantically famous of mid-nineteenth-century western explorers. No longer an Army officer after a scandalous court-martial in 1848, Frémont privately conducted a disastrous fourth expedition in 1848-49. His fifth and final exploration of the West was in 1853-54, on which he employed an innovative method of photographic documentation.

First Lieutenant Edward Griffin Beckwith was a U.S. Army artillery officer who always went by his initials, E.G. Beckwith's first western experience was during the Mexican War, after which he was assigned to travel overland to California as commander of a military escort accompanying Colonel James Collier, who had been appointed the first Collector for the Port of San Francisco. While in the West Beckwith demonstrated a considerable proficiency in the Spanish language, became passably acquainted with that of the Utah Indians, and was able to communicate with other tribes as well. The competence and skill he evinced on the trek to California across this newly acquired, unfamiliar territory led to his being named second in command to Captain Gunnison's 1853 expedition. As a result Beckwith shouldered the responsibility for continuing its mission when Gunnison lost his life at Sevier Lake. The final report on that journey was written by Beckwith and published in two parts: "Gunnison-Beckwith" covers the 1853 portion ending in Utah, then "Beckwith" is concerned with the 1854 segment from Utah to California.

"Schumann," the last name on the title page, is C. Schumann, who prepared illustrations for the Beckwith *Report* on the 1854 exploration from sketches by its topographer, Baron Friedrich Wilhelm von Egloffstein. Egloffstein had at first traveled with and worked for Frémont on his fifth expedition, then after its collapse in February of 1854 went to Salt Lake City. There he encountered Beckwith, who offered him the position of topographer with the expedition to replace the late Richard Kern, which he accepted. Schumann's drawings were engraved for the Beckwith *Report* and published by the government in Volume XI of the *Railroad Reports* of 1855; beyond that no information about Schumann has come to light.

Adhered to the first page of the album is a letter to the otherwise obscure C. Schumann from now Captain Beckwith (Plate 3), who, besides authoring both the Gunnison-Beckwith and the Beckwith *Reports*, had the responsibility of overseeing their final publication.

Transcribed, the letter reads:

No III
Washington D.C.
Jany 18th 1856.

Sir:

The series of landscape drawing executed by you, from

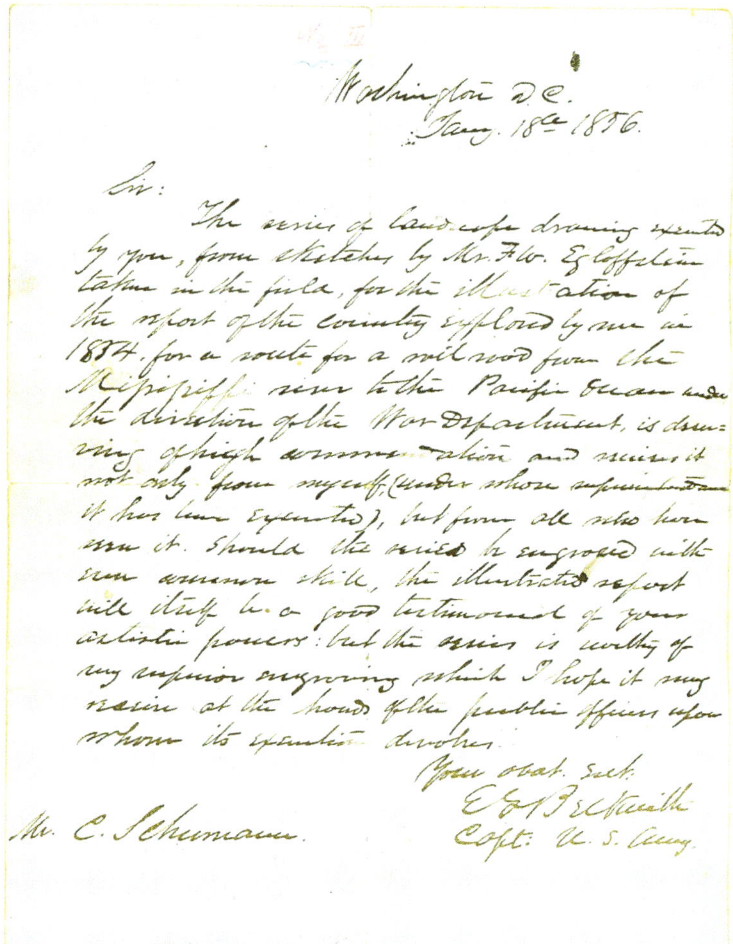

Washington D.C.
Jany. 18th 1856.

Sir:

The series of landscape drawings executed by you, from sketches by Mr. F.W. Egloffstein taken in the field, for the illustration of the report of the country explored by me in 1854, for a route for a railroad from the Mississippi river to the Pacific Ocean under the direction of the War Department, is deserving of high commendation and receives it not only from myself (under whose superintendance it has been executed), but from all who have seen it. Should the series be engraved with even common skill, the illustrated report will itself be a good testimonial of your artistic powers: but the series is worthy of very superior engraving which I hope it may receive at the hands of the public officers upon whom its execution devolves.

Your obnt. Snt.
E G Beckwith
Capt: U. S. Army

Mr. C. Schumann.

PLATE 3. Letter from Beckwith to Schumann

sketches by Mr. F[.] W. Egloffstein taken in the field, for the illustration of the report of the country explored by me in 1854, for a route for a railroad from the Mississippi river to the Pacific Ocean under the direction of the War Department, is deserving of high commendation and receives it not only from myself, (under whose superintendance it has been executed), but from all who have seen it. Should the series be engraved with even common skill, the illustrated report will itself be a good testimonial of your artistic powers: but the series is worthy of very superior engraving which I hope it may receive at the hands of the public officers upon whom its execution devolves.

Your obnt. Snt:
E G Beckwith
Mr. C. Schumann Capt: U. S. Army

What an unlikely treasure—an album thick with either original sketches by Egloffstein, from whose hand very few originals exist; drawings and paintings rendered from them by Schumann; or perhaps both! Turn to the next page and there is a piece of thin, translucent, yellow paper, a slightly irregular rectangle with clipped corners, measuring about 7.9 inches by 4.8 inches. Sketched on it in pencil is a small pond or depression surrounded by trees, behind which in the distance appear some extravagantly rugged mountain peaks. At the bottom an inscription reads simply "Peaks of the Sierra Blanca" (Plate 108). The subject is generic but the style is clear, and the handwriting quite definitive. This drawing is not the work of C. Schumann, nor of Friedrich Egloffstein, but of Richard Hovendon Kern, who was topographer and artist on the Gunnison expedition of 1853. In addition, this sketch is palpably the source of a lithographic illustration, attributed to Kern, that appears opposite p. 42 (Plate 109) of the Gunnison-Beckwith *Report*.

Proceed to the next page and there find a sketch of a river scene with trees on the banks and mesas in the background, titled "Green river Oct. 1" (Plate 338). Egloffstein was nowhere near the Green River on October 1 of any year (he did cross it in January of 1854 with Frémont), but Gunnison's exploring party, including Kern, forded it on October 1, 1853. Every page of the album yields further evidence that the entire collection came from the hand of Richard Kern, with but one exception. Towards the back is a single sheet with multiple views of Mount Shasta (Plate 376) that is unsigned but almost certainly by Egloffstein, who in 1854 would have seen it from many angles while exploring in Northern California with Lieutenant Beckwith.

### THE DESTRUCTION OF THE GUNNISON EXPEDITION

The title page of the Newberry's album promises vicarious yet safe adventure, but its contents endured and survived vicissitudes that repeatedly threatened its existence. The drawings were among the effects of Richard Kern when he fell victim to one of the infamous massacres that occurred far too frequently in that part of the world during the nineteenth century. From an account of the incident by Lieutenant E. G. Beckwith, Gunnison's second in command:

> *October* 25.—Captain Gunnison, with Mr. R. H. Kern, Mr. F. Creutzfeldt, and Mr. Wm. Potter, (guide,) with John Bellows, and a corporal and six men from the escort, left camp at a late hour this morning to explore the vicinity of Sevier lake, supposed to be distant some fifteen or eighteen miles...
>
> *October* 26.—The morning was clear and cold, and Mount Nebo, seen through the Sevier river gap, with its pure mantle of snow, half enveloped in floating misty clouds, mildly reflecting the rays of the rising sun, presented one of the most beautiful mountain scenes I have ever witnessed. Our animals were kept out to graze until a late hour. At 11 o'clock, however, a party was dispatched to ascertain

the practicability of the passage around the mountain and thence north to the Great Salt lake; and, without moving camp again, until the return of Captain Gunnison, it was intended to examine the passage of the Sevier river the following day. But the first party had scarcely proceeded a hundred yards from camp, when it was met by a man, weak and exhausted, reeling breathless into camp, barely able to communicate, by a few broken sentences, as he sank into a seat, the painful intelligence that Captain Gunnison's party had been surprised in their camp by a large party of Indians, and, he thought, all but himself massacred. Orders were instantly given by Captain Morris [commander of the expedition's contingent of Mounted Riflemen], and promptly obeyed by all the men remaining with him of his escort, to replenish their ammunition; and having brought up and saddled their horses, in thirty minutes they were moving rapidly towards the scene of that fatal disaster, hoping to rescue all who might yet survive and perform the last mournful duties of humanity to those who were known to have fallen.

The man who first reached camp was the corporal of the escort, who had made his escape on his horse, and had ridden him until he could go no further, leaving him at our camp of the previous day, whence he ran on foot fourteen miles—twenty-five in all—arriving, without arms, in the condition I have described. Another of the escort reached camp on horseback, before Captain Morris' departure; and two others were met by him in the course of the afternoon, making their way towards camp. The horses of Dr. Schiel, who had accompanied Captain Morris, and of his sergeant and several of his men, gave out during their rapid march, and their riders were left straggling behind; but eventually all arrived safely in camp—the sergeant and some of the men, from their own folly, in a poor plight.

Before Captain Morris' departure…it was…determined to break up the camp altogether, and move towards a convenient point, where Captain Morris and myself could meet on the following or succeeding day…

…The last of our animals were not out of harness when Captain Morris arrived, confirming our worst fears for the fate of our late comrades.

Captain Gunnison had encamped early in the afternoon, while the wind and storm were yet fresh, and doubtless feeling the security which men come to indulge after passing long periods of time surrounded by savages without actually encountering them. The abundant grass and fuel of a little nook in the river bottom, sheltered by the high second bank of the river on one side, and thick willows, distant scarcely thirty yards, on two of the others, with the river in front, offered a tempting place of comfort and utility, which was perhaps accepted without even a thought of danger. It was known to the party that a band of Indians was near them, for we had seen their fires daily since entering the valley; but an unusual feeling of security against them was felt, as Captain Gunnison had learned that a recent quarrel, resulting in several deaths, which they had had with emigrants, had terminated, and that notwithstanding this difficulty they had remained at peace with the neighboring settlers, which had been confirmed and guarantied for the future in a "talk" held with some of the Indians of this band, by an agent of the governor of the territory, during our stay near Fillmore. This information, Captain Gunnison told me before leaving, relieved him from any apprehension he might otherwise have felt regarding this band, and was the reason for his having asked for so small an escort to accompany him, which he as well as his guide, an experienced citizen of the Territory, deemed sufficient.

The usual precaution of a camp guard had been taken, each of the party (including the commander) in turn having performed that duty during the night. At the break of day all arose and at once engaged in the usual duties of a camp preparatory to an early start, to reach that day the most distant point of exploration for the present season. The sun had not yet risen, most of the party being at breakfast, when the surrounding quietness and silence of this vast plain was broken by the discharge of a volley of rifles and a shower of arrows through that devoted camp, mingled with the savage yells of a large band of Pah-Utah Indians almost in the midst of the camp; for, under cover of the thick bushes, they had approached undiscovered to within twenty-five yards of the camp-fires. The surprise was complete. At the first discharge, the call to "seize your arms" had little effect. All was confusion. Captain Gunnison, stepping from his tent, called to his savage murderers that he was their friend; but this had no effect. They rushed into camp, and only those escaped who succeeded in mounting on horseback, and even then they were pursued for many miles. The horse of one fell near camp, tumbling his rider under a bush, where he lay for six or seven hours, while the Indians were passing him on every side, until finally he could no longer hear them near him or in the camp, when he left, and was met soon afterwards by Capt. Morris' party, which reached the fatal spot just before night. Two Indians were seen a mile or two from camp by Lieutenant Baker and Mr. Potter, brother of the guide, but they were not able to come up with them before night enabled them to escape. The bodies of the slain were not all found at dark, and hope still lingered as a bright fire was built to assure any survivor of safety. But the long weary night, rendered hideous by the howling of wolves, wore away, as this little band of armed men, barely larger than that which had already been sacrificed, lay near the fatal spot, and day dawned only to discover the mutilated remains of their recent comrades, none of them being scalped—a barbarity which some of the tribes on this part of the continent seldom indulge. Some of their arms were, however, cut off at the elbows, and their entrails cut open; and, the wolves having had access to them it was not deemed possible to bring them away—not even that of Captain Gunnison, who had fallen pierced with fifteen arrows (G-B, 72-74).

A few of Captain Gunnison's notes, those since October 8th, when we were on the St. Rafael, he had with him, and they were carried off by the Indians; also, some of the topographical notes and sketches of his assistant, Mr. Kern; but I have not been able to ascertain to what precise point, but hope the loss will not be great. I have, through Mr. Call, the president of the settlement, now here, who extends to us all the assistance in his power, sent an express to the chief of the band which was engaged in the massacre, and entertain a faint hope that I may recover these papers and books,* and also the instruments, with which we can ill dispense...

*The notes and sketches were all thus recovered (G-B, 124).

From the account of Dr. James Schiel, geologist and physician with the expedition:

...Among those killed were Captain Gunnison and a number of soldiers. Others were F. Kern, the topographer of the corps and C. Creutzfeldt... The two last named had accompanied Col. Fremont in the 40's on his well-known trip of exploration in the Sierra Madre [Sierra San Juan] and had only barely escaped the fate then which now had overtaken them...

Our most valuable topographical notes and some precious instruments had fallen into the Indians' hands during this sad event. Even if the loss of the latter could be bourne, the loss of those documents meant the loss of a great part of our research which had taken six months, and had only been achieved with the greatest difficulty. Consequently it was deemed advisable to hasten as quickly as possible to the City of the Salt Lake, one hundred twenty miles away, and try with the aid of the Mormons to get those papers back...

...We immediately sent an interpreter with presents to the region of the accident, and thanks to him and even more to the president of the small community of Fillmore we were able to recover the lost objects with the exception of smaller instruments (Schiel, 104-106).

Anson Call, The president of the Mormon settlement of Fillmore, received a visit by Captain Gunnison a few days before the latter's violent end. Call later wrote an account of the massacre, of its prelude, and of his part in recovering the expedition's property from the Indians:

Here I staid three years, during which time what is known as the Gunnison Massacre took place.

The City of Fillmore is one hundred and sixty-nine miles south of Salt Lake City. From Fillmore to the place of the Gunnison Massacre is about thirty-five miles. This massacre took place on the 26th day of Oct., A. D. 1853...during the time of the Indian Walker War... The settlements were in a state of alarm in consequence of the said Indian War, and just previous to the Gunnison massacre a party of emigrants from Missouri, going to California, came to Fillmore and stopped for a while. During their stay they frequently talked about the Indians and made many threats concerning them and declared repeatedly, "that they would kill the first Indian who came into their camp." I remonstrated with them and cautioned them not to follow such a suicidal course. I told them that the Indians hereabout were peaceable and that they would be sure to come into their camps and want to trade with them. After this party had left I learned that some Indians around had gone into their camps, as I had told them that they would, and that they had killed two of them and wounded three others. These outrageous proceedings enraged the Indians, so that they became infuriated and could not be pacified. They were so excited that nothing short of blood would appease their wrath. The settlers became more than ever alarmed and entertained fears for their safety. In this time of excitement, Captain Gunnison and his exploring party came along. The party consisted of about thirty United States soldiers, a guide by the name of Potter, from Sanpete County, and a few others. Gunnison camped about eight miles north of Fillmore for two or three days, during which time he came to Fillmore and I had an interview with him. I told him what had happened and of the excited state of the Indians in consequence. I invited him to rest a while till the Indians became cooled down. At my information he expressed his deep regret and remarked, "The Indians are sure to have their revenge." He continued, "I am going to explore Sevier Lake and then on to Salt Lake City for winter quarters." I entreated him to exercise great caution and disclosed to him my fears that the Indians would if they could have satisfaction from the first white man or men they met, that we for months had kept a picket guard, and that we did not suffer any man to go into the fields or cañons without his fire-arms and company, that our stock was guarded day and night, that I had sought and had succeeded in keeping a number of the Pahvan Indians friendly and out of the Indian Walker War, and was furnishing them labor. I also told the Captain that the Indians were then in pursuit of the party of emigrants who had slain some of their number.

Captain Gunnison, however, did not accept my invitation, but went on, with about twelve others and Potter the guide, to explore the lake. In a few days I heard that he and several of his party, one morning while at breakfast, had been killed by Indians, who were lying in ambush within six rods of the Captain's camp. The party with Captain Gunnison, as I afterwards learned, were assistants Kerr [Kern] and Crifelt [Creutzfeldt], Baylis [Bellows] the cook, Potter the guide, and eight soldiers. While the cook was preparing breakfast, Captain Gunnison was examining his papers. The soldiers had partaken breakfast and had gone to gather up the horses of the party, when almost immediately, or as soon as the Captain and his assistants had seated themselves upon the ground to eat their breakfast, the Captain was fired upon from some willow brush close by, and Kerr and Crifelt were killed instantly and fell within a few feet of where they had been sitting. The cook fell within four rods, and the Captain within nine or ten rods, dead. The Indians then rushed upon the soldiers, who were about forty yards distant, some of whom were by this time on their horses, while others were not and instantly killed four of them and Potter the guide. The other four escaped and returned to the camp north of Fillmore, and reported to Lieutenant Beckwith in command. Beckwith directly sent a number of his men to the scene of massacre, who arrived there between sun down and dark of the same day. They found the dead, all stripped, lying nude, and some books and papers only lying around.

...Lieut. Beckwith deeply lamented the sad end of the Gunnison Expedition and the loss of the papers of the summer's survey. I told him that perhaps all the books and papers the Indians might have that belonged to the expedition might possibly be obtained for a few pairs of blankets and a little calico. Acting upon this suggestion he left me some calico and blankets, which calico I had made into shirts and gave them and some blankets to some friendly Indians, with the understanding that they should procure what they could of the papers, books, instruments, and horses that belonged to Captain Gunnison's command. In a few days three Indians returned with the majority of the horses, the instruments and most of the papers, all of which I immediately took to Lieut. Beckwith, then at Salt Lake City. I furnished three men with horses and provisions to carry the express and hired three others to return to Lieut. Beckwith the property stolen by the Indians from Captain Gunnison's command (Call, 1986, 161-170).

### THE FIRST VISUAL RECORD OF AN EXPLORATION OF THE AMERICAN WEST

The rediscovered collection of drawings by Richard Kern, now in the Newberry Library, is the earliest sequential visual depiction of a trip through the Rocky Mountains, and it serves to illustrate the astonishingly detailed narrative account that is the Gunnison-Beckwith *Report*. In total it is a grand, systematic panorama of the American West that has, against all odds, survived travel, indifference, and neglect and come down to us. The only comparable attempt of the period was a sequence of daguerreotype photographs that Solomon Nunes Carvalho made a few months later on Frémont's fifth expedition, following somewhat the same path as that of Gunnison. The results of Carvalho's revolutionary exploit are for the most part lost, and Frémont never wrote a narrative description of that expedition; it had to be assembled piecemeal from the scanty surviving sources (Shlaer, 2000).

The value of the drawings today is, in part, pure visual enlightenment. To appreciate the appearance of such splendid landscapes, and how the essence of this utterly unfamiliar terrain was conveyed by Kern on small pieces of paper and in only a few pencil strokes, it is only necessary to become immersed in his works, giving every drawing time to assume its full presence in the imagination. By encountering each one on its own terms, studying carefully its nuance and its overall manifestation, and only then comparing it in a leisurely manner to the appearance of the same scene today that is provided by the accompanying photographs, it is possible to gradually decipher the code of subtle nuance that marks Kern's style. The meanings contained in each work, from the hastiest sketch to the most well-worked-out drawing, gradually enlarge themselves in the mind. In this manner one can retrieve Kern's experience of the Rocky Mountains and the western deserts, seeing the world through his eyes, without having to search out the far-flung subjects of his drawings. By combining a contemplative regard for the visual evidence with the narratives from the Gunnison expedition, a reader can re-live the experiences of Kern's, Gunnison's, and Beckwith's journey. For those fortunate enough to travel the West, it is readily possible to visit many of the places from which Kern drew, and share in the excitement of standing where this artist of the 1853 expedition himself once took up his position.

The artistic quality, importance, and purpose of surviving illustrations of the Old West have been recurring subjects for modern scholars (for example, DeVoto, 1947; Hine, 1982; Huseman, 1995; Klett et al., 1984, 2004; Naef and Wood, 1975; Sandweiss, 1991; Taft, 1953; Trenton and Hassrick, 1983; Weber, 1985). But once photography superseded drawing as the preferred method of representation, one point seemed to have been settled: the question of accuracy of representation. Photographs are usually assumed to convey a correct impression, being painted with the mechanical hand of Nature rather than that of a fallible human. As far as I am aware, modern scholars have not detected deliberate alteration to nineteenth—century documentary landscape photographs, with one notable exception (Dingus, 1982). Drawn or painted representations, on the other hand, can hardly escape this consideration.

The question of Kern's accuracy in his artistic transcriptions answers itself. It is evident that the bulk of the drawings were not made directly for a cartographic purpose, although they may have served an ancillary function in that regard, for with one exception none of the drawings are unambiguously precise. That lone anomaly within the collection (Plate No. 31) is fastidiously detailed, covered with compass bearings associated with prominent landmarks, and explicitly intended for the purpose of mapmaking. Of the rest, many are filled with detail, many seem to be almost devoid of it, but most of them so bring out the essence of the landscape through simplification, abstraction, and emphasis as to transport the viewer thoroughly into the field of view. Doubts about the utility of his work dissolve before the power of Richard Kern's art to *make us there*. If we are disinclined to regard "accuracy" in terms of the mathematically defined perspective of a photograph, and hence allow some elasticity in the use of the word, the depictions of the landscape in these drawings are remarkably fine. Neither do distortions and sporadic errors of omission, or the occasional transposition of features, significantly reduce their value.

The intent of the drawings within the context of the Gunnison expedition is unclear. Conveying an aesthetic experience was perhaps not the primary motive behind them, but it was hardly a matter of indifference; those ultimately used for the lithographic illustrations that accompanied the *Report* are certainly among the most attractive of the set. Picturesque views of sublime, unfamiliar landscapes that could be included in a published travelogue appealed to the Romantic sensibility of Victorian-era readers, and a proper set of illustrations might well remain in the minds and consciousness of the public long after the memory of the written narratives had become softened by time. That the sharpness of the public's visual memory would enhance his reputation as an explorer and surveyor must have been a concern of Captain Gunnison's, for some of Kern's drawings were clearly destined to be reproduced and published even as they were being made. It is therefore astonishing to discover that while the drawings are in most cases skilled representations of visual appearances, a rather cavalier attitude governed the content of the captions written on them, presumably added for the purpose of identification by subject, place, and date. The casualness with regard to names and titles suggests that, unlike with maps, considerations of detailed accuracy were a secondary concern, and the evocation of the generalized emotional and physical sense of a place, its *hereness*, the primary one; it was hardly to be expected that any of the future audience for the railroad *Reports*, even those few who might travel west along Gunnison's route, would take the time to evaluate the illustrations that represent the Central Route to the Pacific. The scientific and engineering information contained in the *Report* was within the maps and profiles of the terrain, the tables of observations, and the scientific appendices; tinted lithographic illustrations might convey the nature and appearance of the environment, but their absence would not have seriously inconvenienced a civil engineer whose task was to build a railroad over the route taken by the expedition. The target audience for the illustrations, as well as for much of the descriptive narrative, was a general public that was often concerned with and deeply affected by the romance of distant wilderness.

Despite the sometimes misleading captions it is possible, a century and a half later, to correlate many of the drawings with the narrative text of the Gunnison-Beckwith *Report*; presumably that would have been much easier for its author, Lieutenant Beckwith, since he had firsthand knowledge of the terrain depicted. It is therefore difficult to understand the frequent seemingly gratuitous errors of captioning without concluding that, except for a few scenes chosen for emphasis, Kern's landscapes were minor endeavors within the expedition's larger scheme, and that their production was distinctly secondary to his principal duty as cartographer.

The anomalies in the set of drawings make it impossible to assign to them a consistent rationale, so the purpose of each must be determined individually. It is entirely possible that Kern created most of them on his own initiative and for private purposes, just as in the past he illustrated his diaries and letters. He and his brother Edward had often used such sketches as the basis of finished paintings, and to the extent that the Gunnison expedition drawings were not explicitly requested by his superiors, he may well have intended to retain them for himself after returning home. An aesthetic rather than a rigorous illustrative purpose, along with the demands of his more important duties, might begin to explain the many inconsistent and inaccurate notations that appear on the drawings, even those captioned in Kern's own hand. Although they could have been easily ascertained, the exact names of his subjects must not always have been central to the use for which the drawings were intended. The art of the composition may well have overwhelmed a concern for a precise written description.

Notwithstanding their problems with annotation, the drawings may have been to intended to serve as a visual aid to Captain Gunnison's memory when, as was anticipated, he came to write his report for publication. The notebook would have concurrently provided material from which to choose lithographic illustrations, if they had not already been designated in the field while being drawn. Since it is possible to closely associate many of the drawings with the narrative of the *Report*, I imagine Beckwith used the sketches for just that purpose, but in the course of the expedition may have done less than he might have to familiarize himself with the drawings (perhaps not even having looked them over) than he would have had he known the task of writing the *Report* was going to devolve upon him. But no causal relation can be demonstrated. Even if Beckwith did not refer to the drawings when arranging his diaries for publication as the Gunnison-Beckwith *Report*, and even if the two narratives, one visual and one written, were created in total independence of one another, such a correlation would be the natural outcome for two accounts, dealing with experiences shared at the same places and times throughout the same traverse across half a continent.

Leaving aside the near-miraculous survival of Kern's drawings, it is left for us to marvel at the insight they provide into Gunnison and his companions' adventures in exploration. Their exploits in the summer and early fall of 1853 could hardly be brought more vividly to life.

## THE TROUBLESOMELY HYPOTHETICAL "CENTRAL ROUTE" TO THE PACIFIC

Why in early 1853 did Captain John W. Gunnison find himself under orders from the War Department to explore and evaluate a possible transcontinental railroad route, one that was being advocated almost single-handedly by Thomas Hart Benton, the most powerful and effective polemicist in the country? (In this context "transcontinental" really means just the western half of the continent. The route proposal might be more accurately described as a "Railroad from the Mississippi River to the Pacific Ocean.")

The idea for such a railroad first arose in 1837, when John Plumbe, Jr., construction engineer and later proprietor of a chain of daguerreotype studios, proposed the construction of a railroad from the Midwest to the Pacific at Puget Sound. It was an audacious scheme, since the route could be only vaguely defined, the ownership of the region involved was the subject of dispute with Great Britain, the Mexicans had not been consulted, and the terrain involved had never been explored in a systematic manner. Nonetheless Plumbe spent years promoting his idea without success, and his startlingly American originality is generally overlooked today (Taft 1964, 49-52, 462 n. 61). In 1844 Asa Whitney took up the idea and suggested that its route be from the upper Midwest to the mouth of the

Columbia River. No doubt building on Plumbe's earlier efforts at public discussion, this idea gradually invaded the country's imagination, and it was apparent to many that a railroad to the Pacific Ocean would bring immense commercial and agricultural opportunities to the regions through which it was to pass. Following the creation of the Oregon Territory and the ratification of the Treaty of Guadalupe Hidalgo of 1848 that ended the Mexican War, the need for an efficient line of communication across the continent, one protected by passing entirely through the territory of the United States, was generally recognized and embraced by the government. Because the projected expense of such a monumental undertaking appeared to limit it to a single line, the advocates of various sectional and commercial interests brought forward competing arguments, each favoring their own projected route.

Geographically and politically the United States was in an awkward position, divided East from West and North from South. Great forces of settlement, exploitation, and political power were rising in California and Oregon, while the vastness of the Great Plains, the barrier of the Rocky Mountains, and the deserts of the Great Basin were, with few exceptions, devoid of settlement, and made communication with the established power centers of the East extremely difficult. A different barrier divided the country North from South, where the institution of slavery, with all its moral, social, political, industrial, and agricultural implications, was polarizing the nation.

Stimulated by the Mexican War, the Corps of Topographical Engineers had surveyed much of what came to be known as the Southern Route, from Vicksburg on the Mississippi, crossing Texas to El Paso, running just north of the new border with Mexico, and terminating at the practically nonexistent town of San Diego on the Pacific Ocean. Documented by these fairly advanced surveys and advocated by the Corps of Topographical Engineers and by Secretary of War Jefferson Davis, the Southern Route was the first great claimant for the transcontinental railroad. Thus challenged, Northerners then offered modified versions of Asa Whitney's Northern Route, as well as one aligned with the Oregon Trail over South Pass. Yet another major contender was proposed to cross the western half of the continent at about the thirty-fifth parallel and pass through Albuquerque and Zuñi, New Mexico, finally reaching the Pacific Ocean at Los Angeles. Then there was Senator Thomas Hart Benton's "Central Route to the Pacific," which was to be laid out between St. Louis and San Francisco in the vicinity of the thirty-eighth parallel. This debate could never lead to a resolution, and ultimately Congress handed the issue to the Corps of Topographical Engineers, which was supposed to provide dispassionate scientific evidence by which the choice of a route could be justified.

Benton and his son-in-law, the explorer John Charles Frémont, were natural participants in the discussion. As a member of the Army Corps of Topographical Engineers until his 1848 resignation following his third expedition to the West, Frémont's work for the government had been broadly focused and presumably disinterested geographical and scientific research. He had become known as The Pathfinder for his mapping and detailed descriptions of overland routes, although this was but a fraction of his larger duties and accomplishments. Now the purpose of his exploring activities became narrow advocacy. The questions that intrigued Thomas Jefferson and led to Lewis and Clark's journey—of the habitability of the West and of its general features—were being answered by formal explorations and by the experiences of a rising onslaught of settlers. Although several lines of travel between the Mississippi Valley and the Pacific Ocean were in use by Americans, none of them were easy of passage, nor were any of them at all secure. Senator Benton now proposed that a paved national road to the Pacific, paralleled by a railroad where feasible, be built at government expense. It was to be used freely in commerce and travel by all citizens, with only a small transit fee imposed on foreign merchants.

Benton and the country soon lost sight of the macadamized "road" aspect of this proposal, and his emphasis came to rest upon an unbroken railroad line from San Francisco eastward, where it could connect at the Mississippi River with existing water- and land-based transportation systems. The discussion of where to construct the western half of a transcontinental rail line could not help but mirror the irreconcilable regional interests and conflicting views of American society at the time, which were building towards the Civil War. Senator Benton's position on slavery was clear: It should not be extended to any territory or state where it did not now exist. Equally clear was his notion of where the eastern terminus of the railroad to the Pacific should be: St. Louis, where its commercial benefits would be secured for his home state. This narrow sectional interest coincided in Benton's mind with the idealism of his anti-slavery position. Even though Missouri was a slave state, by promoting its interests he could deny the railroad's economic and strategic advantages to some of the older and much more developed members of the Old South and prevent the spread of slavery west. That a yet more northerly railroad would entirely deny its benefits to the slave states must have been obvious to Benton, but his immensely egotistical personality and the interests of his constituents would not allow him to admit as much, at least in public.

Thus Benton's Central Route to the Pacific joined the fray, contending with both more northerly and more southerly lines for which cogent arguments had already been advanced. The Central Route really didn't exist except in Benton's enthusiastic imagination and that of some of his supporters, but he had a good idea of where it ought to be (which was on a nearly straight line from St. Louis to San Francisco), maintained that it was entirely feasible, and knew that his son-in-law was just the man to prove it. Ironically, on February 7, 1849, while Benton was proposing a bill on the matter of the railroad to the Senate, Frémont on his fourth expedition had grievously failed to prove it, barely escaping from a winter catastrophe in the San Juan Mountains of Colorado.

### THE CENTRAL ROUTE EATS ITS OWN

In 1848, with the aid of Senator Benton and some Missouri businessmen who were also interested in bringing the railroad to St. Louis, Frémont privately organized his fourth expedition. It was a winter reconnaissance, the purpose of which was to demonstrate the practicability of Benton's Central Route. Without the cachet of official sponsorship, and in light of the fierce disputes forming around the railroad issue, Frémont may have felt more acutely than ever the need for authoritative documentation, particularly of the topography and of the meteorological conditions encountered along the route the expedition would take. Considering the limited resources available to him, he took the unusual step of bringing along with his small company a scientific corps that included three expeditionary artist-topographers. Charles Preuss, a veteran of Frémont's first and second expeditions, was there, as was Edward Kern from the third. In addition there was Edward's older brother, Richard, as skilled and intelligent an artist as Edward, but who had never been west. Frémont also recruited a third Kern brother, Benjamin, less of an artist but both a scientist and a physician, and finally rounded out his corps of scientists with the German botanist Frederick Creutzfeldt.

After crossing the Great Plains, Frémont's party ascended the Arkansas River to the settlement of Hardscrabble, where he hired as his guide Old Bill Williams, a well-known mountain man. Despite severe weather the expedition succeeded in negotiating Mosca Pass through the Sangre de Cristo Mountains and arrived in the San Luis Valley, where the snows deepened day by day. Beyond a rapid reconnaissance of nearby Medano Pass, the expedition yielded nothing further of value. It was unable to leave the San Luis Valley and cross the Continental Divide, for on the high frozen ridges of La Garita, trapped by storm after storm, they could go neither forward nor backward. All the mules perished from cold, the baggage was lost, ten of Frémont's men died of starvation and exposure, and one of them was eaten by some of his companions. The argument over who was responsible for missing Cochetopa Pass on the Continental Divide and then leading the expedition to its doom in the San Juan Mountains—Frémont, or his guide Old Bill Williams—will likely never be resolved (Richmond, 1990).

The Kern brothers, Edward, Richard, and Benjamin, survived this catastrophe, but just barely. Frémont dispersed his men into companies, some of which managed to reach settlements in New Mexico and send back help. The Kerns were resigning themselves to death when Alexis Godey, a mountain man from Taos, rescued them. The brothers went first to Questa and then to Taos to recuperate. There they were abandoned and left penniless by Frémont, who along with many of the other survivors continued on to California by the southern Gila route. Adding to their wretchedness, Benjamin Kern and Old Bill Williams (who had become their good friend while acting as guide for the expedition) were soon after killed by Ute Indians when the two attempted to recover some of the expedition's abandoned equipment. Richard and Edward were thus left destitute and disheartened in New Mexico early in 1849.

Despite this inauspicious start, the Kern brothers possessed active intellects that soon led them to find some compensation for their misfortunes and their resulting forced residency in New Mexico. There were unfamiliar cultures, vast scenic landscapes, mysterious ruins, and opportunities for employment with the occupying United States Army headquartered in Santa Fe, to which they moved in the summer of 1849. The Kerns' first employment was with Lieutenant James Hervey Simpson, with whom they formed a close friendship and in whose company they shared many adventures, including exploring and documenting the Ancestral Pueblo ruins in Chaco Canyon. Richard, perhaps under the tutelage of his brother, now acquired fine cartographic skills and traveled widely with the Army to help illustrate and map the newly conquered territory. Richard's time in New Mexico culminated in 1851 with the publication of the monumental "Map of the Territory of New Mexico," also known as the Parke-Kern Map, a huge compilation he made with Lieutenant John Grubb Parke of practically everything that was known about the region at the time. In the summer of 1851 both brothers then left Santa Fe, Edward traveling east on the Santa Fe Trail and Richard going west with Captain Lorenzo Sitgreave's exploring expedition to the Pacific. Significantly, Sitgreave employed as guide the mountain man Antoine Leroux of Taos, who had been one of the most important sources of geographical information incorporated into the Parke-Kern Map. In 1853 Leroux would conduct the Gunnison expedition (with Richard Kern as a member) from Fort Massachusetts in the San Luis Valley to the main branch of the Spanish Trail near its Green River ford. While in California Richard made contact with Frémont, and the two men patched up the angry differences that had arisen between them from the failed expedition of 1848 . From California Richard took ship to Panama, crossed the Isthmus, and finally arrived home in Philadelphia in February of 1852.

While the Kern brothers were stranded in New Mexico and isolated by distance from immediate news of the rest of the country, the debate about where to locate a transcontinental railroad continued in Washington without a break. But once Richard returned to the East, bringing his hard-won knowledge of the geography of the West, he could not help but become embroiled in that controversy. In April of 1852 he moved to Washington, D.C., where he found temporary employment working on maps and illustrations for Lorenzo Sitgreaves, who was there completing his report on the expedition from Santa Fe to San Diego. In Washington Kern discovered that his broad and authoritative knowledge of New Mexico positioned him well to comment on the vexing questions of the railroad, and thus brought him into contact with the power brokers of the Capital. In January of 1853 he responded to a request from Senator William M. Gwin of California and prepared a report for the Senate on the possible lines for a transcontinental railroad, in which he advocated the "Thirty-fifth Parallel" Route, one that would run through Albuquerque and Zuñi, New Mexico, then follow a variant of the path that Kern had taken with the Sitgreaves expedition to the Pacific Ocean. Neither Kern's detailed knowledge of western geography nor anyone else's rhetorical skills were sufficient to persuade a majority of the Senate to adopt any specific route, so the problem was passed off to the Corps of Topographical Engineers, which was supposed to provide a dispassionate, scientifically grounded solution. On March 3, 1853, the Congress passed the Army appropriation bill for 1853-54 with amendments that read:

> Sec. 10. *And be it further enacted,* That the Secretary of War be and he is hereby authorized, under the direction of the President of the United States, to employ such portion of the corps of topographical engineers, and such other persons as he may deem necessary, to make such explorations and surveys as he may deem advisable, to ascertain the most

practicable and economical route for a railroad from the Mississippi River to the Pacific Ocean, and that the sum of one hundred and fifty thousand dollars, or so much thereof as may be necessary, be and the same is hereby appropriated out of any money in the Treasury, not otherwise appropriated, to defray the expense of such explorations and surveys.

Sec. 11. *And be it further enacted,* That the engineers and other persons employed in said explorations and surveys, shall be organized in as many distinct corps as there are routes to be surveyed, and their several reports shall be laid before Congress on or before the first Monday in February eighteen hundred and fifty-four (quoted in Albright, 1921, 37-38).

The thirteen months that Congress allotted the Army to complete the explorations and submit the several reports was excruciatingly short, and Secretary of War Jefferson Davis moved immediately to begin the work. Initially he had before him proposals for four routes about which, through the energetic activities of their supporters, there seemed to be sufficient information to warrant further action. From north to south, they were the Northern, or Whitney, Route to Oregon; the Thirty-eighth Parallel or Central Route to the Pacific advocated vociferously by Benton and Frémont; the Thirty-fifth Parallel Route through Albuquerque and Zuñi, strongly supported by Kern in a letter to the Senate; and finally, the Thirty-second Parallel or Gila Route, which had been largely surveyed by the Army during the Mexican War and so did not require reexamination by an expedition dedicated to the purpose.

Kern fully expected to be assigned to the Thirty-fifth Parallel exploration, and made informal preliminary arrangements to that effect with its commander, Lieutenant Amiel Weeks Whipple. Secretary Davis, however, had other ideas, and assigned Kern to the examination of the Thirty-eighth Parallel under the command of Captain John Williams Gunnison. None of this was to the liking of Thomas Hart Benton, who had lost his Senate seat in 1851 and was now serving a term in the House of Representatives, where he remained an outspoken advocate of the Central Route and a sharp thorn in Jefferson Davis's side. Benton wanted his son-in-law, John Charles Frémont, to command the expedition that was to explore along the Thirty-eighth Parallel, and since Frémont was at the time vacationing in France with his wife, Jessie, Benton sent a cable that called the couple home.

Jefferson Davis was not about to acquiesce in this. He naturally preferred the Army's Gila Route connecting to the slave states of the South, and his conflict-driven antipathy toward Benton precluded an appointment for Frémont to explore Benton's pet route. Nor did Davis share Benton's certitude that the Central Route was in fact practicable, and he certainly found Frémont's abolitionist views abhorrent in the extreme. Politically, however, Benton and his allies could not be ignored, and in hopes of ultimately silencing them Davis did authorize a Thirty-eighth Parallel reconnaissance, but did so on his own terms by placing it under the command of Captain Gunnison, and by assigning Richard Kern as its artist and topographer.

Davis's choice outraged Benton because Kern, far from being a neutral participant, was a firm advocate of the Thirty-fifth Parallel Route, and because Benton and Frémont both imagined that Gunnison was neither dispassionate nor entirely competent, and would therefore do an inadequate job on the survey. As a result, when Frémont returned to the country he and Benton privately organized an expedition that was to be Frémont's fifth and last, and, like the failed attempt of 1848, would attempt to traverse the Central Route in winter.

Thus there were two expeditions planning to leave in the same year and intending to traverse roughly the same Thirty-eighth Parallel Route; but Benton, ever alert to ways to promote his grand plan, arranged yet a third, one that was actually the first to take the field. Edward Fitzgerald Beale, a close friend of the Frémont's and a most resourceful adventurer, had recently been appointed Superintendent of Indian Affairs for California. Beale, who later conducted experiments in the use of camels by the Army in the deserts of the Southwest, (as first proposed by Jefferson Davis,) was an experienced traveler who in three years had crossed the continent seven times. He was now persuaded by Benton to voyage overland to his post in California along the proposed Central Route, rather than taking the more rapid and secure passage by way of steamer and the Isthmus of Panama. Beale engaged his cousin Gwinn Harris Heap as journalist and artist to the expedition, and on May 10, 1853, they left Westport, Missouri Territory, a full month and a half before Gunnison was able to get under way. In order to travel as rapidly as possible the entire party was mounted and their supplies carried on pack animals. They lost most of their stores and equipment in a mishap while attempting to cross the Grand (now Gunnison) River below the mouth of the Uncompahgre River, and had to send back to Taos for replacements. Despite this impediment, they reached Los Angeles on August 22, 1853. Simultaneously, Gunnison's slower-moving party was preparing to leave Fort Massachusetts in the San Luis Valley of Colorado, and Frémont was about to organize his own effort back at Westport. Beale and Heap had accomplished the first uninterrupted crossing along Benton's Central Route from Missouri to California.

To maintain the attention of the public on the Central Route to the Pacific, Heap would periodically send written material back to Benton, who edited and transmitted it in serialized form to the newspapers. At the conclusion of the voyage Benton arranged for a book by Heap to be quickly published, *Central Route to the Pacific* (1854). It was illustrated by a map and thirteen lithographic plates, all from Heap's drawings. In company with his admirable text, the guileless immediacy of his naive illustrations served to reinforce the proposition that he and Beale had crossed the western half of the continent by a route entirely practicable for a railroad. *Central Route to the Pacific* has been reprinted by LeRoy and Anne Hafen, who supplement it with explanatory material, drawn largely from Benton's writings and speeches, that elaborates the thinking behind the Beale-Heap, Gunnison, and Frémont expeditions of 1853 (Hafen and Hafen, 1957).

### 1850-1860, A DECADE OF DILEMMA FOR EXPLORERS: SKETCHPAD VERSUS PHOTOGRAPHIC PLATE

A problem that confronted western explorers during the 1850s was to choose the medium that better represented views encountered during a traverse: supposedly precise, mechanically created photographs, or artistic drawings mediated by the human mind and hand. To judge the issue we have before us more than 100 drawings by Kern, and a similar number of photographs of the corresponding scenes.

The first practical form of photography was invented by Louis Jacques Mandé Daguerre, and first announced to the public in Paris in 1839. Called after its French inventor the *daguerreotype*, it produced high-contrast, finely detailed images on polished, silver-surfaced plates. By the early 1850s the process had become highly refined, and daguerreotype photography had become a tool of, or at least an adjunct to, exploratory and diplomatic travel. In 1850 William C. Mayhew made daguerreotypes of camp life and of the members of a survey expedition led by Lieutenant Lorenzo Sitgreaves to Indian territory (Naef and Wood, 1975, 30). In 1851 John Wesley Jones traveled from California to St. Louis making a series of daguerreotypes of the landscape. The results were used to create an immense panoramic painting of the West, the *Pantoscope*. Jones's original daguerreotypes were never exhibited, and, along with the enormous painting derived from them, are now lost (Naef and Wood, 1975, 32-33; Rudisill, 1971, 142-149; Sandweiss, 1991, 104-106; Taft, 1938, 257-258).

In 1852 Commodore Matthew C. Perry sailed for Japan, taking along the daguerreotypist Eliphalet Brown, Jr., as well as the artist William Heine. Many of the lithographs and woodcuts that grace the report of that momentous voyage are based on Brown's work, which was apparently confined almost entirely to portraiture. It was rather Heine's pencil that illustrated most of the exotic scenery the expedition encountered in the Far East (Hawks, 1856; Rudisill, 1971, 108-112).

No fewer than four American explorations departed in 1853 with plans to exploit photography. Elisha Kent Kane brought daguerreotype equipment to the Arctic, where it proved useless (Kane, 1857, 1:155, 2:46). He ultimately made the polished daguerreotype plates into a solar reflector that helped warm and illuminate his crew's cramped, icebound shelter. The artist John Mix Stanley took daguerreotypes while on another of the government-sponsored railroad expeditions, this one under Isaac I. Stevens, which explored a route to the Pacific Northwest. Stanley seems to have made only a few daguerreotypes, all of them Indian portraits, and all of them now lost. He relied instead on his artistic skills to illustrate the appearance of the lands he traversed with Stevens (Stevens, 1855, 87, 103-104; Taft, 1938, 261-262). Richard Kern's brother Edward, who worked as an artist and topographer for Frémont on both his third and fourth expeditions, now became a seafarer by accompanying Commander Cadwalader Ringgold on the North Pacific Exploring Expedition, where he acted as both artist and daguerreotypist. Edward took with him a supply of 432 blank plates that he employed with mixed success (Hine, 1982, 99-126; MS, Cron Collection, Beinecke Library, Yale University). One daguerreotype, apparently by Edward Kern, survives in the collection of the International Museum of Photography in Rochester, N.Y.

The last of the 1853 attempts at expeditionary photography was the most ambitious. Bringing an idea from his first expedition back into the field for a reprise of his failed fourth expedition, Frémont hired the Baltimore daguerreotypist Solomon Nunes Carvalho as photographer and artist, along with the Bavarian immigrant Baron Friedrich Wilhelm von Egloffstein as topographer, to accompany him on his fifth and last expedition to the West. Still an innovator, Frémont intended to make a systematic photographic document of the terrain in order to prove its practicability as a railroad route to the Pacific. This was a novel idea at the time, and the attempt was apparently quite successful up to the point where the expedition, mired in deep snows and paralyzed by freezing temperatures in the Wasatch Mountains of central Utah, had to abandon Carvalho's photographic equipment. With one member dead of exposure, the rest of the company barely managed to reach the Great Basin, where they received succor first from the Indians and then from Mormons in the new settlement of Parowan. In the face of these immense obstacles Carvalho's daguerreotypes, numbering some 200 to 300,

improbably survived. They were ultimately taken by Frémont to San Francisco, then back to New York City. Unfortunately this monumental achievement remained practically unknown because Frémont's efforts had not been sanctioned or supported by any governmental body, and because he never wrote or published a report of the expedition. Of the daguerreotypes, only one badly damaged plate survives in the Library of Congress, the rest probably having been destroyed in an 1881 fire at Morrell's "Fireproof" Warehouse in Manhattan (Shlaer, 2000).

Photography was associated with at least three explorations in the last half of the 1850s, even though their leaders were probably unaware of Frémont and Carvalho's successful innovation. In each case, however, it was the skill of artists, not of cameramen, that provided documentary illustrations. In 1857 Lieutenant Charles Christmas Ives organized an expedition from Fort Yuma, near the Gulf of California, to determine the navigability of the Colorado River by steamboat, on which Americans for the first time encountered the Grand Canyon (Ives, 1861). Lieutenant Ives had with him Heinrich Balduin Möllhausen and Friedrich Wilhelm von Egloffstein, two of the finest and most skillful artists ever to be hired for a government-sponsored expedition (Huseman, 1995), so it would be no surprise if photography and its accompanying limitations were totally ignored. Yet there was photographic equipment taken along too, and during a time of inactivity near the mouth of the Colorado River Lieutenant Ives himself gave it a try.

> *December* 14.—... The northwester of last week exhausted itself at the end of three days, and since then there has been an uninterrupted succession of the delicious weather experienced before. There being a little photographic apparatus along, I have taken advantage of the mild and quiet interval to experiment, and having constructed out of an India-rubber tarpaulin a tent that entirely excluded the light, have made repeated efforts to obtain a view of camp and the river. The attempt has not met with distinguished success. The chemicals seem to have deteriorated, and apart from this the light is so glaring, and the agitation of the atmosphere near the surface of the ground so great, that it is doubtful whether, under any circumstances, a clear and perfect picture could be secured (Ives, 31-32).

Despite uncertain chemicals and the "heat-waves" that blurred his impressions, Ives did succeed at least once, however poorly, for a lithographic illustration in his report captioned "Robinson's Landing, Mouth of Colorado River" reads at the bottom left: "J. J. Young, from a photograph by Lieut. Ives." The reference is to the artist John J. Young, who back in Washington, D.C., prepared a drawing or painting from the photograph for the use of the lithographers. Even with the elaborations that Young undoubtedly added for purposes of compositional and narrative interest, this plate comes off poorly when compared with the magnificent works of art that fill the Ives report. Apparently there were no further photographic attempts, and the equipment was soon damaged by a windstorm.

> *December* 21.—On the morning of the 18th a north-wester set in, and, with the exception of a short lull yesterday, has been raging furiously up to the present time. The river has been overspread with a thick haze, a high sea running, and the spray driven by the gale over the flats. The tents were strongly secured, particularly the observing tents, for the transit was in good adjustment, and I hoped that it would not be disturbed. For one day and night the result was doubtful, but yesterday morning a gust came that settled the business, and put an end to a very unpleasant state of suspense. One rope and tent-peg still held on, forming a fixed center, about which the tent was whirling and waving like a handkerchief, thumping against the transit stand, and undoing the labor of many a long night. The photographic tent made a clean thing of it, apparatus and all, but that was comparatively of little importance (Ives, 34).

It is unclear whether Ives was using the well-proven daguerreotype method or was experimenting with the new wet-collodion process on glass. Invented by Frederick Scott Archer in 1851, the wet-plate, as it came to be known, was by 1857 well on the way to displacing the daguerreotype entirely in photographic practice. It had a particular advantage over daguerreotypy in that instead of a one-of-a-kind positive, it produced a photographic negative from which positive images could be multiplied indefinitely by printing on sensitized paper. It is this negative-positive process, perfected for field use by Mathew Brady, his employees, and his competitors while documenting the Civil War, which was afterwards exploited successfully by those conducting the great surveys of the West. On Ives's Colorado Exploring Expedition of 1857-8, however, whether it was by daguerreotype or by wet-plate, photography could not begin to compete with the work of his two artists.

Lieutenant Ives made clear his opinion of photography by mostly neglecting it. Captain James H. Simpson (the Kern brothers' old friend from Santa Fe) explored the Great Basin in 1859, where he gave photography full consideration yet found it wanting:

> To Mr. Von Beckh I am indebted for the original sketches of scenery, and to Mr. John J. Young, of this city, for the very handsome manner in which they have been elaborated and perfected in the office for my report. I carried out with me a photographic apparatus, carefully supplied with the necessary chemicals by Mr. E. Anthony, of New York, and a couple of gentlemen accompanied me as photographers; but although they took a large number of views, some of which have been the originals from which a few accompanying my journals have been derived, yet, as a general thing, the project proved a failure. Indeed, I am informed that in several of the Government expeditions a photographic apparatus has been an accompaniment, and that in every instance, and even with operators of undoubted skill, the enterprise has been attended with failure. The cause lies in some degree in the difficulty, in the field, at short notice, of having the preparations perfect enough to insure good pictures, but chiefly in the fact that the camera is not adapted to distant scenery. For objects very close at hand, which of course correspondingly contracts the field of vision, and for single portraits of persons and small groups, it does very well; but as, on exploring expeditions, the chief *desideratum* is to daguerreotype extensive mountain-chains and other notable objects having considerable extent, the camera has to be correspondingly distant to take in the whole field, and the consequence is a want of sharpness of outline, and in many instances, on account of the focal distance not being the same for every object within the field of view, a blurred effect, as well as distortion of parts. In my judgment, the camera is not adapted to explorations in the field, and a good artist, who can sketch readily and accurately, is much to be preferred (Simpson, 1876, 8-9).

It is probable that in 1859 Simpson's photographers (whom he does not name) were using the new wet-plate process, the term "to daguerreotype" notwithstanding, for the word had become a generic term for photography—just as today "to film" reflects a process that is more often purely electronic rather than photochemical. Simpson's report demonstrates his extraordinary interest in and command of the history of exploration in the region, reproducing long extracts from the journal his friend Edward Kern kept on Frémont's third expedition. He also included summaries and excerpts from the diaries of Fathers Francisco Atanacio Dominguez and Francisco Sylvestre Velez de Escalante (translated from the Spanish by Philip Harry of the Topographical Engineers), and a map by the friars' cartographer, Don Bernardo Miera y Pacheco. In 1776 these adventurous Spaniards had attempted to reach California from New Mexico, an effort that, with its detailed descriptions of the terrain and accompanying map, receives Simpson's highest accolades.

Simpson's report was not published until 1876, and although it contains scientific illustrations there are no scenic views by either the artist von Beckh or the unnamed photographers, even though paintings by J. J. Young from von Beckh's sketches are in the National Archives. Because more than 25 years had elapsed since the exploration itself, time in which photography had secured its place as the preferred means of illustration, the contents of these "pictorial sketches" may not have been considered important enough to warrant the expense of including engravings or lithographs.

While Simpson's opinion of the relative virtues of artists versus photographers in western explorations may have been the one generally held at the time, it was not quite the last word of the decade. In 1859 and 1860 Colonel Frederick West Lander surveyed a new road from Fort Kearny to Honey Lake in California. Lander was joined for part of the way by a group of artists and photographers who were not in his employ. The most notable among them was Albert Bierstadt, who both photographed and sketched extensively on this, his first trip to the Rocky Mountains. Bierstadt was soon to make his reputation and his fortune as a painter of monumental scenes of the West, some of the material for which he collected on his travels of 1859. The photographs that so positively impressed Colonel Lander were apparently all of nearby subjects, not distant landscapes.

> A. Bierstadt, esq., a distinguished artist of New York, and S. F. Frost, of Boston, accompanied the expedition with a full corps of artists, bearing their own expenses. They have taken sketches of the most remarkable of the views along the route, and a set of stereoscopic views of emigrant trains, Indians, camp scenes, &c., which are highly valuable and would be interesting to the country. I have no authority by

> which they can be purchased or made a portion of this report (Lander, 1861, 5).

Chapter 4 of *Albert Bierstadt* by Gordon Hendricks (1988) contains reproductions of some of Bierstadt's work from his 1859 excursion.

### THE ALBUM

I was not the first to notice the drawings in the Newberry Library and question their attribution to Egloffstein. That honor perhaps belongs to David H. Miller, then of Cameron University in Oklahoma. William H. Goetzmann must have at least seen the sketches, for he reproduced without comment three of them, one at the beginning of each of three parts of his *Army Exploration in the American West, 1803-1863* (1959). On page 1 is "Arkansas Plains," on page 63 "Bents Fort." page 339 displays "Uniontown, Kaw River." Their use is decorative, not illustrative, and for this purpose they appear to have been redrawn; it is probable that neither their origin nor their significance was entirely understood. Goetzmann makes direct reference to the Newberry album in his later book, *Exploration and Empire* (1966). Its short final chapter, titled "A Note on the Sources" (649-656) was included to call additional material to the attention of "scholars and interested readers who wish to proceed beyond the beginning that I have made." Entry 24 is "Newberry Library; F. W. von Egloffstein Drawings." Goetzmann does not appear to have treated the material or put the drawings to any use, but he did note their existence, and placed that information before his readers.

I first attributed the Newberry drawings to Richard Kern on the basis of their style, and because the handwriting on most of them appears to be his. Evidence in support of this opinion is readily found in the printed Gunnison-Beckwith *Report* of 1855: Bound within it are thirteen colored lithographic illustrations. Each of twelve of these lithographs corresponds in a quite obvious way to a particular composition found within the Newberry album, and often bears a similar caption. In the lower left-hand corner of these lithographs is usually the attribution "J. M. Stanley from a sketch by R. H. Kern." That would be the artist John Mix Stanley, whose contribution to the Gunnison-Beckwith *Report* was to take Kern's field sketches and transform them into finished works of art (either in oil or in watercolor) that could be used by lithographers to create a printing plate. If Richard Kern had not been killed he would likely have performed the work himself. The next best choice would no doubt have been Edward Kern, Richard's younger brother and frequent close collaborator, whose artistic style and understanding was so similar to Richard's that it is often impossible to distinguish visually which of the two is responsible for a particular work. Unfortunately Edward was shipboard with Commander Cadwalader Ringgold's North Pacific Exploring Expedition, so Stanley became the natural third choice. A well-known artist with broad experience in the West, Stanley was highly skilled and possessed firsthand experience with the sorts of landscapes depicted in Kern's drawings. Stanley and the lithographers with whom he worked did a superb job of rendering the illustrations of the expedition into printable form with little distortion, although the anonymous person responsible for the captions accompanyingthe lithographs will not always be found deserving of the same accolades.

The caveat frequently met with in this context—that the copyist and/or the lithographer distorted the artist's intention—is here without merit. The lithographs are all reasonably precise transcriptions of Kern's originals, despite being embellished in accordance with nineteenth-century taste by the introduction of figures, foliage, and foregrounds that add human interest to the scenes; the only objection to this practice is that it can unknowingly distort a viewer's sense of scale. Stanley was expert at detailing small human and animal figures in the foregrounds of his oil paintings; when he does so they are exquisitely rendered, appropriately sized, and of a quality well beyond what can be accommodated by the relatively coarse lithographic process. Because he had not directly observed the subject matter at hand, it is hardly surprising that Stanley's additions sometimes fit awkwardly into the actual landscape. Occasionally he has altered foliage or added figures in ways that might change the interpretation of place or subject, while leaving the actual landscape details unaltered.

An additional source of variation arises because the House of Representatives and the Senate ordered the printing of more than 20,500 copies of the railroad *Reports*, so the lithographs were reproduced in huge numbers. Multiple firms were engaged to work on the images, and the unprecedented numbers required meant that either several lithographic stones were prepared to print the same image, or stones had to be reworked to allow further use. As a result, in some samples the foreground figures may change and the inscription acknowledging the artistic source may read differently or even be absent. But where they are present, all the published examples agree in attributing them to Richard Kern. We cannot be absolutely certain that we have here the actual material that was placed in Stanley's hands; but if not, these sketches might be earlier versions of the compositions provided to Stanley, or, even more unlikely, both the lithographs and the drawings might be derived from a common but as yet unknown source.

Disappointingly, the Newberry Library has no information on the provenance of Ayer MS 794a. Why the material disappeared from Washington, who assembled it into an album, where it had been before it reappeared in the hands of a Chicago collector, all are total mysteries. It can be judged only by its present state, and its history must be inferred entirely from its contents and appearance. The album consists of the title page on its inside front cover, and 87 bound pages that for reference were all numbered sequentially in pencil by the staff of the Newberry. The first page holds the letter from Beckwith to Schumann. With the exception of five that are empty, each of the remaining pages has adhered to it one or more pieces of paper on which are found the sketches. Next to each piece of tipped-in paper is a lightly penciled number starting with "1" on page 2 (the letter on the first page is not a drawing and was left without an adjacent number), and, because there is often more than one piece of attached paper per page, ending at "122" on page 87. I have compared the numbers on the album pages next to each of the sheets with some samples of numbers in the hand of John Mix Stanley (*Papers*, Smithsonian Archives of American Art). He is the one person who certainly had the drawings in his possession and who might have been somehow responsible for the creation of the album, but the handwritings simply do not match. Unlike the reference numbering on the pages, these lightly penciled numbers are not recent additions, because two of them correspond to vacant places that once held sketches. Page 18 is empty, but the number by the sketch on page 17 is 21, while that on album page 19 is 22; the sequence is unbroken, so page 18 probably never held anything. Page 78 has lightly written on it the number 109, and page 82 has the number 115. Both pages are now empty, but the numbers they display are in the correct sequence relative to those that precede and follow them; each presumably held a single sheet of paper. Pages 83 and 84 are empty and blank, but the next drawing on page 85 again takes up the sequence correctly from page 82 with 116, so it appears that neither of these two pages ever had anything affixed to them, either. I conclude that two sketches once present, and given the numbers 109 and 115, are now absent from the album.

Most of the sketches are on pieces of a thin, translucent paper resembling modern tracing paper, and drawn in pencil. They are not at all uniform in size, and have been cut into quadrilateral shapes that usually approximate a rectangle but sometimes are quite irregular. A fairly typical piece, adhered to page 2, measures approximately 20.1 cm wide by 12.4 cm high (7.9 in. x 4.9 in.), and is titled "Peaks of the Sierra Blanca" (Plate 108). It is cut somewhat irregularly, the corners are trimmed off, and the right side is cut so close to elements of the drawing as to have barely avoided removing some of it. This thin paper upon which the majority of the sketches appear is of a yellow appearance but varies in depth of color from very pale to nearly orange, a range great enough and irregular enough to suggest that there were multiple batches of paper differing in their original tint, or multiple batches that aged differently, or individual sheets that were subjected to dissimilar environmental influences. The largest single sketch in the album is mounted on page 15 and was given the number 19 (Plate 48). It bears the title "2d Huerfano Butte—Upper Huerfano R," is 30.0 cm wide by 20.0 cm high (11.8 in. x 7.9 in.), and is a fairly clean, regular rectangle; we might at first imagine therefore that the size of Kern's sketchbook or sketchpad was about 12 in. by 8 in. Upon close examination, however, the right edge of the paper cuts off one line from Kern's pencil, so unless Kern brought his pencil to the very edge of the paper and perhaps beyond, this largest of the surviving individual thin sheets was trimmed after it was drawn upon. It is probable that the same is true for all the others, for there is no standard size; they are all to differing degrees smaller than this one example, and often somewhat irregular. It appears likely, therefore, that the sketches were cut from larger sheets in order to be placed conveniently in the album.

Glued into three of the album pages are sketches in a rather different form—panoramic views made up of multiple pieces of paper attached to one another, and arranged to fold out so as to completely, if inconveniently, display their contents. On page 7 is one that is 160.2 cm (63.1 in.) wide when folded out (Plate 82), on page 9 is another that measures 181.3 cm (71.4 in.) extended (Plate 105), and on page 11 is a third folded panorama (Plate 99) with a full length of 193.3 cm (76.1 in.). They are all made up of multiple pieces of paper end to end, all are of different sizes, and the largest of them is 55.8 cm long by 14.3 cm high (about 22 in. x 5.6 in.); so Kern's paper supply originally included pieces of a much larger size than would appear at first glance. A few sketches are on other sorts of paper, and this variation will be noted in the discussion of each where it occurs. When captioned in the text, each drawing will be accompanied by the width and height of the sheet in centimeters; these measurements will be of the larger dimension if the shape of the paper is irregular.

A vast quantity of visual matter was produced by the railroad explorations of 1853 and later brought back to Washington, used for the lithographic and engraved illustrations that accompanied the reports, and then subsequently discarded. Most of it has vanished without a trace. Once the originals from the field had been redrawn and made into printing plates, they ceased to be of enough value to the War Department to warrant an effort at maintaining their integrity. Whatever the reasons may have been for mounting and preserving Kern's sketches for Gunnison, they could hardly have survived in such numbers or in such good condition without their protective album. Someone obtained them, was able to recognize their value, and went to considerable trouble to assemble them into their present form. The letter from Beckwith that was incorporated with them and that led to the misattribution of the drawings to Egloffstein seems to be a matter of innocently preserving all the materials at hand, rather than a deliberate effort to deceive. It was able to mislead only because nowhere on any of the drawings is there a signature or other written indication of the identity of the artist. Here, as elsewhere in his surviving works, Richard Kern was disinclined to sign sketches, although he usually wrote his name on his more finished works. The style of the grandly lettered title page of the album reflects a substantial regard for its contents on the part of the unknown compiler, and the attribution of the contents to Schumann simply reflects a logical conclusion from a reading of Beckwith's letter. That letter may have come into the collection by association with the single sheet containing multiple views of Mount Shasta, presumably by Egloffstein, and the presence of these two items suggests to the more optimistically inclined that hiding somewhere there yet may be an album of original sketches by Friedrich W. von Egloffstein, perhaps containing a letter from Captain Beckwith to John Mix Stanley praising his work in preparing them for publication. The Newberry Library does not have this hypothetical assemblage, but as a result of the title page and the Beckwith letter, Ayer MS 794a was initially cataloged as: "Schuman. The Far West Drawings from Sketches by F. W. Egglestein." It was this understandable mistake that initially led me to the collection.

### THE ARRANGEMENT OF AYER MS 794A AND ITS RELATION TO THE *REPORT*

The order of the sketches in the album has no clear thematic, geographical, or topographic significance; there does not appear to be a unified organizing principle. For example, what is clearly the first in the sequence is a view titled "Camp No 1, June 20-53, near Westport" (Plate 4), but it is attached to page 20, and the number penciled in next to it is 23. Sketches of the same subject or related subjects are at times grouped near each other, but such juxtapositions are not extensive enough to make inferences about their meaning. Perhaps the occasional relatedness among adjacent sketches in the album arose because associated sketches, not otherwise having been put to any use, fortuitously remained in close proximity within a detached pile of papers. It may also be that the anonymous compiler, faced with a presumably disordered collection of material, was, on occasion, able to recognize and respond to similar characteristics or logical affinities among a few samples, but the preservation and mounting of the sketches appears to have been the primary concern and the particulars of their organization somewhat secondary. The sequence of the sketches as they have come to us suggests that the compiler had little if any detailed knowledge of the expedition, or else chose not to reflect that knowledge in mounting the drawings. It would therefore be a hindrance to treat the sketches in the order found within the album, for our subject is not the album *per se*, but the drawings it contains. I have instead arranged them, as best as I can determine, in geographical and therefore temporal sequence from east to west along the path of the expedition. Their placement corresponds to the order of the main text of the Gunnison-Beckwith *Report*, forming a day-to-day narrative of the progress of the expedition, the terrain it encountered, the conditions under which its men labored, and the sights they saw.

The format and style of exposition in the *Report* is very much modeled after the approach pioneered by John Charles Frémont in the narratives of his first two expeditions over the Oregon Trail, a style that was generally embraced by the many authors of the railroad reports and that became its standard in practice. In the introduction to his account Beckwith explains to Secretary of War Davis why he adopted the narrative method of presentation:

INTRODUCTORY LETTER.

Washington, D. C. *November* 25, 1854.

Sir: In submitting to the department the accompanying report of the explorations for a Pacific railroad, conducted, up to the time of his death, (at the hands of the Indians,) by the late Captain J. W. Gunnison, Topographical Engineers, it is proper that I shall state that I have preferred the journal form in which to embody the labors of the party and the minute and general descriptions of the country, required by the specific object of the survey, as affording greater facilities for introducing the observations and conclusions of Captain Gunnison, in his own language, than could have been secured in any other form. I have intentionally adhered to details and repetitions, however monotonous, by which alone a faithful description of this great interior country can be presented; for, monotonous as it is in itself, and far removed from general fertility, no general description not made up of facts, constantly repeated can convey a true picture of the country explored—an object deemed of the first importance in this report, in which I have endeavored to exhaust the material obtained for it, for which too much credit cannot be given to Captain Gunnison...

I am, sir, most respectfully, your obedient servant,
E. G. Beckwith
*First Lieutenant 3d Artillery.*

Hon. Jefferson Davis
*Secretary of War*
(G-B, 3)

Beckwith is a bit too modest in describing his own contributions. He defends his narrative form as the best method of presenting Gunnison's thoughts and words, but little of those thoughts occur in the text of the *Report*. Perhaps unsure of his authority to describe topographical matters and concerned that he would be challenged on some points because he was not a topographic engineer, Beckwith may have thought to deflect such objections by presenting himself as a subordinate offering tribute to his fallen superior officer, whom he humbly acknowledged as the major source of the work. Gunnison is quoted on occasion, and sometimes sections of his diaries are reproduced, almost always with a careful attribution; but Gunnison's notes from the trip have not survived, while Beckwith's have, and they are now in the Huntington Library. A comparison of Beckwith's diary with the text of the *Report* quickly establishes that the major voice in the body of its text is Beckwith's, not Gunnison's. Except for the few places where Gunnison is explicitly referenced and quoted, we are reading the mildly edited words of Lieutenant Beckwith, not "the observations and conclusions of captain Gunnison, in his own language."

Beckwith's narrative is an astonishing document, and because he did not presume to judge what information might or might not ultimately come to be of use, that "monotonous" presentation is one of thoroughgoing completeness: Nothing has been left out. This concentrated but relatively unselective attention to detail reflects Beckwith's belief that he was not particularly qualified for the task that fell to him. The beginning of the *Report* is again addressed to Secretary Davis and expresses a pained surprise at the duties that, against all expectations, he had been forced to assume:

Sir: In order that you may be put in possession, at as early a day as practicable, of the result of the investigations of the exploring party organized under your order of the 20th of May, 1853, by the lamented

> Captain J. W. Gunnison, of the corps of Topographical Engineers, who was barbarously massacred by the Pah Utah Indians, on the 26th of October, on the Sevier river, and near the lake of that name, in the Territory of Utah, while in the performance of the duty assigned to him, I deem it my duty, as his assistant, to report the same—a duty upon which I enter with unusual diffidence; the more so as it is not contemplated, by the instructions referred to, that this duty should devolve upon me. There being with the party, however, no other person upon whom it can be devolved, and the importance of its being submitted within a specified time, seems to render this report necessary... (G-B, 9).

In company with the narrative text of the Gunnison-Beckwith *Report* of 1855, the progress and positions of the expedition are established by its exquisitely detailed maps, prepared by Friedrich Egloffstein from Richard Kern's notes, and published later in Volume XI of the *Reports of Explorations and Surveys...* (1855-1861). This cartographic triumph displays the topography of the regions traversed and the names of geographic features, while threading among those plains, mountains, and valleys is a dotted line of the expedition's path, marked out continuously from start to finish. On that line is noted the position of every camp, each one identified by the date of arrival and of departure. It would be possible to number the camps by starting the count at Westport and moving west, but that task is rendered unnecessary by the table of observations incorporated into Chapter IX of the *Report*: "Barometric and Meteorological Observations and Table of Altitudes and Distances for the Profile of the line of survey from Westport to Great Salt Lake City" (G-B, 94-107). It is filled with daily information about the terrain and weather conditions encountered, and from Camp 18 onward juxtaposes the dates and camp numbers for easy reference.

Utah historian Robert Kent Fielding exploited these published maps and tables to locate all of the Gunnison campsites in Utah (Fielding, 1994). This text includes detailed instructions on how to best approach each site, and since I revisited most of these places I can attest to both the accuracy and the utility of Fielding's account. He also discovered that Lieutenant Beckwith's diary from the expedition was still in the possession of his family, and arranged for it to be deposited in the Huntington Library. Gunnison's diaries no longer exist, but by comparing Beckwith's *Journal* to the portion of the Gunnison-Beckwith *Report* dealing with the time the expedition was in Utah, Fielding demonstrated that the printed version is in the main a transcription of Beckwith's own field notes, with occasional modifications, additions, and deletions. I have drawn the same conclusion from my own (admittedly incomplete) comparison of Beckwith's *Journal* with the printed text of the portion of the *Report* that describes the expedition's traverse of Kansas and Colorado. The exact contribution from Captain Gunnison "in his own language" is small in proportion to the whole; the largest segment occurs where the expedition was divided in two in eastern Kansas, for which two separate but parallel accounts covering the same time interval, one by Gunnison and one by Beckwith, were published. Later on Captain Gunnison occasionally left the main body of the expedition to make short forays, and on those occasions Beckwith's text typically includes isolated quotes from Gunnison's notes, yet the main account remains substantially in Beckwith's words. As commentary on the terrain the expedition traversed, and which is depicted by Kern in his drawings, the printed text of the Gunnison-Beckwith *Report* can be relied upon, with few exceptions, to be entirely satisfactory. Some letters from Captain Gunnison regarding the expedition are in the Huntington Library, and these will be quoted when they are relevant, as will occasional passages in Beckwith's private diary, which he did not see fit to publish.

### WHAT TO DO WITH IT?

The survival of such a trove of original sketches from a western exploration is virtually unprecedented. The artistic works created on an expedition under the direction of the War Department were the property of the United States Government, and could be used by it for any purpose. No historical or documentary importance seems to have been attached to these originals that might have resulted in their placement in an archive or other repository. This had not always been the case with government-sponsored expeditionary art, for illustrative watercolors survive in the National Archives from the Maine-Canada boundary determinations of 1841. There is a difference here, for beyond their illustrative purpose the products of that survey were primary documents used by the State Department to negotiate with Great Britain over the location of the border between Canada and the United States. The surviving Kern-Gunnison sketches do not have a diplomatic import, but are rare, fragile, and of such historical interest that despite being discarded by the War Department they deserve publication and an interpretive commentary adequate to place them in their context.

A simple question was posed by David Weber: "How accurately did Kern draw what he saw?" (Weber, 271). From the point of view of a topographic artist, accuracy of representation might be paramount, the end to which all other considerations of artistry and aesthetics must be subordinate. To evaluate Kern in this regard, all that is required is to locate the scenes that he sketched and compare them directly with the drawings. If the viewpoint is accurately positioned and the scene then properly photographed, the results can be put to the judgment of all, by juxtaposing sketch and photograph. This seems straightforward enough, but was exact representation the requirement that Gunnison made of Kern? To what extent is such a thing possible? What did Kern demand of himself? Is there more to be learned by comparing the sketches with the found scenes than simply evaluating their precision of representation?

Kern had at least two roles to fill while with the expedition; Beckwith refers to him as "topographer and artist." It was common to assign these closely related duties to one person; Charles Preuss held that dual position when traveling with John C. Frémont, as did Richard's brother Edward, who signed on to Frémont's third expedition at first simply as artist, but was trained in astronomical and cartographic techniques by Frémont while in the field. Friedrich Egloffstein was both topographer and artist for Frémont's fifth expedition, and after Kern's death was engaged to perform the same duties with the remnant of Gunnison's expedition under Lieutenant Beckwith. He later served in both capacities while with the Ives expedition that explored the lower Colorado River and the Grand Canyon in 1857-58, although Heinrich Balduin Möllhausen was its primary artist.

## RECORDING NATURE IN UNFAMILIAR, DISTANT CLIMES

The great Prussian naturalist Baron Alexander von Humboldt held that the truth in nature is best communicated by a judicious amalgam of literal accuracy and poetic expression, whether by verbal or pictorial means. Man's place in nature and his innate response to its sublime beauty demand that an observer not be passive and detached. To succeed fully, a description must convey both the literal truth and the ardent passions aroused by the proximity of that truth.

> Ought any means to be left unemployed, by which an animated picture of a distant zone, untraversed by ourselves, may be presented to the mind with all the vividness of truth, enabling us even to enjoy some portion of the pleasure derived from the immediate contact with nature? The Arabs express themselves no less truly than metaphorically, when they say that the best description is that by which the ear is converted into an eye...

> Descriptions of nature, I would again observe may be defined with sufficient sharpness and scientific accuracy, without on that account being deprived of the vivifying breath of imagination. The poetic element must emanate from the intuitive perception of the connection between the sensuous and the intellectual, and of the universality and reciprocal limitation of all the vital forces of nature (Humboldt, *Cosmos*, 1849, 2:437-438).

Such sentiments are profoundly Romantic, and suited the age of western exploration in America perfectly. What was literal accuracy to Richard Kern? A tool for map-making, but otherwise perhaps literalism was not by itself the best means to convey the splendor and the terror evoked by a sublime and unfamiliar western landscape. If we admit the pervasive nature of Humboldt's thought, perhaps a more liberal idea of what Kern set out to accomplish will free us from a rigid demand for simple accuracy and open us to a broader and much more generous evaluation of these newly uncovered fruits of Kern's labor. In the context of Gunnison's expedition, with its nineteenth-century sensibilities, when might literal accuracy be called for, and when might a more responsive and perhaps more evocative and emotionally charged representation be required? What might Gunnison have intended to convey to a reader by the included illustrations? It appears that while in the field, and for reasons about which we can only speculate, particular views were taken down more carefully than others, with finer detail and enhanced nuance, and these often were turned into lithographic illustrations complementing the final published account. Otherwise we may suppose that Kern chose to draw some views more fully than others, and the higher quality of these sketches led to their being ultimately chosen for publication. Either way, a subset of the drawings is clearly of a superior quality, and many of those better ones were ultimately made into lithographs. Are the rest of the drawings simply rejects, or were they conceivably intended not for publication but for another more private use, perhaps as cues for the memory in writing the final account?

Attempts to retrospectively illustrate the course of western explorations began almost as soon as they became "historical" and people took an interest in them as such. Those who traveled the Oregon or the Santa Fe Trail after they fell into disuse, and who then wrote about the adventure, might, if so inclined, accompany their efforts with artistic or photographic illustrations that added immensely to the sense of the escapade. Humboldt maintained that such pictures gave a sense of immediacy to the narrative without requiring the descriptive gifts of a literary genius. On occasion serious artists seeking adventure have tried their hand at it as well; an especially fine example of this is Briggs and Hurley (1976) on the route of the Dominguez-Escalante expedition of 1776. Lately such records have been more often photographic, for landscape photographers seem particularly vulnerable to the Siren songs of long-ago travelers, whether or not the original trip was illustrated.

More closely related to the present work are attempts to replicate (more than a hundred years after their creation) some particularly fine landscape photographs of the West, with an eye to the changes wrought upon the subjects by an intervening century. The exemplar of this form is *Second View* by Mark Klett and four of his associates (Klett et al., 1984). Klett has even reprised the project in a second book, *Third View* (2004). I believe that *Second View* was the inspiration for and provided the impetus to a rising wave of such rephotographic activity, the results of which can be found on the shelves devoted to photography in libraries and bookstores. *Second View* was also the immediate stimulus for my own *Sights Once Seen* (Shlaer, 2000), in which I attempted to re-create Solomon Nunes Carvalho's now-lost landscape daguerreotypes from Frémont's fifth expedition of 1853-54. The core of the effort was to discover and daguerreotype nineteen scenes represented in steel engravings that were originally intended for publication in a book on the expedition, one that Frémont ultimately never wrote. The daguerreotypes and the engraved plates are lost, but the compositions survive in a unique proof set in the Bancroft Library (Benton-Frémont, 1886[?]), and most were published in a prospectus for and/or in the first volume of Frémont's *Memoirs of My Life* (1886). It was possible to demonstrate that these illustrations are based on the missing daguerreotypes, and such was the quality of the work that all of the scenes were ultimately located.

Much less common are attempts to re-create photographically scenes that were the original sources for work by artists who wielded the brush and the pencil. I know of only three. In *Retracing Major Stephen H. Long's 1820 Expedition* (1995), George J. Goodman and Cheryl A. Lawson followed the route of Long's exploration, the first of its kind in the West to include artists in its entourage. In order to document precisely where the expedition had been and demonstrate their argument to readers, the authors located and photographed the scenes taken down for Major Long by the Philadelphia artist Samuel Seymour. Goodman and Lawson were interested in the botanical observations made by members of Long's expedition, and in the changes that might have occurred in local flora over the intervening years. Their reconstruction of the expedition for this purpose is nothing short of marvelous. Granted that their method was to use pictures as a tool and not to create a photographic work of art, the just-adequate quality of printing in their book remains unsatisfying.

A recent study that *is* primarily about landscape art in the nineteenth- century West is Ben Huseman's *Wild River, Timeless Canyons: Balduin Möllhausen's Watercolors of the Colorado* (1995). Möllhausen was a protégé of Alexander von Humboldt, and in 1988 the Amon Carter acquired an album of Möllhausen's watercolors, titled "Original Sketches for the United States Survey of the Territories."

> Inside the volume were forty-six watercolors each measuring approximately 8-1/2 x 11 inches, signed "Möllhausen," and tipped onto a folio-size blank sheet of paperboard, with the title of each painting penciled below. The pictures included a depiction of a steamboat, topographical landscapes along a river, views of deserts, mountains, and canyons, studies of trees, and an intriguing view of a group of natives along a riverbank. The watercolors were signed by Heinrich Balduin Möllhausen (1825-1905), a Prussian adventurer, traveler, writer, artist, and naturalist who made three lengthy trips to the United States in the 1850s...
>
> The subjects of these watercolors clearly relate to Möllenhausen's third and last American trip, in 1857-58, when he accompanied Lieutenant Joseph C. Ives' expedition to determine the navigability of the western Colorado River (Huseman, 9).

The circumstances of discovery and the nature of the material immediately bring to mind the mysterious Newberry album, but with one distinct difference: The Möllhausen volume contains not simple drawings but finished paintings in watercolor that were probably completed anywhere from months to years after making the field sketches on which they must be based. Unlike Richard Kern's, Möllhausen's life did not end on the Ives expedition; he returned to Germany, and using his experiences in the American West forged a successful career as a writer. He also created and sold multitudes of paintings based on material from his adventures in the United States and its western territories. Huseman focuses primarily on Möllhausen's development and skill as a landscape artist, and includes an enormous amount of supplementary visual material that enables a broad discussion extending well beyond the initial set of forty-six watercolors. The book also contains a trove of useful information on Friedrich von Egloffstein, who was on the Ives expedition too. In the course of his researches Huseman had occasion to follow Ives, Möllhausen, and Egloffstein over part of their route, one that took them up the lower Colorado River, across Arizona south of the Grand Canyon, down to the canyon's floor and out again, then finally eastward into New Mexico. In the process Huseman located many scenes depicted by Möllhausen and took photographs of them, sometimes from the exact same vantage point, and sometimes, of necessity, from only as near as was possible. The result is astonishingly gratifying to my eye, but the photographs are treated as lesser objects in the book, where they are not reproduced on a sufficiently large scale or printed with a tonal range that would allow them to be fully appreciated in comparison with Möllhausen's gorgeous pictures. The visual material consists of reproductions of watercolors completed by Möllhausen in Germany after he concluded his travels in the West, and of illustrations by Möllhausen and Egloffstein that accompany the Ives report for which the originals are now lost. Leaving aside simple precision of representation (which appears for the most part to be very good), a comparison of Huseman's photographs with the drawings, engravings, and watercolors reveals Möllhausen as a mature artist who created sharply evocative and fully recognizable depictions of the unfamiliar landscapes he encountered while traveling with Lieutenant Ives.

The only other systematic attempt of which I am aware that photographically compares landscape views with artistic representations of them involves the work of a twentieth-century painter who clearly took inspiration from the western landscape, who has received far wider recognition than is ever likely to be accorded Samuel Seymour, Balduin Möllhausen, Friedrich von Egloffstein, or Richard Kern, and of whom the most intimate biographical details, artistic and personal, continue to fascinate authors, historians and critics: Georgia O'Keeffe. Traditionally held to have worked within a convention of modernism and abstraction, O'Keeffe lived her later life in northern New Mexico and used the stark landscape forms of the region as a starting point for many of her paintings. The places where she worked are now regarded with something akin to spiritual reverence by her many admirers, so it is only natural that the extent to which the origins and content of certain of her paintings depended upon her surroundings would become a topic of study and discussion. It was inevitable that a critical examination of the relationship of O'Keeffe's paintings to the literal forms she saw around her in New Mexico would be undertaken, and Barbara Buhler

Lynes, former curator of the Georgia O'Keeffe Museum in Santa Fe, has done just that (Lynes et al., 2004).

> When I first visited Ghost Ranch ... I immediately recognized some of the sites that had inspired paintings O'Keeffe made there more than seventy years ago, and I became aware of the varying degrees to which the forms in these paintings refer with seeming realism to the sites' contours, proportions, and colors.
>
> Moreover, when I explored these sites, walking in and around them, I found I could pinpoint where O'Keeffe had positioned herself to achieve the configurations in several of her paintings. These observations made me want to explore further the degree to which she re-created the forms in her New Mexico landscapes exactly as she saw them; in other words, the degree to which the forms in her drawings and paintings of these subjects were specific to the sites that informed them... Certainly, at first glance these works appear to be site-specific—and thus far removed in concept from the landscape-derived abstractions of her early career...I wondered if these works were truly site-specific, and if so, how this realization might affect my perception of the larger body of O'Keeffe's work, which I perceived as having strong abstract underpinnings (Lynes et al., 12).

What more could be desired of a landscape illustration than that its subject be immediately recognized by a perceptive visitor to the place where it was painted or drawn, and that the emotional and aesthetic response to the illustration be on a par with that experienced by viewing the scene itself? Could Baron von Humboldt have asked for more? Lynes was compelled by the immediacy of her responses to frame the description of her discovery in the first person, and place herself directly in the landscape to which she responded. A Romantic sensibility has broken through the facade of modernism, as the author wonders if she will ever again be able to regard O'Keeffe's paintings with a less visceral and more intellectual appreciation of their abstract qualities.

Lynes ultimately commissioned professional photographers to document the sites she located and mounted the results of some of their efforts side-by-side with the corresponding paintings as an exhibition at the Georgia O'Keeffe Museum in Santa Fe in 2004. An illustrated catalog of the exhibition accompanies her essay and makes this remarkable presentation generally available (Lynes et al., 2004). In it she finally responds to her disquiet by reaffirming her personal sense of the overriding strength of abstracting qualities in O'Keeffe's landscapes:

> In almost all of her landscape paintings of the 1930s and 1940s, O'Keeffe's reliance on contour as a descriptive device permits her to present specific, recognizable landscape configurations as sharply focused, fixed entities. This infuses her work with a sense of precision that, regardless of her inventions, gives it a quality of verisimilitude. It is not surprising then that others have noted this and, in analyzing the phenomenon, have suggested that this seemingly heightened "realism" represents a development distinctive to her landscape paintings of these decades.
>
> Yet these works are the opposite of verisimilitude. Paintings that may appear at first to adhere faithfully to their subjects are, in fact, highly subjective explorations that are as dependent on the manipulation of color and shape as they are on the forms that inspired them. And in spite of the fact that almost all of these paintings depict certain components of specific sites with amazing accuracy, they as consistently use the sites as a framework for exploring various formal devices with which O'Keeffe had experimented for years. In so doing, she selectively manipulated the forms she saw in New Mexico landscapes to achieve some of the most inventive and imaginative works of her career. In what follows, I compare a number of paintings to the site photographs in order to demonstrate that, in spite of their apparent specificity, O'Keeffe's New Mexico landscapes reveal her lifelong commitment to abstraction (Lynes et al., 13).

Lynes comes to O'Keeffe with a history of understanding and appreciation that, as she admits, colored her reactions, and she ultimately affirms her perception of O'Keeffe as strongly leaning towards abstraction in these landscape paintings. My own response to the exhibition and book was quite opposite, and of course reflects my own history, experience, and predilections. I saw O'Keeffe capturing and enhancing a "sense of place" in the most wondrous manner. Rather than regarding her alterations of the landscape as a form of abstraction, I saw her transformations and omissions as distilling out and emphasizing the pure form of the view, heightening its impact and defining more surely its essential components—a form of editing, refining, simplifying, and strengthening, if you will. The effect was in every case intensified when I compared each painting with the literal documentary photograph that accompanied it. My first impression on viewing these pairs was, like that of Lynes, astonishment at the extent to which painting and photograph could be matched with seeming precision. That soon gave way to a certain sense of dismay, for the different photographers Lynes employed seem to have varied in their dedication to carefully positioning their cameras, framing their subjects, and using their skills to evoke the spirit of the terrain as it appears in the paintings. There did not always appear to be a marked concern for the lighting conditions that would best emulate O'Keeffe's rendition, probably because waiting for the right light, or returning at a more promising moment, is time consuming and often frustrating for a photographer. After so many years there may have been extenuating circumstances, invisible in the picture, to make compromises necessary, but if so these have been passed over without comment. What is made obvious by this comparison is that often O'Keefe so precisely delineated the contours, outlines, and positions of her subject that the failings of the photographs as landscape documents and as works of art stand out in glaring contrast. Granted, the supposed imprecision of the living hand of the artist or a taste for anamorphic distortion may make it impossible to locate the original vantage point with perfect confidence. Nor is it always clear that a single viewpoint is represented in all of O'Keeffe's paintings, for the artist had the luxurious freedom to vary the position of her eye during creation.

Once past my astonishment at the extent to which the paintings and the photographs do correspond to each other, another phenomenon became painfully clear: the inadequacy of straight photography to represent the essence of a scene in the face of subtle color nuance, tonal merging, atmospheric haze, extreme contrasts of light and shade, foreground obstacles, excessive but near-meaningless detail, uncertain points of view, and the limitations of linear perspective. So an advantage accrues to the artist, who by pencil and brush and with the freedom to elaborate through abstraction creates a profound representation of the landscape rather than a mere linear transcription, an enhanced result that only the very finest landscape photographers can regularly achieve. This is not to claim that accuracy is of secondary importance, but that mere photographic accuracy may convey less of the subject than can a work derived from a practiced eye, one that can abstract and alter the view at hand to heighten its emotional impact, and yet by focusing upon the essential maintain or even enhance a viewer's ability to immediately recognize and fully appreciate the whole.

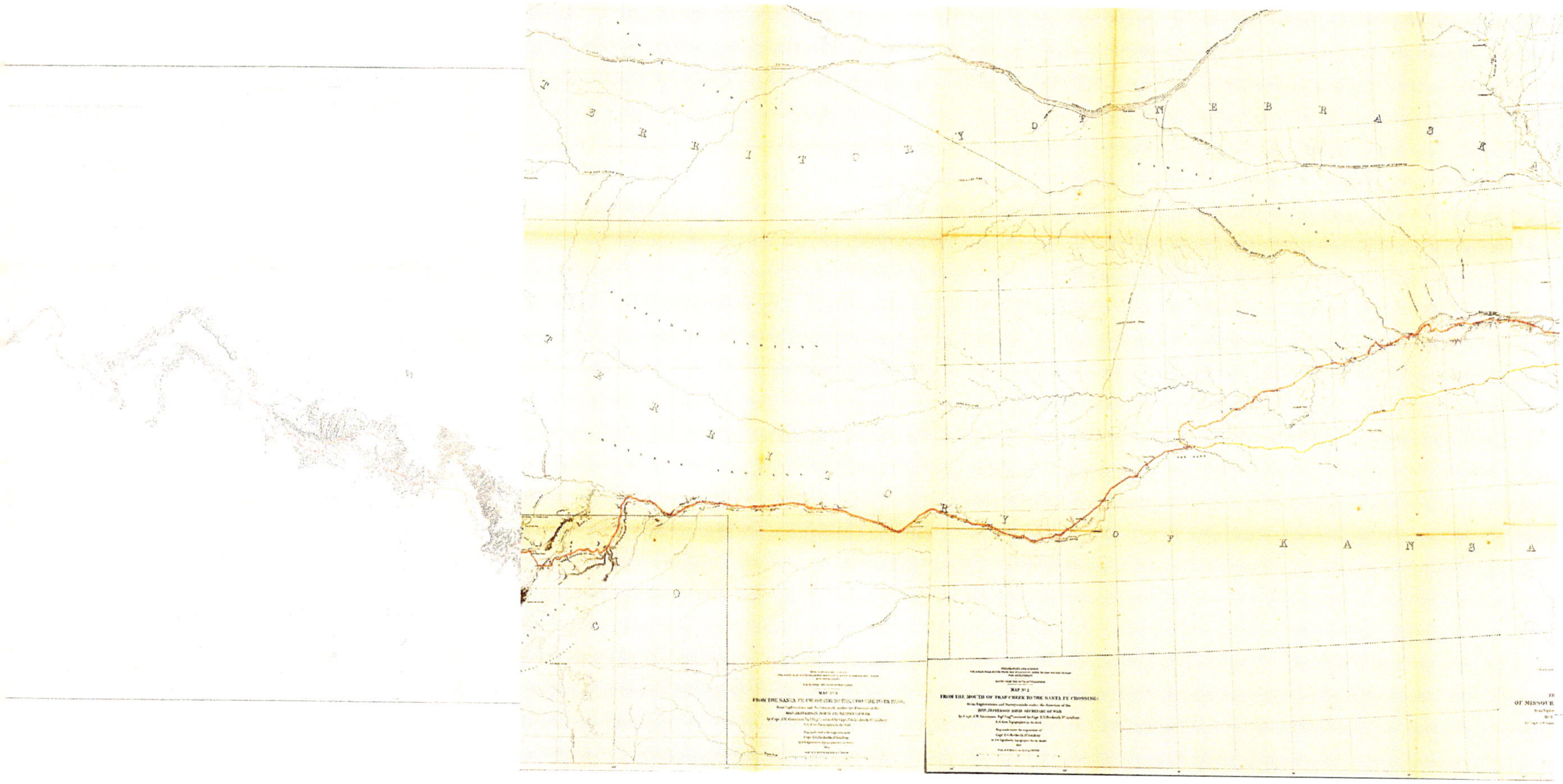
T E R R I T O R Y O F N E B R A S K A
T E R R I T O R Y O F K A N S A
MAP No 2
FROM THE MOUTH OF TRAP CREEK TO THE SANTA FE CROSSING:
OF MISSOUR

# 1

# The Great Plains

## WESTWARD FROM WESTPORT, WITH HIGH HOPES

*From Fort Leavenworth, via Westport, Fort Riley, and Smokey Hill Fork, to Pawnee Fork; also, via Santa Fé road to Council Grove and Walnut Creek—June 15th to July 13, 1853 (G-B, 9).*

ON JUNE 15, 1853, Captain Gunnison and Lieutenant Beckwith took a stage from Fort Leavenworth to Westport, Missouri, and made their way into Kansas Territory, where their expedition was assembling. Beckwith described the beauties of the region:

> The day was fine, and the high, beautiful rolling prairie...was covered with luxuriant grass, and profusely sprinkled with flowers... The creeks and rivulets were lined with timber, in which oak largely predominated... Arriving near Westport we fell in with our camp, and with pleasure alighted from the wretched stage to begin our arduous march. Our encampment was some five miles from Westport and the western line of the State of Missouri, selected by Mr. Kern in a fine grove near a spring, and surrounded by fine grass and an open prairie, and in the midst of the various Shawnee missions, which appeared well... On the 20th, Brevet Captain R. M. Morris, first lieutenant, and Second Lieutenant L. S. Baker, with some thirty non-commissioned officers and men of the regiment of Mounted Riflemen, with the necessary subsistence train, joined us as escort. The 21st of June was spent, as the previous two or three days had been, in breaking in wild mules; no others could be obtained on short notice, so large had been the demand by emigrants going west of the mountains. Nor were we more fortunate in procuring capable teamsters, the large trains which annually cross the plains having preceded us; but by industrious drilling, and replacing incompetent men by the trial of the skill of others, we deemed ourselves at evening in a condition to move forward the following morning. But at an early hour it began to rain in torrents, and continued during the day, so that it was impossible to do more than to harness up a few of the wildest mules to habituate them to their labors. On the 23d the creeks and branches were still swollen by the rain of the previous day... The advance, however, was ordered...
>
> The party, (the escort having been already mentioned,) which this day made its first marching essay for the exploration of the Central Pacific Railroad route, was composed of Captain J. W. Gunnison, Topographical Engineers, commander; First Lieutenant E. G. Beckwith, Third Artillery, assistant; Mr.

> R. H. Kern, topographer and artist; Mr. Sheppard Homans, astronomer; Dr. James Schiel, surgeon, geologist, &c.; Mr. F. Creutzfeldt, botanist; Mr. J. A. Snyder, assistant topographer, &c.; and Mr. Charles Taplin, wagon-master; besides the necessary teamsters and employés for the performance of the labors of the route (G-B, 11-12).

Three members of the expedition were already well acquainted with each other, for Kern, Creutzfeldt, and Taplin were survivors of Frémont's disastrous fourth expedition. Once again they were joining together near Westport with a band of explorers for the purpose of surveying the line of Senator Thomas Hart Benton's Central Route to the Pacific, the very course that they and Frémont spectacularly failed to traverse in the winter of 1848-49. Taplin would leave the expedition in the San Luis Valley because of ill health; Kern and Creutzfeldt were both to lose their lives in Utah, victims of the Gunnison Massacre, perpetrated on October 26, 1853, by Pahvant Indians.

Westport, Missouri Territory, in 1853 was the frontier, the limit of civilization from which many an expedition organized itself before traveling west. It provided easy access to two major wagon routes, the Santa Fe Trail and the Oregon Trail. It was well watered and had abundant grass so that livestock and beasts of burden could be fed and fattened before starting on the arduous journey. It could be reached overland or by steamboat from St. Louis up the Missouri River to Westport Landing, and it was here at a campsite he had selected that Richard Kern made his first surviving sketch of the expedition. It is typical of the majority of those collected in the album: The paper is yellow, thin, and translucent, while the marks on it are in places so faint that some of the details are difficult to see. The sketch of Camp No. 1 (Plate 4) is first reproduced unaltered, in approximately its original color and contrast.

Computer image processing as used here can improve the intelligibility of a faint drawing by increasing its contrast (see Plate 5), and I have done this without comment whenever it seems necessary. When a drawing is to be compared directly with a black and white photograph it is best to convert the sketch into black and white as well (see Plate 5), because the juxtaposition of a colored drawing and a monochrome photograph is visually jarring.

This first scene that Kern has sketched is indeed a bucolic one, with trees, bushes, and, in the distance, low hills. On the

PLATE 4. Camp 1, June 20, 1853, near Westport. 22.9 x 13.5 cm

PLATE 5. Two treatments of "Camp No. 1": contrast enhanced, and monochrome

left in front of the hills is a row of vertical lines that suggests fenceposts; centered in the picture are the tents of the expedition's first camp, and in front of them stands an object hard to identify, perhaps a cart. Frederick Creutzfeldt (also spelled Kreutzfeldt), the German botanist of the expedition, noted:

> We camp on the so called Indian Creek, together with the soldiers... From the 18th - 22nd we camp under Populus alba [white poplar] (Creutzfeldt, June 23).

This fast-growing, invasive tree is common in Europe, where Creutzfeldt would have been familiar with it, and from where it was first introduced to the Americas as an ornamental planting in 1748. Because it is well adapted to conditions in North America and hybridizes readily with native aspens, it is now found throughout the United States. Because white poplar has a distinctive pattern in its bark, it is doubtful that Creutzfeldt was mistaken. This implies that in just 100 years it had spread halfway across the continent. Kern was interested in the sense of place provided by botanical subjects, but the trees he drew immediately behind the tents of the camp are perhaps too tall and narrow to suggest pure white poplar, which has a more spreading character.

The inscription at the lower right informs us of the date, the location, and the subject matter, at the same time as it illustrates a perplexing mystery woven throughout the album and its drawings. "Near Westport" is in a right-leaning cursive that is recognizably the hand of Richard Kern, but two other hands are present as well: a slightly left-leaning, hasty scrawl with thin, light lines reads "Camp No 1," followed in a firmer and clearer script by "June 20-53," telling us that the sketch was made after the camp was well established but before the expedition was ready to depart, which it finally did on June 23. As will become apparent, the written information on the sketches must be approached with some caution and often cannot be relied upon; the indications of place, date, or subject can at times range from mildly to wildly misleading, even when clearly in Kern's own hand. The nature of the errors often implies that the drawings were not always titled and dated immediately on site; sometimes several days or even weeks passed from the time of their creation until written information was added. Kern may have taken them up in batches to be identified and labeled as circumstances allowed and in the process sometimes confused adjacent drawings, or sometimes found his memory wanting. Other than that belonging to Kern, the different hands on the sketches have defied identification. It would have been useful to know who among his companions were annotating his work, and why some notes were added long after the fact, perhaps even back in Washington.

Two men of the expedition are likely candidates to have been annotating the drawings, both of them members of the "scientific corps" whose duties would have kept them in constant contact with Kern. Sheppard Homans was the expedition's astronomer, a Harvard graduate with a flair for mathematics whose observations were critical to the construction of the expedition's maps. When the expedition was over Homans joined an insurance firm, for which Beckwith provided him with a letter of reference, and used his mathematical skills to rise in the field and become a well-known actuary. As a result I was able to locate two signed letters Homans wrote that are now in the Maryland Historical Society. Eben Dennis provided me with photocopies, and these samples of Homans's handwriting are so palpably different from those under consideration as to exclude him entirely. James A. Snyder's position on the expedition as "assistant topographer" implies he worked closely with Kern as his subordinate, and after Kern was killed in Utah Snyder wrote a pathetic letter to his father praising Kern, describing how close they had become over the miles of travel, and bemoaning his loss. It was published in several newspapers, but I have not been able to turn up the original or any other sample of Snyder's handwriting, so no matter how likely it is that Snyder as Kern's assistant helped to annotate the sketches and perhaps occasionally drew on them, it remains to be demonstrated. Others in the Scientific Corps who may have occasionally helped Kern out were James Schiel and Frederick Creutzfeldt, but I can find no writing samples for either of them. Creutzfeldt's memorandum book from the expedition is in the National Archives along with a typescript translation from the German, but the cursive original appears to be a fair copy and not in Creutzfeldt's own hand. Neither is any of the text on the drawings a match to the hand of either Gunnison or Beckwith. There is another confounding possibility: The sketches were trimmed from larger sheets of paper before being mounted, a process that may have removed portions of their annotations. It is possible that those responsible for compiling the album on occasion transferred information that was lost in the trimming process onto the remaining piece of paper.

The markings by unknown persons sometimes display a measure of indifference to the material by overwriting details of the sketches themselves, something Kern very rarely did. Not being very confident of my skill at handwriting recognition, and having failed to classify and/or identify the various hands that appear on the drawings, when I must refer to them I shall generally identify them as "not Kern's," with one exception: The sprawling, left-leaning script of "Camp No 1" occurs often enough and is so likely to be that of James Snyder that I may identify it as such purely for convenience. He was Kern's assistant, this particular handwriting appears again and again on drawings, and often it conveys useful information otherwise lacking, or supplies a corrective when Kern is in error.

Providing a photograph by which to compare each scene with its corresponding drawing is impossible for much of the work made on the plains of Kansas and eastern Colorado, and so it is with this first example. The area that Kern chose as a campsite for the expedition, and where they spent a week outfitting themselves for the coming trek, is now a part of Kansas City, dominated by paved streets, large houses, decorative trees, and well-maintained yards. Today the foliage of the district can in no way be compared with that in the sketch, and the gently rolling terrain Kern depicted would be difficult to locate.

The Great Plains present such a uniform appearance and possess so little detail of the sort that might attract an

PLATE 6. Mission & Kansas Rivers [June 29]: 23.1 x 12.8 cm

PLATE 7. Photograph of the scene

PLATE 8. Composite of drawing and photograph

artist like Kern that the beginning of his series of landscape views contains little of visual interest and few details that can be matched to the scenery of today. A sequential method of presentation requires that I begin with the relatively uninteresting views of Kansas, but fortunately there are not very many of them in the album, and only two can be precisely located and photographed. The rest of this set may more logically belong in the chapter of scenes unfound, but because I could sequence them and know roughly where each was made I have placed them here at the beginning with a little commentary. This way the reader can skip rapidly over the Plains and on to Bent's Fort (Plate No. 18), after which the breathtaking appearance of the

PLATE 9. Kansas R. [scene unlocated, June 29?] 23.1 x 12.8 cm

Rocky Mountains provided Kern with an abundance of subjects to which his sketches can make strong visual references.

On June 26 Captain Gunnison divided his party, sending most of the company along the Santa Fe Trail under Lieutenant Beckwith with instructions to wait for him at Walnut Creek, while Gunnison proceeded up the Kansas River towards the Smokey Hill Fork with a small mounted company that included Richard Kern, the astronomer Sheppard Homans, just one wagon for the scientific instruments, and a few pack mules. Beckwith quoted from Captain Gunnison's journal entry two days after the expedition was divided:

> "*June* 28. At 3 o'clock p.m. we arrived at Mission creek, where there are all the requisites of wood, water, and grass, for encampments, for a long time to come" (G-B, 14).

Gunnison's band camped that evening on the east side of the creek, which enters the eastward-flowing Kansas River from the southwest at an acute angle. The low hills depicted on the right side of the sketch are along the south bank of the Kansas River east of the mouth of Mission Creek. In the sketch the Kansas River enters from the left and disappears in the center, beyond and to the left of the two hills, while there is a strong

PLATE 10. Uniontown, Kaw River [June 29] 27.4 x 11.2 cm

suggestion that Mission Creek enters diagonally from the right. These are the only hills in the vicinity, and Kern must have captured them from the west bank of the creek. Because the starting time for the expedition was normally 7:00 a.m., Kern would have made his drawing shortly afterward, so the time notation "from 82.0 on" on the drawing (in Snyder's hand) should probably be amended to "8.20," or 8:20 a.m. in modern notation.

My attempt to photograph this view involved me in the most difficult approach to a vantage point I have ever encountered—on foot but not really walking; through, over, and under the brush along the Kansas River to its junction with Mission Creek. Nothing could have induced me to undertake this crawl through the woods except that I had already ascertained the location of the hills in the sketch, and could find no other approach to where Kern must have viewed them. When, after climbing and crawling, weaving,

PLATE 11. Fort Riley at the junction of the Smokey Hill and Republican rivers [July 3?] 27.2 x 13.3 cm

ducking and bobbing through low-hanging branches, dense scrub, and driftwood, and covering myself with burrs, I finally reached my goal, the vegetation on the opposite side of the creek obscured my view almost entirely. In the photograph the slope of the farther of the two hills is visible in the haze over the river, but to the right everything else is hidden behind a crush of trunks, branches, and dead but not yet fallen leaves. If the plants on the opposite bank of the creek were somehow removed, the contour of the hill farthest to the right would become visible against the sky, for by shifting my head from side to side I could perceive its presence through the trunks and branches; the barest hint of that form is discernible in my stationary photograph. If a sketch artist were to do the same thing, or were to integrate multiple points of view into a single representation, the outline of this hill could be straightforwardly represented. In the center of the photograph there is less obscuration of the horizon by trees, and the outline revealed there against the sky is close to that in the drawing.

Kern's sketch of the "Kansas R." (Plate 9) has no defining characteristics by which to locate it. "Uniontown, Kaw River" (Plate 10) is from today's Willard, Kansas, the modern successor to Uniontown; there is nothing today at the site to correspond with the details of Kern's drawing. "Kaw" is an alternative nineteenth-century name for the Kansas River. The expedition passed through here but did not stop, and Uniontown was given only the slightest mention in Captain Gunnison's journal for that day.

> "*June* 29.... At Uniontown, to which we came after a ride of 7½ miles, there is a street of a dozen houses..." (G-B, 14).

Richard Kern had traveled for miles over terrain that did not present much in the way of defining features; coming across a small town with buildings and fences that could give detail to a sketch must have been a welcome relief. The undated inscription is not in his hand.

Kern's view of Fort Riley (Plate 11) was from high above the river, but the dense foliage there today forced me to work much lower and close to the riverbank. This point of view alters the perspective. The hill on the left, where Kern places some barracks buildings that are still there but hidden in the photograph, appears higher than the more distant one on the right, which is almost invisible behind the trees. Railroad and highway bridges are just out of the frame to the left.

The hill with the barracks is on the left, but no structures can be seen in this photograph. Kern's sketch is a view to the northeast. The Republican Fork (now the Republican River) flows in from the left; from the lower right the Smokey Hill Fork (now the Smokey Hill River) enters on the diagonal; then the two streams merge and exit to the right as the Kansas River. On the rounded hill in the center of the drawing the unfinished barracks can be seen outlined against the sky, with a flag flying to their right. "Green" is written in two places to guide the colors of the finished painting, and the closer "green" perhaps indicates that the bank extends in front of the wooded area, or that there is a small island in the middle of the river.

PLATE 12. Photograph, junction of the Smoky Hill and Republican rivers.

PLATE 13. Composite of drawing and photograph

When Gunnison and his companions left Fort Riley they crossed the Republican Fork (also called the Pawnee River) so that they could explore the north side of the Smokey Hill Fork, which Gunnison sometimes mistakenly calls the Kansas River. After a difficult crossing of the Nepeholla River they struck the Saline Fork (both tributaries to the Smokey Hill), a stream from the north and west that was in a flood stage and almost impossible to ford.

> *July 7.*—A cool, delicious morning, the [Nepeholla] river still rising... After riding seven miles we struck the Saline fork in the meadow. This stream is also swollen by a flood, and looks like the boiling Missouri. Continuing on our course for two miles, we halted on one of the bends of this stream and cut two dry cottonwood logs, which we lashed to the sides of our wagon wheels, and thus made a ferry-boat of our carriage. With this we ferried over the stream, which is 150 feet wide and 9 feet deep, with a rapid current. The guide represents it as being usually 20 feet wide and 2 feet deep. It is surprising to see such a freshet without any visible cause. Stretching away to the west for some hundreds of miles, the river has no doubt received the product of heavy rains. The Nepeholla

PLATE 14. Crossing Saline Creek, July 7th, 1853. 28.1 x 16.5 cm

PLATE 15. Crossing Saline, July 7th, 1853. 22.5 x 14.8 cm

> rose six inches yesterday, and this river as much during the seven hours we were most laboriously engaged in crossing it (G-B, 17).

If Gunnison had brought his entire party with its wagons, they would have either had to wait for the Saline Fork to subside or turned back to Fort Riley. While the men of the expedition were laboring to bring that single wagon across, Kern made two sketches of the stream. An artist who was primarily interested in the human element might have depicted the dramatic efforts of his companions as they struggled to cross the raging torrent, but in keeping with his task as topographic artist to illustrate the nature and conditions of the terrain the expedition encountered, Kern instead drew the inundation caused by the swollen watercourse. It is evident that the stream was unusually high because most of the trees in Plate 14 (Crossing Saline Creek) have their trunks partially submerged by the water, though just how deeply cannot be said. The spare idiom of his sketches does not allow for "the boiling current" to be distinctly represented on the surface, yet there is a suggestion of the agitated surface patterns such a flow would make as it passed around the flooded tree trunks. The banks are ill defined, and if we regard his sketches literally it will take

PLATE 16. Elk Island, Arkansas River, July 20th 17.0 x 2.8 cm

an effort of the imagination to see this as a stream "150 feet wide and 9 feet deep," but by keeping in mind that Kern has a tendency to compress his sketches laterally, the view may be correspondingly expanded in imagination, restoring a sense of its width that Gunnison described in his journal.

The second of these two sketches (Plate 15. Crossing Saline) evidently was cut to size after the paper was drawn upon. Close examination of the word "Crossing" shows that the tail of the "g" extends to the edge of the paper as if the end of it has been trimmed off. The same observation extends to one of the vertical lines representing foreground reeds or grasses and over which the "C" in "Crossing" has been written. As is the case here, captions by unknown hands are occasionally careless of details in the sketches. The two drawings were attached to adjoining pages of the album and numbered 44 and 45. Either this is a coincidence, or else on this occasion the compiler of the album consciously juxtaposed the sketches properly when mounting them.

### FROM PAWNEE FORK TO THE CROSSING OF THE ARKANSAS RIVER AT THE MOUTH OF THE APISHAPA. —JULY 14 TO AUGUST 2, 1853. (G-B, 24).

On July 13 Captain Gunnison and his companions rejoined the main force of his expedition at Walnut Creek, and the entire party continued up the Arkansas River along the Santa Fe road. The featureless landscape that gave Kern's artistic skills so little upon which to fasten probably led him to an opinion close to the one Beckwith expressed in the *Report*:

> *July* 21.—Nothing can exceed the dull monotony of a journey along the Arkansas. Neither in the character of the country nor in any department of science, do

PLATE 17. Arkansas Plains. 22.7 x 7.4 cm

> we find a variety in a day's march of twenty miles. A gradual change is going on, however of which we feel sensible; the vegetation of the rolling prairie being already parched and dry, and the earth of the hills is so compact and hard that it rings under our horses' feet, and it is often impossible to drive a tent-pin of wood into it (G-B, 26-27).

This tiny sketch of Elk Island (Plate No. 16) displays evidence of having been cut down before mounting because the cloud in the upper left is incomplete, but it is hard to imagine that anything of consequence has been lost. The subject is identified in Snyder's hand, but the date is by Kern. If July 20 is correct, it was made while the expedition was between the present-day towns of Charleston and Garden City, Kansas. There is no mention of Elk Island in the text of the Gunnison-Beckwith *Report*, but Beckwith does refer to it in his private diary for the day of July 21. The island is noted on the map of the expedition and shown to lie between the camps for July 20-21 (Camp 23) and 21-22 (Camp 24), which is just where Beckwith recorded his brief discourse on the monotony of the scenery along the Arkansas River, but one day later than the date on the drawing. This is the first clear example of the sort of conflicting information found in the inscriptions on the drawings that occurs with dismaying regularity. Here the inconsistency is of no real consequence, for, as Lieutenant Beckwith so morosely noted, the topography of the valley of the Arkansas is so uniform that a difference of perhaps 20 miles would hardly affect its appearance. Low, nondescript hills are in the distance, while sparse trees line the banks of the Arkansas River and constitute the only indication of its presence.

The next sketch ("Arkansas Plains," Plate No. 17) of the plains is very similar to "Elk Island" (Plate 16), but the distant hills are higher and the trees along the river better worked out; the scene is probably between Elk Island and Bent's Fort, and is the last in the collection that Kern made before first Bent's Fort and then the Rocky Mountains came into view.

# 2

# The Sangre de Cristo Mountains

*From Bent's Fort up the Arkansas to the Mouth of the Apishapa River, across to the Huerfano Valley, then over Sangre de Cristo Pass and down to Fort Massachusetts in the San Luis Valley*

PLATES 18, 19, AND 20 SHOW BENT'S FORT (now Bent's Old Fort National Historic Site), an immense adobe structure near the town of La Junta, Colorado. Built by William and Charles Bent in 1833, it was the principal way station along the Mountain Branch of the Santa Fe Trail, became the busiest of the trading forts on the Great Plains, and then was abandoned and destroyed in 1849. There are several versions of what happened: The fort may have been invaded by Indians, then scavenged and sacked; it may have been deserted because it had become so infested with vermin as to be uninhabitable; or, most colorfully, perhaps William Bent demolished it himself with explosives rather than be forced to sell it to the U.S. government at what he believed was a confiscatory price (Lavender, 1972, 338-340, 443-444). Charles Bent had been murdered in Taos during the rebellion of 1847, but after the destruction of the original fort his brother William continued commercial activities from three trading houses located thirty miles downriver from the old fort, in a stand of cottonwood trees called Big Timbers. There he began in 1853 to erect another fort, this one of stone. It was still in such a preliminary stage of construction that it did not receive any notice from the Gunnison expedition, although the trading houses did:

PLATE 18. Bent's Fort [July 29]. 17.6 x 9.8 cm

> *July 27.*—... A mile from camp we passed two or three log-houses, occupied as a trading station by Mr. Wm. Bent, during the past winter, but now left vacant, and, as yet, undestroyed by the Indians (G-B, 28).

On the other hand, Bent's "Old" Fort was so monumental an edifice that it was impossible to ignore, and provoked comments by all the travelers. The Bent brothers located it on the Arkansas near the mouth of the Purgatory River because the site was well defended yet could be readily visited by the many Indian tribes with whom the Bents traded, a business from which they derived an immensity of fortune and influence. Beckwith noted the virtues of its location when he proposed the site be adopted for a military fort:

PLATE 19. Photograph, Bent's Fort.

PLATE 20. Composite drawing and photograph

*July* 29.—Between camp and Bent's Fort, grass was very abundant. We spent an hour in examining the river at the fort for a practicable ford, but the excellent one which formerly existed here was found impracticable to cross, in the present stage of the water. Mr. Bent abandoned his fort about four years ago, but not until he had destroyed it. Its adobe walls still stand in part only, with here and there a tower and chimney. Here, beyond question, would be one of the most favorable points for a military post which is anywhere presented on the Plains. There is an abundance of pasturage, fuel, and building material in the neighborhood, for the use and building of the post. It is of easy access from its central position, from the east, from Santa Fé, from Taos through the Sangre de Cristo Pass, and from Fort Laramie. It is on an emigrant road from southern Missouri and Arkansas, either by the North Park or Coochetopa Pass; and it is in the heart of the Indian country, accessible to the resorts of the Comanches, Cheyennes, Arapahoes, Kioways, some bands of Apaches, and even occasionally of the Utahs of New Mexico (G-B, 28).

> We passed by in the morning Bents Fort or rather its ruins, since it is burnt out and desolated (Creutzfeldt, July 29).

> Bent's Fort had been abandoned by its possessor and its walls were largely destroyed; there was, of course, no trace of a roof... (Schiel, 55).

The inscriptions on the sketch are first "BENTS FORT" in block letters, followed by something else in cursive that has defied my attempts to decipher it, although the last part may be either "fort" or "ford." My best guess is "near Sta (Santa Fe Trail?) River ford." Since Kern's visit the ruins of the fort have been rebuilt by the National Park Service, so only an intact reconstruction presented itself for comparison. The Arkansas River is behind it, and the trees along its banks now obscure the distant hills that Kern was able to see when he drew his sketch.

The expedition did not camp at Bent's Old Fort, and after the men determined that there were no usable fords across the Arkansas River in the area, they continued up its north (left) bank. They were given a brief glimpse of the Spanish Peaks, a welcome landmark for travelers on the Santa Fe Trail because it was a visible marker of the boundary of what was once Spanish and then Mexican territory, and thus portended the approaching end of a long and arduous journey. For the Gunnison expedition it was no such thing, but a view of it kindled expectations of a future more interesting than the tedious days spent on the Great Plains following the road along the Arkansas River.

> *July* 29.—(continued)... The atmosphere for many days has been so cloudy that we have seldom had a distant view; and for the last two or three, smoke has quite obscured the whole country, so that we could see but a very few miles. A small opening in the clouds and smoke, however, an hour ago, gave us a first but not very distinct view of the Spanish peaks, bearing nearly southwest; but it was only a momentary view, and we were again left to gaze on barrenness and a circumscribed horizon (G-B, 28-29).

At this point the task of the expedition was to find where the Huerfano River emptied into the Arkansas. The orders to Gunnison from the War Department stated explicitly that he was to ascend the Huerfano, so he would naturally have been intent on locating its mouth. In his introduction to the *Report* Beckwith quotes extracts from these documents:

> "...the War Department directs a survey of the pass through Rocky mountains, in the vicinity of the headwaters of the Rio del Norte, by way of the Huerfano river...
>
> "The party...will repair with the utmost dispatch to Fort Leavenworth, and with the escort proceed to the Huerfano river...
>
> "The more minute reconoissance will continue up the Huerfano into the San Luis valley..." (G-B, 10).

This recurring insistence on a Huerfano River route may have caused Gunnison some apprehension about locating it. Unfortunately, but as will be seen, understandably, he mistook the Apishapa River for the Huerfano, and at the mouth of the former the expedition spent several days resting, crossing the Arkansas with great exertions, and resting again. Then he and his men ascended the Apishapa for several days before their error was discovered.

> *July* 30.—... our departure was delayed for an hour, which Captain Gunnison and myself, with a number of men, spent in search of a ford, but without any favorable result...we were anxious to reach the Huerfano, that astronomical observations might be taken while we found the means of recruiting our animals and of crossing the Arkansas. According to the maps we had with us, and in the opinion of several men of the party who had passed here before, the Huerfano was believed to be already in sight, and, after ascending two or three high hills in the vicinity and obtaining a distant view of a broken line of trees in the direction in which this stream was believed to be, we turned toward the river and encamped... Captain Gunnison, whom I accompanied, went in search of the mouth of the river, which we found in a bend of the Arkansas immediately south of the camp, and of a ford by which to cross the latter stream: in this, however, we were unsuccessful, and it was not until the following day that Captain Gunnison found one, on the northern bend of the river, half a mile west of our camp... The $31^{st}$ of July was passed in camp, and on the following morning... Captain Gunnison...built a raft of logs... It was only by the greatest labor and difficulty that a rope could be carried across the stream... The raft, once in successful operation, lightened the wagons of half their loads or more, which were safely landed on the opposite bank at sundown, and the

> wagons thus laden were crossed at the ford before the twilight rendered it unsafe... (G-B, 29-30).

Among the maps Gunnison had with him must have been a copy of the comprehensive *Map of the Territory of New Mexico* (Parke-Kern, 1851), one that Kern helped to compile and then drew for Lieutenant Parke while employed by the U. S. Army in Santa Fe. It was the most recent and also the most authoritative to be had, but unbeknownst to Gunnison the names of the Huerfano and the Apishapa rivers on it are interchanged! The "several men of the party who had passed here before" were Charles Taplin, the wagon master, Frederick Creutzfeldt, the botanist, and Richard Kern. In the winter of 1848 they had come up the Arkansas River with Colonel Frémont on his fourth expedition. Passing by both the Apishapa and the Huerfano rivers, Frémont continued up to Hardscrabble Creek before turning into the Sangre de Cristo Mountains. In a letter to Jefferson Davis from near Fort Massachusetts, Gunnison placed the responsibility for the error on "...those in my command who had been in this country in winter, [and] could not recognize places and streams in a different season" (quoted by Weber, 1985, 223 and footnote 32, 332). Everything conspired to ensure that Gunnison would mistake the Apishapa for the Huerfano, and it seems that Kern was the one mainly responsible.

Sunday, July 31, was "passed in camp" because Gunnison's practice was to rest both men and animals on the Sabbath whenever possible. As was the case at the crossing of the Saline Fork in Kansas, the laborers of the expedition here struggled to bring wagons and animals across the Arkansas River while Richard Kern was occupied with his art. In fairness, Kern's responsibilities were far more extensive than just creating a few sketches now and then. He would have been continually collecting and organizing the data from which he intended to construct maps of the terrain through which the expedition passed; the quantity of his observations, the quantity of his data, and the precision with which he worked is reflected in the superlative maps that his successor, Friedrich W. von Egloffstein, produced from those field notes. Here both astronomer and topographer made the observations and calculations to precisely locate the junction of the supposed Huerfano with the Arkansas, by which Gunnison could demonstrate that his orders had been carried out exactly. Creutzfeldt took note of the scientific activities going on near the camp.

> Remain on the same place and look out for a ford; is apparently found and to be tried probably tomorrow.

Here special astronomical observations are made and Kern is surveying the principal points... (Creutzfeldt, July 31).

*August* 1.—We were gratified this evening by a clear and beautiful view of the Spanish peaks and of the Greenhorn mountains, with others just rising above the horizon to the north and south. From the summit of the bluffs on the north bank of the river, James' [Pikes] peak is distinctly seen; and upon all the high ranges the snow is visible, accounting for the high water in the streams which rise in them (G-B, 30).

Schiel also valued the beauty of the views now that the air had cleared.

From the camp which we occupied on the first of August on the right bank of the Arkansas we saw the rocky Mountains for the first time lying clearly before us. It was in the evening. The Spanish Peaks and their northern neighbors the Greenhorn lay directly before us on the horizon and from a nearby peak we could see James' Peak, whose summit was covered with snow. It was an enjoyable sight for the whole crowd, for we had all grown tired of the monotonous prairie. A sojourn on the prairie of a few weeks is quite agreeable... But when the sojourn became protracted...then the monotony of the prairie became noticeable, you grew tired of the eternal grass and it was a treat to see the gigantic mountain peaks. It was almost like a holiday (Schiel, 59-60).

PLATE 21. Plains [August 1?]. 28.0 x 14.9 cm

There are three sketches by Kern from the time spent at the confluence of the Apishapa and Arkansas rivers, all of which were made from the north (left) bank of the Arkansas. The undated "Plains" (Plate 21) shows three segments of landscape and is the first example of a format that Kern uses

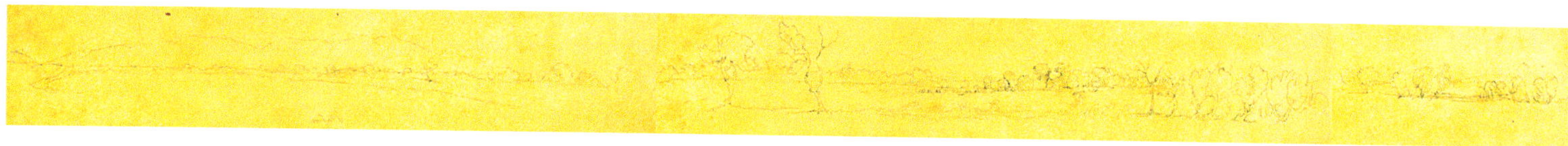

PLATE 22. Continuous panoramic drawing

PLATE 23. Photograph of plains south of Olney Springs, CO.

PLATE 24. Composite drawing and photograph

repeatedly, a broad panorama that is broken down into parts and represented by several rows in the sketch, so the whole can be compressed onto a single sheet. That all three segments are in fact contiguous and that from top to bottom they represent a scene from left to right was at first only a supposition, but one that could be tested by locating Kern's point of view. The simple inscription "Plains" is not much help, but the general area was not hard to identify because two of the subjects that Beckwith was "gratified" to see and that Schiel "enjoyed" are clearly present: the Spanish Peaks are the double bumps in the middle of the second line of the drawing, and the broadly outlined distant contours in the bottom segment are recognizably the Greenhorn Mountains. The problem is that these two landmarks retain their general appearance from a wide expanse of the plains south of the Arkansas River and east of Walsenburg, Colorado, so that pinning down Kern's point of view depends on identifying the hills outlined in the upper left corner of the sketch. These multiple peaks gave a sense of being Fisher's Peak south of Trinidad, on the Colorado-New Mexico border. My mistake here was abetted by one of the limitations inherent in Kern's representational methods, where depth is represented mostly by superposition and obscuration. The effects of the atmosphere on distant views can hardly be shown, except perhaps in a limited way by weaker, thinner lines and perhaps a reduction in detail. As a result the remoteness of the hills on the left is difficult to interpret. Since the expedition pursued a course south and west for many miles after crossing the Arkansas, I was able to find many putative matches for the scene that were marred only by the fact that Fisher's Peak, which is far to the south, presented only two prominences, not three. If I had been a bit wiser I could have saved several days by reading Beckwith more carefully:

> *July* 30.—(continued) Opposite to our camp of July 30$^{th}$, and to the east of the stream which here enters the Arkansas from the south, are three hills, two conical and one oblong, rising some 250 feet above the river, and 100 above the general level, distinguishing land-marks for the stranger. The bluffs to the northwest of that camp rise still higher above the adjacent hills (G-B, 30).

This experience taught me to look more closely at the text of the *Report* for correspondences between it and the sketches such as occurs here. The correct viewpoint for "Plains" is from just south of the town of Olney Springs, CO, which is on the north side of the Arkansas River. I used Photoshop to digitally cut and stitch the panoramic drawing into a continuous whole. The ends are not well matched, so my joining of the parts is by simple juxtaposition, but there is little doubt that they were intended to be in continuity with one another and to represent the entire view. On the right end of the top (first) segment and on the left in the second segment, Kern drew large ovals, probably to signify that the two portions should be adjoining, although they are not specific enough to show how the parts align. Later on Kern used a small "x" on separate parts of a drawing to indicate their configuration more distinctly. From south of Olney Springs I made a corresponding panoramic photograph with infrared film.

Despite some disparities and discontinuities the drawing and the photograph can be placed together satisfactorily,

PLATE 25. Bluff on Arkansas—August 1. 23.8 x 8.9 cm

PLATE 26. Photograph of bluff near Arkansas River.

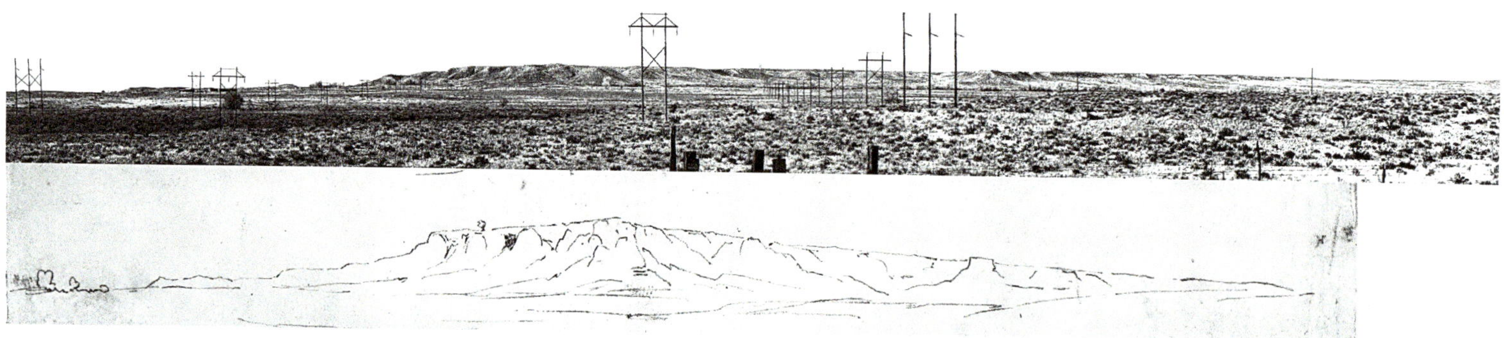

PLATE 27. Drawing and photograph juxtaposed

with both the Spanish Peaks and the Greenhorn Mountains in their correct positions. Beckwith's "three hills, two conical and one oblong" on the left side of the scene are today called the Apishapa Bluff, and lie only eight miles to the south.

Kern's propensity to exaggerate the vertical is here clearly in view, and will be found so universally in his work that going forward I will rarely comment on it.

The sketch "Bluff on Arkansas" (Plate 25) was also made near the mouth of the Apishapa while the expedition was crossing the Arkansas River, and it is of the second distinctive landmark that Beckwith observed here, "The bluffs to the northwest of that camp rise still higher above the adjacent hills." It appears that when dating this sketch Kern began with a capital "J" that suggests he was about to write "July," a mistake he corrected by overwriting with a capital "A" and then completing "Aug." The viewpoint he used is within a mile of where "Plains" was drawn; my maneuvering to find the best possible match was constrained by a prison located just west of Olney Springs.

The sketch becomes less and less detailed to the right, and it is unclear where in the scene it ends, so I have included more of the right side of my photograph than is perhaps warranted. It is evident that Kern exaggerated the small but defining particulars of the scene such as the "steps" downward to the left in the outline, the gap on the horizon just to the right of the closest double power pole, and the flat-topped hill that sticks up to the right of the triple power pole. The effect is to increase the recognizability of this important but rather nondescript scene without having to spend time and effort working in all of the details of its appearance. The same device appears in other works by Kern as well. In the same vein, Kern often sharpens the crests of hills in a way that makes their presence more obvious, as he did with some of the tops of the low hills farthest to the left. An artist friend suggested to me that the effect may be a by-product of Kern's technique, wherein it appears he would start his pencil strokes from the crests of hills, make a stroke first in one direction and then return to the crest and draw a line in the other. This is a natural technique to correctly place the peaks and summits along the horizon in a drawing, but may not render their outlines in a perfectly correct manner; thus the discontinuity at the highest point represented in this sketch. Under magnification Kern's drawings show many such breaks in his lines where, I imagine, he halted the motion of his pencil, glanced up at the scene, then returned his eyes to the paper and continued to draw.

Plate 28 is the third sketch Kern made from the north side of the Arkansas River near the Apishapa. The lower inscription is entirely in Kern's hand, but its parenthetical

PLATE 28. (Mouth of the Apishapa River) Ferry, Arkansas, August 1, 1853
Top sketch of two on paper, 13.3 x 19.1 cm

PLATE 29. Photograph near site of the Arkansas River ferry at the mouth of the Apishapa River, Arkansas

beginning, "Mouth of the Apishapa R," cannot have been put to paper when the sketch was made because the location of the expedition was presumed at the time to be at the mouth of the Huerfano River, a geographical error that Gunnison did not discover and correct until several days later. This is the first clearly defined example of what is here a too-frequent and often error-inducing practice: Kern did not annotate his sketches immediately but instead did so at irregular intervals after he created them. On the right the date is repeated in a different but firm and elegant hand as "Aug 1-53," inscribed so as to handsomely accommodate the curling line in the foreground that defines the near bank of the river. Just to the left of center in Snyder's hasty-appearing cursive is the notation "dark," superimposed on some details of the foreground, or, more likely, of the water in the river. According to its caption, this drawing was made from the place where the expedition forded the Arkansas River, and looming above the trees on its banks is the clearly identifiable outline of the Spanish Peaks. Because of their distance they are marked out lightly compared with the foreground trees, but they are the vital subjects of the drawing. Plate 28 shares a single piece of paper with a second one placed below it (Plate 54), inscribed "Sierra Mohada from 2.30 Camp 40," though not in Kern's hand; the two sketches have no obvious

PLATE 30. Composite drawing and photograph

relation to each other. Camp 40 was at the base of the Sierra Blanca in the Huerfano Valley, from which the expedition began to cut a road to the crest of Sangre de Cristo Pass. It was occupied the night of August 10-11, which is some ten days after the date of the upper sketch on the sheet. Drawings separated in time and place but juxtaposed on a single sheet of paper are to be found throughout the album, and many others may have been that way originally but later were cut apart before mounting. On occasion such multiple sketches are part of an intentional form of presentation, but more often, as in this case, it seems as if Kern just found a partially used sheet and drew on it, irrespective of what else it contained.

**FROM THE MOUTH OF THE APISHAPA, VIA THE SANGRE DE CRISTO, TO ROUBIDEAU'S PASS.—AUGUST 2 TO 25, 1853 (G-B, 33).**

The expedition would ultimately follow the Apishapa River south for several days, during which time it became increasingly obvious that they were not on the Huerfano.

> *August* 4.—... We have been forced, in searching for a passage, nearly to the summit of the divide between the waters of the creek at our morning camp, and of the Arkansas river; and it is becoming more than doubtful if we are not following some other than the Huerfano river...
>
> *August* 5.—...Captain Morris and myself ascended a small butte...and through an opening in the hills, a few miles to the W. N. W., were seen the green leaves of the cotton-wood...we proceeded at once to the cotton-woods, and found, as we anticipated, a fine stream, larger than that we had been attempting to

> explore; and it was at once evident, from the position and course of this, and the great southern bend of the former that it could not be the Huerfano… (G-B, 32-33).

As might be expected, the maps created by the Gunnison expedition corrected this error and show the two rivers in their proper relation.

> *August* 6.—… we…struck a wagon trail leading from the Raton Pass to the Pueblo on the Arkansas river, and Fort Laramie on the Platte. This we followed to the Cuchara, which is forty feet wide and two deep at the ford which we crossed. Encamping two miles above the ford, Captain Gunnison ascended a neighboring butte, and thus describes the view: "Pike's Peak to the north, the Spanish Peaks to the south, the Sierra Mojada to the west, and the plains from the Arkansas—undulating with hills along the route we have come, but sweeping up in a gentle rise where we should have come—with the valleys of the Cuchara and Huerfano, make the finest prospect it has ever fallen to my lot to have seen" (G-B, 33-34).

Plate 31, an elaborate rendering of Gunnison's "finest prospect" was made while the expedition rested at Camp 37 on the Cuchara River from August 6 through 8. It is of a type unique to the album because of its precision and the compass readings recorded on it. A detailed panorama of the front range of the Rockies starts on the left with today's Mount Mestas and swings northward past the Sierra Blanca and the Sierra Mojada to cover an expanse that ends with Pikes Peak, which is barely visible in the distance on the right. It depicts a significant portion of the view that Captain Gunnison is quoted as having seen in Beckwith's entry for August 6. The drawing is plainly for cartographic rather than just illustrative purposes, and is the only one of its kind that has come to us, though there must have once been many more of this sort. Several factors set it apart from the rest of the collection. First, the paper is different—relatively opaque, of a pale blue tint, and ruled with light vertical lines spaced a bit less than 3/8 inches apart across its entire width. Second, the drawing, which is in four parts and covers both sheets, is an exceptionally well detailed and accurate panorama of the eastern slopes of the Rocky Mountains seen from near the Cuchara River. Third, practically every unambiguously recognizable geographic formation is clearly delineated and marked with its magnetic compass bearing. Fourth, several such landmarks

PLATE 31. August 6 [with magnetic bearings] Four related drawings on two sheets, each 19.7 x 16.5 cm

have bearings observed from other points of view, in particular from camps of the expedition of both earlier and later dates. Making such intricate compilations of data and observation is the sort of thing Kern would likely work on when the expedition was stationary, such as for noon break or at camp, and since mapping was his primary responsibility he may have remained behind the expedition to complete such work when necessary. Creutzfeldt observed that Kern was working at "surveying the principal points" while the men of the expedition were struggling to ford the Arkansas River. The compiler of the Newberry album attached these two contiguous drawings to adjacent pages and in the proper order. Slightly overlapping the right edge of the second drawing is attached a separate sketch of Pike's Peak, one that was almost certainly made from the same exact place. The August 6 panorama can be digitally cut into four parts and assembled into a continuous panoramic representation.

Both its breathtaking splendor and its wealth of detail are immediately obvious. The little x's on the right of the first pane and the left of the second are a device Kern began to use here to indicate the correct alignment of a continuous panoramic representation that was drawn in parts. The convention by which compass bearings are notated on the drawing is not that of today. Modern usage designates north as 0°, then proceeds by degrees clockwise around the dial; after a complete rotation of 360° the return to north can be denoted

PLATE 32. Drawings arranged as a continuous panorama from Mount Mestas to Pikes Peak

PLATE 33. Photograph of the scene of August 6 drawings

either by 0° or 360°. In Kern's drawing a typical compass bearing is "S63W," which means the compass needle pointed 63° west of south (read as "south sixty-three west"); in modern notation it would be 180 + 63 = 243°. Again, the marking farthest to the right on the drawing, "N44," means 44° west of north (the "west" here is understood because nothing to the east is shown, so it reads as "north forty-four west"), which in modern notation is 360 —44 = 316°. "C.34 S84W" means that Badito Cone seen from Camp 34 of August 2-3 had a bearing of S84W, (read as south 84 west, or 264°). This datum was recorded while the expedition was still on the Apishapa River and was in all likelihood transferred from notes or from a similar topographic view made at that earlier time. Similarly, a notation like "Camp 40 S63W" refers to the bearing of the left end of Sheep Mountain taken several days later from Camp 40 of August 10-11. At the far left of the panorama is an inscription over today's Mount Mestas, "El Bota," but apparently erased. "La bota" is Spanish for "boot," and just to the right over Silver Mountain is "Boot" or "Root."

Spread out along the foreground are three formations each marked with its magnetic bearing and with the date "Aug 6," accompanied by what can be read as either the number "9" or the letter "q." Also marked at these places are, in order, the notations "N41," "N39," and "N34." These last bearings are plainly not of the formations with which they are associated, and the only sense I can make of them is to suppose that they correspond to the magnetic readings for Pikes Peak as it would have appeared from each of the three hills, although I did not take a compass and climb them to test the notion. Pikes Peak appears at the far right of the panorama, but no compass reading is given for it; when I was at Kern's vantage point I found it to be at 334°, but because of the shift in magnetic declination over the years Kern would have obtained about 331° or N29W. Perhaps a member of the expedition ascended the foreground hills and took readings on the famous but distant Pikes Peak so Kern could make triangulation points of the distinctive landforms in the foreground, which stand isolated on the plain and can be identified from

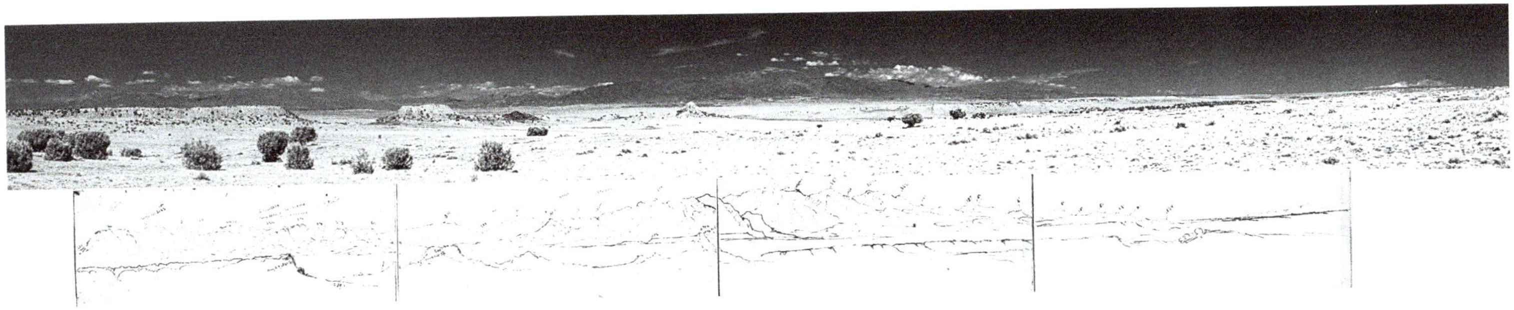

PLATE 34. Composite drawing and photograph

great distances. As the expedition moved on, Pikes Peak soon disappeared from view and was never again visible.

The photographic correspondence with the scene is excellent except for the position of Pikes Peak. The magnetic bearings were of no use in locating Kern's vantage point, although in principle it should have been easy to take two widely spaced features, find them on a map, and draw through each of them a line at the angle corresponding to their notated bearing. The point of intersection would then be where the measurements were taken and from where Kern drew his panorama. Even after correcting for the change in position of magnetic north since 1853, small errors produced a wide area of uncertainty, a difficulty not helped by the need for more than one Geological Survey map to cover the territory in sufficient detail. Abandoning that idea as fine in theory but impossible in practice, I reverted to my usual method of visually aligning nearby and distant features. In a sketch that encompasses such a broad view this process is conceptually easy, but often laborious in actuality. Exhaustion and multiple physical barriers prevented me from reaching the right spot by approaching from the east, so the next day I started from the south, which turned out to be much easier walking. Once close to the proper place I located the point of view by moving around over several hundred feet to adjust as best I could the alignments in the landscape before me. From that spot I mounted a precision compass with a sighting device on a tripod of brass and wood, so I could take readings on the distant landmarks. The expedition's map gives the magnetic variation at the mouth of the Apishapa River as 12° 15' E, while the National Oceanic and Atmospheric Administration website calculates it for 1853 as 13° 34' E. In 2002, when I made my observations, the NOAA value for magnetic declination was 9° 23' E. As was to be expected, my readings were 3 to 5 degrees higher than those Kern obtained in 1853.

Some of the more prominent landmarks and the names they bear today are, from left to right: S64 is Mount Mestas; S66 is Silver Mountain; S69 is Mount Lindsey (Blanca Peak is behind it and cannot be seen); S70 is an unnamed peak north of Lindsey, attached to it by a high ridge and approximately 13,760 feet high; S74.30 to S77 is Sheep Mountain; S79 to S81 is Little Sheep Mountain; S86 is Mount Zwischen; S88 is Medano Pass; W, Mount Herard, also called Mount Seven; N88W is Badito Cone; N72W is Greenhorn Mountain.

A modern-day controversy in art history and criticism is whether artists of the past privately made use of optical drawing aids, such as the *camera obscura* or the *camera lucida* (Hockney, 2001). This drawing (Plate 32) is the most finely detailed and precise of the whole collection, and one could argue that a *camera lucida* was the means by which Kern attained his astonishing accuracy. Optical aids to drawing were carried along and used by many nineteenth-century expeditions, although there is no evidence that Gunnison's had this particular piece of equipment. The anamorphic distortion so characteristic of Kern's style is obviously present here, for the mountains are represented as perhaps 1.5 times higher in the drawing than they appear in the corresponding photograph, making it unlikely that a *camera lucida* was used. The regularly spaced vertical lines on the paper, the multiple compass readings, and Kern's keen eye are a more probable explanation for the precision exhibited in this drawing. When matched to photographs, others of Kern's drawings, though less detailed, are often similarly precise. Again, the anamorphic distortion in all of them argues for their having been drawn free-hand.

Many more representations with such high precision and cartographically appropriate detail must have existed. The very last item in the Gunnison-Beckwith *Report* is Appendix B, an exhaustive disquisition by Beckwith on the expedition's work of mapping titled "Explanations of Map and Illustrations." Strategically placed between the two reports that Beckwith wrote, it relates equally to both of them, embracing the skilled participation of Friedrich von Egloffstein in 1854, but also looking backward to the work done by Richard Kern for Captain Gunnison in 1853. It is at once an epilogue to the work of the first year and a prologue to the following year of the reconnaissance. This wide-ranging discussion of the expedition's topographic methods usefully informed readers of how the task was pursued as well as what to expect from and how to interpret the resulting maps and illustrations.

To show to what extent our topographical work may be depended upon as correct, I deem it proper to explain the manner of its execution, when it was immediately under my charge, after the experience of the first year's field-work under Captain Gunnison, assisted by Mr. Egloffstein, both in the field and in the office. Proper astronomical observations for the determination of geographical positions, and of the variation of the [compass] needle, were, of course, frequently made; the distances traversed were measured by odometers, two being used upon the same trail wherever it was practicable, for comparison, and barometric observations made at regular hours daily, as well as at all considerable changes of level, for altitudes. The party daily proceeded on its duties in such order as circumstances required, it being frequently necessary to locate our trail with accuracy, for a portion of it to keep a greater or less distance in advance of the topographer to enable him to take accurate bearings upon their successive positions on extensive plains, where no trees or prominent objects afford natural marks for this purpose; and to facilitate the taking of back-sights, if possible to discover any local attraction, or other source of error, smokes and camp-fires left behind were often found useful. In connection with the trail the topography adjacent to it was constantly laid down with great care, and the first favorable locality near it assumed for making observations of the country to a greater or less extent, and as accurate profile or outline sketches of it as our skill enabled us to execute, on which every prominent feature and landmark was noted with especial care, together with their magnetic bearings; and if distant snowy peaks were visible, angles of elevation were taken to the lower lines of snow, the general altitude of this line for the section of country and season of the year being once determined, affording great assistance in estimating the height of all other mountains in the vicinity, and were subsequently used for determining their distances from the point of observation, and the adjacent and middle ground portions were laid down with fidelity. Proceeding, then, for two, three, or four miles upon the trail, the distance, of course, varying with the formation of the country, the topographer again assumed the most favorable position in the vicinity for his purposes, and repeated the labors of the previous hour. In addition to this constant labor along the trail, it

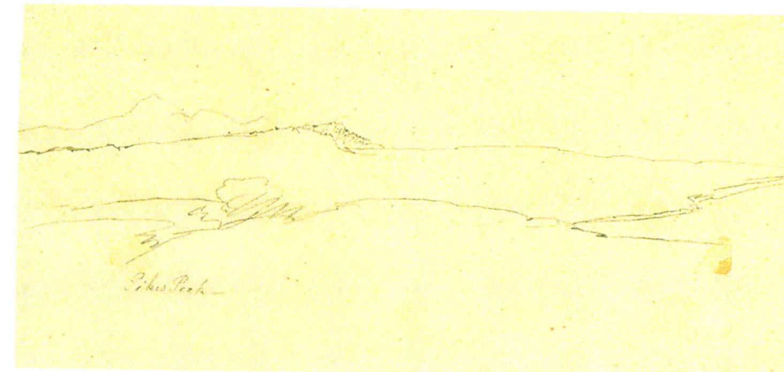

PLATE 35. Pikes Peak [August 6] 17.2 x 10.2 cm

frequently, almost daily, became necessary to leave it and make distant side trips, ascending elevated mountain peaks and ridges to obtain correct and distant views of the country, and I cannot speak too highly of the fidelity, zeal, and ability with which Mr. Egloffstein always performed these onerous labors. [Egloffstein was something of a mountain goat with a taste for climbing, perhaps acquired during his youth in Bavaria. He received a similar accolade from Lieutenant Joseph Ives for his work on the exploration of the Colorado River and the Grand Canyon in 1858.] In starting for such points, forward bearings were, of course, taken, and verified on his arrival by back-sights, and barometers read for altitude, both on his arrival and departure. It is not necessary here to describe the beauty, extent, and grandeur of the scenes which from these positions, in the pure atmosphere of this portion of our country, greeted him, frequently embracing an area equal to that of some of our Atlantic States, and presenting a multitude of plain and mountain outlines, with snow-capped peaks rising just on the verge of the horizon, and frequently remaining in sight for days, serving as points of reference, and all of which were carefully traced and noted for the delineation of the country. This labor done, those on the trail were resumed and continued to camp, where the mountain curves were filled up with shading lines, and every item of importance to the correct construction of the map recorded; for, in prosecuting for months labors of this kind in a mountainous country, it will not do to trust to the memory for its character on successive days. For field use a continuous map of the country was daily kept up, and the field-work, as here described for a day, was continued to completion (G-B, 127-128).

Plate 35, "Pikes Peak," is attached to and slightly overlaps the second sheet of the panoramic topographic drawing of the

PLATE 36. Photograph, Pikes Peak in the distance

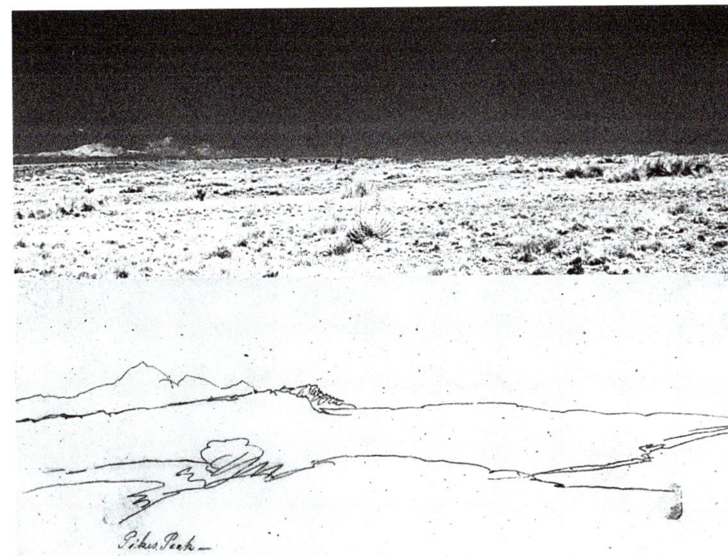

PLATE 37. Composite drawing and photograph

front range of the Rockies (Plate 31), and was most likely made from the same place. It has been cut so that the left side of the sheet ends exactly at the edge of the drawing, but nothing seems to have been removed. The grouping in the album here demonstrates again that on occasion, and for whatever reason, its compiler recognized the relatedness of three sketches and kept them adjacent to one another. Unfortunately for my own view of Pikes Peak, the hazy air, the obscuring clouds near the mountain, and the distance to the subject resulted in a most unsatisfying representation on film. To match the alignment of the cliff on the bluffs in the middle distance would have required an impractically long movement of the camera to the right and would have greatly distorted the foreground by omitting the slope (barely visible in the photograph) under the peak. It appears that Kern simply moved that cliff to the left and increased its stature to enhance what is otherwise a view that, aside from the outline of the distant peak, contains very little of artistic or topographic interest. It does contribute to the narrative, however, by demonstrating that Pikes Peak was in fact visible.

PLATE 38. Spanish Peaks, from near the Cuchara River, August 6, 1853, 20.1 x 11.6 cm

PLATE 39. Photograph, Spanish Peaks

The left end of Kern's elaborate drawing of the Front Range (Plate 31) goes only as far south as Mount Mestas, but standing in comparative isolation farther to the south are the Spanish Peaks, of which Kern made a beautiful drawing (Plate 38). Part of my general search method was to start with the easily found subjects, of which the Spanish Peaks are a prime example. Once located, such viewpoints would indicate the path or position of the expedition, and other more obscure or difficult subjects might turn out to be visible from nearby. This time, searching for the exact location from which Kern sketched the Spanish Peaks occupied me for days, without success.

These distinctive peaks can be identified without difficulty and their general appearance from the plains to their northeast remains about the same over a very wide area, but the emphatically drawn foreground in Kern's representation is another matter. While looking for his viewpoint I kept near the Cuchara River, but here the path of the expedition was more or less toward the peaks, so moving along it did not change their appearance very much. Despite my best efforts I could not find a location where the proper foreground was present and in the correct relation to the distant mountains, but when I finished my photographs of the preceding panorama (Plate 33) and

PLATE 40. Composite drawing and photograph, Spanish Peaks

PLATE 41. Lithograph by John Mix Stanley, Wah-Ha-Ta-Gas, or Spanish Peaks. From near the Cuchara River, August 6, 22.6 x 15.4 cm

of Pikes Peak (Plate 36), I turned to the southwest and compared the view with that of Kern's sketch of the Spanish Peaks. Everything fell into place, and it was apparent that all three drawings had been made from the same spot!

The of the rendering two peaks (Plate 38) is not on the thin yellow paper found most often in the album, but on a heavier, opaque white material. It is well-worked-out, with shading on the distant peaks and heavy markings characterizing the foreground, as though Kern were anticipating that he would eventually adapt it for use as an illustrative plate in the final publication. It is the first of twelve sketches by Kern that ultimately became lithographic illustrations in the Gunnison-Beckwith *Report*, this with the title "Wah-Ha-Ta-Gas or Spanish Peaks. From near the Cuchara, Aug. $6^{th}$. " (Plate 41).

This plate by John Mix Stanley is palpably based on Kern's sketch. "Wah-Ha-Ta-Gas" is a transliteration of an Indian name for these mountains, sometimes seen as "Wahatoyeh," that roughly means "Breasts of the World." Stanley redrew this sketch, as well as most of the others that appear in the Gunnison-Beckwith *Report*, and prepared them for

PLATE 42. Composite drawing and lithograph, Spanish Peaks

reproduction by lithography while maintaining a remarkable fidelity to the originals. Stanley had seen the Spanish Peaks during his own trip to New Mexico during the Mexican War, and as a result seems particularly sensitive to the spirit and the nuances of this dramatic pair of mountains.

Minor details are reinterpreted, softened, or otherwise altered, and a foreground added to balance the composition. The Indian on his horse with a lance adds human interest but detracts somewhat by providing an incorrect sense of scale. To the right are some of the far-off peaks of the Culebra Range, whose greater remoteness is indicated by means of atmospheric perspective; as distance increases, the scattering of light by the air changes the appearance of objects by softening their outlines, reducing their contrast, and shifting their color cast towards the blue. This strikingly handsome illustration is an example of a "tinted" or "toned" lithograph, created by using multiple lithographic stones to achieve a sense of color. Probably the method of placing the image on the stones used for printing was "transfer lithography," which, like almost everything else about the process, was first described by its inventor, Alois Senefelder (1819). The technique required that an original be traced or redrawn in waxy pencil on a sheet of transfer paper, which was much like a heavy tracing paper in texture. If the original was not of the desired dimension it could be outlined ina different size with a pantographic device, or a skillful artist could just redraw it free-hand. This drawing was then placed face down on a prepared lithographic stone and the greasy markings transferred to its surface by pressure and heat. A print taken by this method from the stone would be reproduced in its original orientation, and the process could be repeated to create multiple stones if a larger edition was needed than could be obtained from just one of them before it deteriorated through use. To achieve the effect of color, a "tinted" or "toned" lithograph such as this one required one or two additional stones that carried colored ink:

> Many...views published after the middle of the nineteenth century were printed with the basic design in black and with a second color added to provide cloud and shadow details. The most common colors were yellow brown or gray green...
>
> In the hands of a skilled lithographer, this one color could give the impression of a range of tonal values and even suggest other colors when used by itself, combined with blacks of varying intensity, or omitted altogether to produce highlight effects.
>
> Nearly as popular...were those printed with three stones. Normally, the printer used black, yellow-brown, and blue. Overprinting the two colors created green as a derivative. Thus the blue stone carried ink for the sky, water, and any grass or other vegetation to be green in the finished print. Yellow-brown appeared on...the shadowed sides of structures, and also in the areas of grass and trees to create green when combined with blue. The lithographer might also use yellow brown for bare earth and unwooded portions of distant hills and mountains.
>
> Such three-stone lithographs apparently came from the press with fairly intense colors. On many impressions today, however, the color is faded and appears less distinct because of general age-toning of the acidic pulp paper on which most were printed. In some cases one or both colors are so badly faded as to be discernible only after careful inspection (Reps, 29-30).

PLATE 43. Superimposition of Kern's sketch and Stanley's lithograph

Finally, the precision and respect with which Stanley treated Kern's field sketch can be verified by juxtaposing the two pictures (Plate 42), and then by digitally resizing and superimposing the sketch onto the lithograph (Plate 43). The general outlines have been adhered to almost as if they were traced, though not with a slavish attention to detail. It cannot have been merely traced, however, because, as is the case for all the lithographs in the Gunnison-Beckwith *Report*, this one is larger than the drawing. It could have been enlarged with a pantographic drawing machine or copied to a different size with a *camera lucida*, but more likely an artist of Stanley's skill would just redraw it free-hand. The simple lines of the sketch have been enhanced and transformed into the gradations and expressive qualities of a toned lithograph, with gentle contours rendered in place of Kern's penciled indications. The overall impression the lithograph gives is of a superior representation that fully expresses the grandeur of the scene, and leaves out nothing of importance. Some of the middle-ground details are altered in their character, such as the line of exposed rock just in front of the left peak that extends from the left edge of the drawing and descends slightly toward the right. This structure appears as a faint dark band in my photograph, and is today called the Big Dike. The Spanish Peaks are surrounded by hundreds of such dikes, walls of igneous material that were extruded upwards through fissures in softer sedimentary matter that later eroded away, leaving the magmatic ramparts standing free. I emphasize this detail because the Spanish Peaks retain their peculiar outline and character over a wide range of viewpoints, but the proper alignment of the Big Dike occurred only from the place where the broad panorama of the Front Range was drawn (Plate 31). In retrospect, I made a mistake in first pursuing the Spanish Peaks, for although it was an easily located subject it gave few clues to Kern's specific vantage point. I expected the viewpoint for the Front Range panorama of the same date to be difficult to pinpoint, but in fact the drawing contained so much explicit information that the only hardship was the amount of walking required.

PLATE 44. First chain of Rocky Mountains, Eastern base [August 6], 19.8 x 7.4 cm

Kern made yet another sketch from near the same spot (Plate 44). This, the fourth sketch of the day, is drawn on the same sort of paper as the Spanish Peaks (Plate 38), mounted on the same page of the album, and titled "First chain of Rocky Mts Eastern base." It is a view of the Culebra Range that seems to connect the Spanish Peaks to Mount Mestas, although the Culebras are in fact much more distant. The sketch was probably not intended to be in direct panoramic continuity with the right side of the "Spanish Peaks" (Plate 38) or the left end of "August 6 [Magnetic Bearings]" (Plates 31, 32) because it is a very exaggerated anamorphic representation. The heights of the mountains are drawn more than three times their width, whereas Kern depicted the two surrounding scenes with a ratio of less than two to one. The drawing is a rather simple outline sketch, in contrast to the well-worked-out views that it connects, and the mountain range it depicts is so far away that it is very hard to match details either visually or with a photograph. No foreground is present, so there is nothing in this drawing specific enough to determine an exact vantage point. Ultimately I photographed it (Plate 45) opportunistically on a clear day from a position about a mile from where I made the pictures for the Spanish Peaks, Pikes Peak, and the large topographic drawing, with its notations on the bearings of landmarks.

It is impossible to correctly scale the photograph to the drawing because of the latter's "elasticity." "First chain" appears to be an afterthought. Perhaps Kern drew the magnificent Front Range panorama that starts with Mount Mestas and stretches north; recorded the appearance of Pike's Peak in a separate sketch; turned to the southwest and delineated the Spanish Peaks, then filled in the gap. It is much less dramatic than either of the two drawings it connects because the Culebra Range it encompasses lacks distinctive shapes or dominant peaks, and is so much more distant that it cannot be seen clearly enough to define its makeup convincingly. Kern's sketch is lightly worked out and has a sort of irregularity in the lateral placement of details, so that it requires a great deal of concentrated study, both in the field and in the photographic comparison, to convince oneself that my

PLATE 45. Photograph, first chain of Rocky Mountains

PLATE 46. Composite drawing and photograph, first chain of Rocky Mountains

identification is not purely a creature of imagination. Kern's habit of sharpening the crests of peaks is disturbing here because none of them appear that jagged in actuality, but the device serves to indicate where he means to place each summit.

On August 6, while Kern was making his drawings from near the Cuchara River, Lieutenant Beckwith and a small escort rode northward to the settlement of Greenhorn looking for a guide. During his trip he passed the Huerfano Butte, which stands apart on the plain and next to the river to which it lends its name.

> *August* 6th.(continued)—Ten miles from the Cuchara we descended from the table-land to the valley of a stream evidently rising in the position laid down on some maps for the Huerfano, and on whose southern bank we had an hour before had a fine view of an isolated butte in its bottom—a feature of this valley marked and unmistakable. It is from this butte, from its isolation known as the Huerfano or Orphan butte, that this river derives its name (G-B, 34).

Beckwith succeeded in this quest, and on Sunday, August 7, while the expedition was taking its Sabbath rest in the camp near the Cuchara, he returned with Massalino, an experienced mountain man, and several of his companions. On August 8 the expedition followed the early portion of the route Beckwith had taken to Greenhorn, and, confident of finally being in the valley of the Huerfano, camped near its defining landmark.

> *August* 8.—We crossed immediately over to the Huerfano butte by the route which I had followed the previous day. This butte is one hundred and fifty feet in height, as determined by Mr. Homans, standing in the river bottom quite detached from the adjacent hills. Its diameter at the base is equal to twice its altitude, sloping up to its summit, which is about twenty-five by forty feet across. Its base is strewn around with prismatical blocks of granite rocks, of from one to six feet across, and its surface is also covered with these prisms, which are very dark—containing iron, perhaps, as a coloring matter. A narrow way, leading over the summit from the southeast, is nearly destitute of these rocks, on either side of which they are arranged in regular order... (G-B, 35).

Schiel also noted the appearance of Huerfano Butte, and commented on the maps as well:

PLATE 47. Second Huerfano Butte, Upper Huerfano River [August 8], 20.9 x 10.8 cm

PLATE 48. Second Huerfano Butte, Upper Huerfano River [August 8], 30.0 x 20.0 cm

On the 8th of August we moved our camp over into the vicinity of the Huerfano Butte, close to the foot of the mountain range. The Huerfano (orphan) butte is visible from a long distance. It is an isolated hill about 150 feet high, consisting of black granite quartz, glimmer (mica), and pebble slate... It is from this butte that the Huerfano or Orphan River, which flows past within gunshot, has received its name. The Huerfano is a raging mountain torrent eighteen feet wide and one foot deep. Its source is a narrow valley formed by the Sierra Mojada Blanca in the north and a foothill of the Sierra Blanca in the south. It flows into the open country and about twenty miles to the west of Apishapa, erroneously called Huerfano on the maps, it empties into the Arkansas (Schiel, 61-62).

Two sketches of Huerfano Butte with identical titles (Plates 47, 48) are attached to adjoining pages of the album. The smaller is the less well worked out of the two. The second drawing is a much more detailed version of the same scene. In the larger one, a series of light, vertically oriented lines along the horizon are of uncertain meaning but perhaps

PLATE 49. Juxtaposed drawings of Huerfano Butte

PLATE 50. Photograph, Huerfano Butte

indicate rain, although the meteorological observations indicate only dark clouds. Juxtaposing the two drawings (Plate 49) makes it clear that they represent the subject from precisely the same point of view.

I imagine that Kern began with the smaller of the two sketches, but because of its distinctive appearance and prominence as a navigational landmark, it must have been suggested that the scene would ultimately become a lithograph in the published report of the expedition. Kern then created a more suitably detailed work (Plate 48) that indicates the Huerfano River with a line of trees and takes in a wider field of view to better place the Butte in the context of the landscape. The tree in the left foreground is superimposed over details of the sky and background, so it was probably drawn in afterwards as a compositional accent and to close the composition on the left, something Kern does in other of his more highly elaborated sketches. Yet despite the attention lavished on this fine production and the importance of its subject as a marker, it was never used as an illustration in the Gunnison-Beckwith *Report*.

Since Kern's two drawings portray the subject from identical vantage points, I have juxtaposed only the larger, more detailed of them with the photograph. Mount Mestas is to the left and partially obscured by Silver Mountain, some of which is in turn covered by the Huerfano Butte.

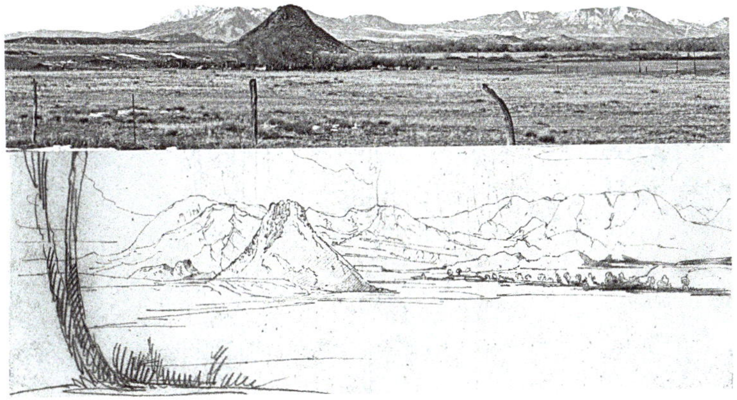

PLATE 51. Composite drawing and photograph, Huerfano Butte

PLATE 52. Huerfano Butte, lithograph based on a drawing by Gwinn Harris Heap

The loaf-shaped form off to the right is Sheep Mountain. Interstate 25 goes across the frame just behind the Butte but can hardly be seen.

It is not clear why the titles on both drawings refer to this as the "second" Huerfano Butte. If there were a "first" butte farther downstream the expedition would not have encountered it, because when they inadvertently went up the Apishapa they bypassed that part of the Huerfano River Valley. However, there is another striking formation some twenty miles up the Huerfano that is today called Gardner Butte, and that on the maps of the Gunnison expedition is marked "Black Butte." Gunnison and his men turned away from the Huerfano River just within sight of that butte, but not before Kern made a drawing of it (Plate 57). Kern had also passed by it and commented on its dramatic appearance while he was with Frémont's fourth expedition of 1848. By being upstream, Black Butte perhaps would be considered the "first," making the formation illustrated here into the "second" Huerfano Butte.

Other travelers also found the Huerfano Butte a compelling subject; earlier that summer Beale's expedition passed by this way, and Gwinn Harris Heap sketched it from a direction

PLATE 53. Huerfano Butte engraving based on a daguerreotype by Solomon Nunes Carvalho, re-oriented to match the scene

PLATE 54. Sierra Mojada, Camp 40 [August 10] Bottom drawing of two on a sheet of paper 13.2 x 19.0 cm

opposite to Kern's, so that the Huerfano River is seen in the foreground. The next year he and Thomas Hart Benton published the drawing as a tinted lithograph (Plate 52, "Huerfano Butte") in Heap's *Central Route to the Pacific* (1854, op 29).

A few months after the Gunnison expedition's visit to the area, Frémont's fifth expedition came up the Huerfano Valley, and Solomon Carvalho made a daguerreotype of the Butte from a position not far from the one Kern used. An engraving derived from that picture is in Frémont's *Memoirs of My Life* (1886, op 569). Because it was made from a daguerreotype, the engraved illustration was inadvertently printed reversed, as a mirror image of the scene (Shlaer, 2000). Here is Frémont's illustration reversed again, to show the view in its correct orientation (Plate 53. "The Huerfano Butte," engraving from a daguerreotype by Solomon Carvalho, and reoriented to match the scene.).

Two days' travel away from Huerfano Butte, the expedition made Camp 40 in the foothills of the Sangre de Cristo

PLATE 55. Photograph near the expedition's Camp 40

PLATE 56. Composite drawing and photograph, near the expedition's Camp 40

Mountains (Plate 54, "Sierra Mohada from 2-30 Camp 40".), from which they were to leave the valley and begin cutting a road southward up to Sangre de Cristo Pass. According to the table *Barometric and Meteorological Observations and Data for Profile* for August 10 (G-B, 97), the early morning was characterized by "Dark clouds"; at 2:30 p.m. it is noted to be "Stormy," and at 3:00 p.m. "Rain." I located the viewpoint, a place that overlooks today's Badito Crossing at the foot of Badito Cone, where I encountered a fortuitous rainstorm while making my photograph (Plate 55).

The not very distant Sierra Mojada, or Wet Mountains, still display enough detail to be a convincing match to the drawing. The hill sketched at the far left is in the photograph and plainly in front of the distant range of the Sierra Mojada; Kern shows it simply outlined against the horizon, probably because the rainstorm to which he was subjected so obscured it that he couldn't be certain of its position.

The central feature in Plate 57, "Wet Mountains," is the Gunnison expedition's "Black Butte," today Gardner Butte, near the town of Gardner, Colorado. Beckwith noted its appearance in a lengthy review and discussion of the entire Huerfano Valley and the approaches to Sangre de Cristo Pass that he wrote a few days later.

> *August* 13.—... Twelve miles above this gorge [of the Huerfano] stands the Black butte, an immense mass

PLATE 57. Wet Mountains [August 10], 19.0 x 15.1 cm

PLATE 58. Photograph, Wet Mountains

> of rocks with irregular points shooting up 100 and 200 feet (G-B, 37).

As was the case for the previous sketch "Sierra Mojada, Camp 40," (Plate 54), this view would have been drawn on August 10 and in the rain. The peculiar shape of Gardner Butte and its position adjacent to Colorado Highway 69 makes locating the subject relatively easy, while the backdrop of mountains are distinctively those of the Sangre de Cristo Range as they appear when looking up the Huerfano Valley to the northwest. The point of view aligns Gardner Butte with the most rugged of the mountains on the horizon (which turns out to be Crestone Peak), and this does not allow a lateral motion of more than a few feet. The "dip" in the foreground cannot be found anywhere and seems to have been rapidly penciled in as an afterthought. My search for the foreground was cut short by the discovery that I was sharing a pasture with a bull. When he was gone I went back, and ascertained that the foreground "dip" is entirely spurious. The site is a little bit north of Colorado 69 along 620 RD and near the town of Farisita, marking the farthest that Gunnison's expedition traveled up the Huerfano River before turning into the mountains. The view is roughly to the west-northwest, and the mountains in the distance are a part of the Sangre de Cristo Range that separates the Huerfano from the San Luis Valley. The closer

PLATE 59. Composite drawing and photograph, Wet Mountains

PLATE 60. Main chain of Sierra Blanca (eastern slopes), August 10 Bottom sketch of two on a sheet 20.1 x 15.1 cm

mountains and the high valley beyond them are sometimes considered to be part of the Wet Mountains; they are connected with those in the previous drawing that are here off to the right and out of the field of view (Plate 54). However slippery geographic names were in the nineteenth century, Black Butte is at the very least in the foothills of the Wet Mountains.

Many of the high peaks seen from here can be identified. The rugged one directly over Black Butte that looks dark in my photograph because of a cloud shadow is Crestone Needle, and beyond it Crestone Peak (14,294 ft.). They are practically one behind the other from this point of view, and so are difficult to identify separately. Barely visible against the sky and just to the right of the two Crestones is Kit Carson Peak (14,165 ft.), the summit of which is barely discernible between two closer mountains. Because of its greater distance Kit Carson seems to be much lower than Crestone. In the drawing Kit Carson is merged with the nearer and seemingly higher peak to its right, Marble Mountain, but Marble is much closer and some 900 feet lower. The high rounded mountain farthest to the right seen silhouetted against the sky is Humboldt Peak (14,064 ft.). Crestone Peak, Crestone Needle, Kit Carson, and Humboldt, closely grouped and each exceeding an altitude of 14,000 feet, were collectively known as "Les Trois Tetons," although exactly which three make up the group depends on the position from which they are viewed.

Plate 60, "Main chain of Sierra Blanca (eastern slopes") is almost the same view of the Sangre de Cristo Mountains as in the previous drawing (Plate 57), and it was made on the same day. The distant peaks are readily visible from much of the

PLATE 61. Photograph, Sierra Blanca

PLATE 62. Composite of drawing and photograph, Sierra Blanca

Huerfano Valley, but the foreground implies a viewpoint up in foothills, perhaps along the route the expedition was using to cut a road to Sangre de Cristo Pass. I have not been able to locate the steep wooded hillsides of the foreground; drawn in a much more emphatic line than the background, it creates a strong sense of depth through superposition plus a feeling of atmospheric perspective, and because it is superimposed on some background details it may have been added later for artistic purposes. Giving up on the foreground, I then concentrated on representing the distant mountains, which in my photograph include some of Mount Zwischen on the left and all of Black (Gardner) Butte on the right.

The view is similar to what is seen in the previous drawing, (Plate 57), but extends farther leftward. The highest peak is Mount Herard, and rising to the left before it is the slope of Mount Zwischen. Concealed between Mount Zwischen and Mount Herard is the trail to Medano Pass (also called Sandhill or Williams), one of the ways through the Sangre de Cristo range that had been suggested as an alternative to the route Gunnison was going to take. He later entered it from the floor of the San Luis Valley and explored it for a short distance, but did not think it promising enough to continue.

Today the proper name of a pass is typically placed on maps at its literal high point, which usually would be the saddle on a ridge connecting yet higher mountains on either side. This, the summit of a pass, is by its nature a tiny fraction of a vast landscape, and pointing signs are frequently needed in maps because the printed name occupies too large and ill-defined an area. In common nineteenth-century usage, however, a pass consists of a much broader extent, one that

PLATE 63. View eastward from El Sangre de Cristo Pass (Huerfano River). [August 10?] 28.0 x 15.0 cm

PLATE 64. Photograph, looking east from El Sangre de Cristo Pass

includes the totality of the crest and its approaches from both sides. In the Gunnison-Beckwith *Report*, in its maps, and in the notations on Richard Kern's drawings, the word "Pass" refers to the entire traverse from beginning to end. Thus when the expedition first left the relatively level Huerfano

PLATE 65. Composite drawing and photograph, looking east from El Sangre de Cristo Pass

Valley and began to ascend through the Sierra Blanca to the south, it had entered "Sangre de Cristo Pass." On the map that accompanies the *Report*, the pass is identified by snaking text along the length of two valleys, one on either side of the crest. (Tellingly, the path the writing on this map follows up from the Huerfano River is not the route where Gunnison had his men cut the road, but along an easier course that was discovered later, from information provided by the guide Massalino.)

Plate 63, "View eastward from El Sangre de Cristo Pass - (Huerfano R.)" is looking to the east from somewhere along Gunnison's road to the summit of Sangre de Cristo Pass.

PLATE 66. Huerfano River (near Camp 40) [August 10], 19.8 cm x 11.7 cm

PLATE 67. Photograph, near Camp 40

PLATE 68. Composite drawing and photograph, near Camp 40

Just to the right of center is the Huerfano River, flowing away from the viewer. On the left are some fairly close slopes behind which is a flat-topped prominence, perhaps a foothill of the Sangre de Cristo Range, but I can find nothing in the area that approaches its steepness and distinctively symmetrical silhouette. Private property boundaries curtailed the search, so in the photograph I have appropriated the Sierra Mojada to create the slope in the composition, even though it seems much too far away. Huerfano Butte is clearly present in the sketch as a small symmetrical form out on the plain, one-third of the way in from the right edge and not quite reaching up to the horizon. It cannot be seen at all in the photograph and was only barely visible in the distance when I was at this site.

On August 10 the expedition was at Camp 40 ("Huerfano River (near camp 40)" Plate 66), and the weather was mostly cloudy and rainy. Again I was fortunate to be near the campsite on a rainy day and so could make a photographic view that may approximate what Kern was seeing. As has been the case with most of the drawings from this day, I was unable to locate the appropriate foreground, and had to make do with an approximation. It is the last of the many small sketches

Kern made on the rainy day of August 10, and they all seem to have peculiar, hard-to-locate foregrounds. I am more certain here of the distant view despite Kern's extreme exaggeration of the vertical. It is looking across the Huerfano Valley to the Sierra Mojada where the crest of Greenhorn Mountain is obscured by clouds, Badito Cone is to the far right, and the foothill in the middle of the drawing is outlined in my photograph by ground fog rising behind it. Schiel described August 10 as a day of general discomfort.

> We...sought to gain the height of the Sangre de Cristo Pass, but were forced to put up our tents once more in a luxuriant field because of heavy rain (Schiel, 65).

In rain and fog Kern could not make detailed observations of distant landmarks, nor could he readily work on meticulous topographic drawings. Perhaps he used the time between downpours to create small, rapid sketches, after which he may have returned to his tent and filled in foreground details from memory, not always correctly.

The next sketch (Plate 69), Titled "Wet Mountains__ Huerfano R." includes within its view the position of Camp 40 of August 9-10, so it probably dates from the following day, August 11, when the weather must have cleared. There is no weather entry for "Camp 41—in Sangre de Cristo Pass" (G-B, 97), but the altitude is given as 8757 feet, some 1300 feet higher than Camp 40. It seemed that the simple way to find the viewpoint was to locate Gunnison's road or its remnants, and then follow it up the mountain. There were several candidates for the route, but I was prevented from continuing high enough on any of them by private holdings, fences, locked gates, "No Trespassing" signs, dogs, and landowners who could not be identified or located. The roads beyond the fences looked as though they would be impassable for my vehicle, and even if I obtained permission to enter, walking for miles along each of several candidates up their steeply inclined ways in order to determine the correct one did not seem practical. Abandoning the bottom-up approach, I started instead from the top down. A wedge of land belonging to what was then the Forbes Trinchera Ranch separates US 160 from the high ridge of Sangre de Cristo Pass, over which Gunnison built his road. I visited the ranch headquarters near Fort Garland, where I met Ty and Alicia Ryland, who manage it. From them I obtained permission to explore the area, and when I did so the next day I found a primitive road that climbed toward the crest, went through a gate in a fence, then down the other side. It looked as if it was still in occasional use for ranching purposes, but there were no "Keep Out" signs, so I

PLATE 69. Wet Mountains—Huerfano River [August 11?], 26.9 cm x 12.5 cm

PLATE 70. Panoramic photograph, Wet Mountains—Huerfano River

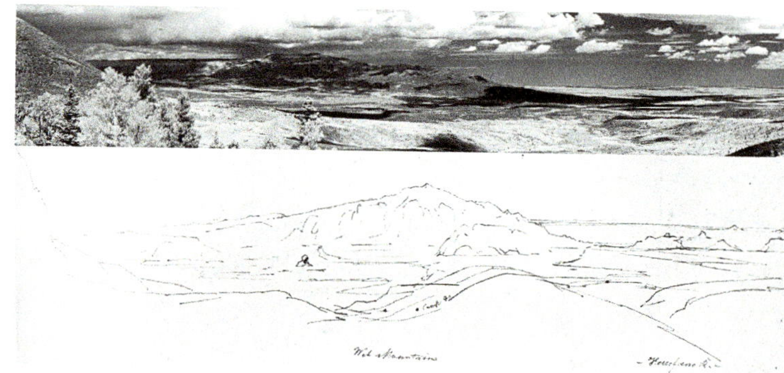

PLATE 71. Composite drawing and photograph, Wet Mountains—Huerfano River

PLATE 72. Les Trois Tetons in the distance (Sierra Blanca) [August 11], 19.2 x 12.3 cm

crawled under the barrier and was on my way! Soon I found myself in a dense forest where I could only occasionally see far enough to reassure myself that I was traveling in generally the right direction. I was actually searching for two scenes that I suspected had been made from along the road. By going at it in the reverse of the expedition's progression I first found and photographed "Les Trois Tetons in the distance (Sierra Blanca)" (Plate 72), which confirmed that I was on the correct track. I then arrived at a fairly satisfactory location for "Wet Mountains —Huerfano River" (Plate 69). If I could I

PLATE 73. Photograph of "Les Trois Tetons in the distance"

would have gone somewhat lower and more to the right, but was prevented by a fence with a locked gate and a "Keep Out" sign, beyond which dense woods and rough terrain rose up to block my view. The usual afternoon thunderstorm was rapidly approaching, encouraging me to act quickly and get out of the woods, climb back over the crest of the pass, and descend to relative safety before it struck.

PLATE 74. View of Sangre de Cristo Pass looking northeast from camp north of summit, August 11. Lithograph by John Mix Stanley.

In the drawing, (Plate 69), Gardner (Black) Butte is emphasized as a small, darkened shape about a third of the way in from the left and at the base of the Wet Mountains, the high point of which is Greenhorn in the center. In the photograph, the Butte cannot be seen, probably because my position was not ideal so the slopes to the left obscure it. Kern's Huerfano River is vaguely represented by curving lines, that turn away from the viewer as it passes to the right of Greenhorn and out into the plains. Camp 40 is present as a point of reference from the

PLATE 75. Composite drawing and lithograph

day before; it was probably located by leaving a smoky campfire burning at the site, a mapping technique that Beckwith mentions in his Appendix B (G-B, 125-128). Despite appearances this practice did not recklessly place the entire forest at risk, for not only had it rained for most of the day before, but also the whole mountain had already been largely burned off in the great fire of 1851.

Plate 72, "Les Trois Tetons in the distance (Sierra Blanca)," is the second drawing for which I expected to find the viewpoint along Gunnison's road, but because I was traveling backwards in the sequence it is the one that I came upon first. The sketch has been tightly trimmed on its sides, and a small amount of material appears to have been lost at the left edge. "Les Trois Tetons" are the three distant, sharp, and closely spaced peaks lightly depicted on the horizon about one-third of the way in from the left edge. They can be easily seen from just above Sangre de Cristo Pass, as this detail in a photograph made from higher up illustrates (Plate 73).

While I descended along Gunnison's road I was able to see "Les Trois Tetons," but by the time I reached a point from which I could correctly visualize the scene in the drawing, gathering stormclouds obscured them. Of the most distant peaks in Plate 73, the one farthest left is a somewhat rounded-looking Kit Carson Peak, then comes the double-pointed Crestone Peak, with the single sharp summit of Crestone Needle to its right. The broad, curved mountain at the right edge is Humboldt Peak. Aside from these remote mountains, the sketch is of what appears to be a winding road in a valley

PLATE 76. Panoramic photograph

among the close-in mountains. A lithograph derived from the drawing and printed in the Gunnison-Beckwith *Report* reinforced my supposition that this is Gunnison's road (Plate 74. "View of Sangre de Cristo Pass looking northeast from camp north of summit, August 11").

Stanley has smoothed the distant mountains and entirely omitted the lightly penciled "trois Tetons," perhaps because he did not understand the import of those little bumps in the distance. The nearer hills are well copied, but the "road" is shortened at both ends. Only a small amount of foreground with rocks was added, along with the requisite figures, among whom is a mounted rider facing an Indian on foot, who is in turn gesturing towards the zigzag "road" upon which interpolated men and animals are heading away from the viewer and up a seeming slope. Trusting the expanded title of the lithograph (view of Sangre de Cristo Pass looking northeast from camp north of summit, August 11) meant that by following Gunnison's road from the crest I would arrive at the site of Camp 41 and readily locate this view, which is just what happened; but I was not forewarned of what I would actually see.

The tiny drawing (Plate 72) encompasses a wide panorama that overlooks the Huerfano Valley and reaches to Sheep Mountain on the right ("Panoramic photograph," Plate 76). I could not retreat far enough nor climb high enough to quite duplicate the relations depicted in the sketch because of encroaching forest, but the basic aspect of the scene is clear enough. Because the sketch is so highly compressed laterally there was no reasonable way to juxtapose the drawing with the photograph, so instead I have reproduced the drawing several times under the photograph, along with the photographic detail that shows "Les trois Tetons" from higher up, placed beneath the spot where these peaks would appear on

PLATE 77. Composite photograph and repeated drawings

the horizon had they not been obscured by gathering clouds (Plate 77).

When I arrived at the site, I also discovered that the apparent "road" in the drawing and in the lithograph is actually a streambed! The passage that Gunnison constructed and that I was following is not visible because it was here roughly parallel to the plane of the photograph and almost under my feet. This was in August of 2003, a year of such extreme drought that the channel of the stream was empty of water except for a small pond and the whole forest was tinder-dry, making me slightly nervous about lightning strikes that threatened later in the afternoon, possibly igniting fires. At 9,100 feet I must not have been far from Camp 41, the elevation of which was given as 8,800 feet.

> The weather till noon fine and cool, then we get thoroughly wet by a rain we have to encamp in… We are through the wet mountains and are passing the so-called Sangere [Sangre] de Cristo (Creutzfeldt, August 11).

> *August* 11.—We…encamped, in a shower of rain, amidst luxuriant fields of blue grass (of the mountain men) and flowers. Quaking-asp covers the moun-

tains around us, interspersed with small pines. Fire, however, swept over these mountains two years ago, destroying much of the timber...

*August* 12.—A working party was engaged during yesterday afternoon in opening a road through the forest to the summit of the pass, and much of to-day has been spent in the same manner and in working on the opposite side-hill, along which it is necessary to descend from the pass. The teams, too, were engaged all day in making the ascent as the road advanced, and at dark the most of them had reached the summit, and a few had descended to El Sangre de Cristo creek; and all were obliged to encamp where night overtook them, on a line of two or three miles, on the summit and either side of the pass. The examination of the various depressions in the mountains also went on to-day, to ascertain their elevations and practicability for roads. The scenery around us is very fine—the views from various points extending far back over the plains, buttes, ridges, and streams, on which we have for so many days laboriously pursued our march. The bold, rocky mountain peaks tower loftily above us—whitened here and there with lines of snow—around which, at mid-day, dark masses of clouds gather and the lightning plays, while torrents of rain pour down their sides with irresistible fury...

*August* 13.—The labor of crossing the ridge was completed this morning, and just in advance of the 1 o'clock shower we encamped in, but near, the head of the southern descent of the pass, on the Sangre de Cristo, which is a small stream of clear, cold water, in a beautiful little park or valley. The labor of crossing this summit has been very considerable, which is partly owing, however, to the rarified atmosphere at so great an elevation. Both men and animals were soon exhausted and obliged constantly to stop and rest, where at a lower altitude no rest would have been required. Our teams were all doubled, without being then able to do the ordinary work of a single one, and the strongest men sat down out of breath after a few moments' exertion (G-B, 36-37).

Beckwith describes an expedition that was assaulted by daily cloudbursts, weakened by lack of oxygen, and stretched out for miles along the mountain road it was building. Kern must have gone with the crew that was sent ahead on August 11 and then reached the crest of the pass with them, because

PLATE 78. In Sangre de Cristo Pass (August 11) 19.9 x 15.2 cm

that is where the drawing "In Sangre de Cristo Pass" (Plate 78) was made.

The characteristic late-summer mountain rains would have both limited visibility and made it difficult for Kern to work while keeping his materials dry, circumstances that may account for the odd nature of his sketch. At the top of the sheet is a view with one easily identified landmark: Mount Lindsey, the high peak to the left with a notch at its apex. To its right is a slightly lower peak with "gn" on it, probably an abbreviation for "green." Below the title there

PLATE 80. Continuous panoramic drawing

PLATE 79. Photograph, Sangre de Cristo Pass

PLATE 81. Composite drawing and photograph

PLATE 82. Part of Sangre de Cristo Pass Panorama; Sierra Blanca and El Sangre de Cristo Creek (Valley); Sierra Blanca; Wet Mountains and Sangre de Cristo Pass Panorama [August 15?] 160.2 x 14.1 cm

is a vague sketch of mountainous shapes with an uncertain relation to the better worked out upper portion. There are four possibilities: First, that the sketch portrays a single scene from a high point of view, and the lower portion is of hills and valleys nearby but far below; second, the drawing is a panoramic view with the lower portion belonging on the left of the upper; third, the same, a panoramic view, but with the lower portion belonging to the right of the upper; and fourth, the two are unrelated, but just happen to be on the same sheet of paper. The only way to choose among these alternatives was to locate the scene and compare it with the drawing. Since the upper portion of the sketch has the distinctive outline of Mount Lindsey and of the adjacent peak to the right of it, this was not difficult, and the point of view turns out to be on the ridgeline high above and to the east of Sangre de Cristo Pass.

83. Panoramic Photograph of the Sangre de Cristo Pass.

Once found, two alternatives could be eliminated: The lower part of the sketch does not fit on the left end of the scene, and there is nothing below (and closer) than what is portrayed in its upper portion to indicate that the whole drawing is correct as it stands. If the bottom is of something else entirely, its minimal contours do not bring to mind anything with which I am familiar, so for the sake of argument I have digitally attached it to the right of the upper portion with Photoshop® (Plate 80).

Since there are no alignment marks I have assumed what I think is the best of three possible configurations, one that aligns the horizon, but it remains difficult to see how the sketch represents the right-hand portion of the scene. Because of this uncertainty I retained an extra measure of my panoramic photograph at each end so that readers can form their own opinions. I have been unable to make even a marginally satisfactory alignment on the right side, no matter how I altered the relative magnification and lateral relationship of the photograph to the drawing. Instead I have adjusted sizes to match the photograph to the left-hand part of the drawing, with its superior detail, then let the right-hand portion fall where it may. My thought here is that the bottom of the sketch was hastily done in the rain and is incomplete, with some of the higher mountains that should be seen against the sky partially omitted. I can see some details within the bulk of the mountain on the right that suggest a correspondence to bits of the sketch, but never clearly or consistently enough to assert it with confidence. It is possible that the peaks drawn farthest to the right are not close by but rather a part of the distant range seen in the photograph, in which, if it had been extended a bit more to the right, the tiny shapes of Les Trois Tetons would show their silhouettes against the sky.

Plate 82 is an immense panorama in four parts with multiple notations written upon it, the first of which is "Part of Sangre de Cristo Pass Panorama." A broad range of dates are possible for this drawing because the expedition remained near Sangre de Cristo Pass for days while finishing Gunnison's road up to its crest and down the other side. The only clue that narrows the time frame a bit is a simple marking of "Camp" located in the valley along Sangre de Cristo Creek. According to Table II, this would be "Camp 42, Sangre de Cristo Valley" (G-B, 98), which was located at the spot shown on the drawing, was first occupied on August 14, and was maintained there through August 17. This outsized panoramic drawing is the first of three large foldouts in the album; it is a little more than five feet long and encompasses a horizontal field of view of about 270°. The whole is made up of four sheets of paper, each numbered at the top, of which "1," the leftmost, is 25.9 cm wide, "2" is 55.8 cm, "3" is 35.1 cm, and "4" 44.3 cm in width. At the extreme left and right ends of the panorama there are short horizontal lines, each with a small "x" drawn through it. These marks suggest the ones Kern uses on occasion to indicate the correct alignment of separate segments of a sketch that he intends to join into a continuous panorama, but when he does that the lines marked with an "x" are a part of the sketch and correspond to elements in the scene. These pencil marks do not relate to any detail in the sketch, and one of them is drawn over some of its content. On closer inspection there are three more of these, one at the far right side of the first sheet where it joins the second, one that is just a small cross (+) without a line through it at the far left edge of the third sheet where it joins the second, and one in the middle of the fourth sheet between a lone burned tree and Sheep Mountain. From their positions and their uniform placement vertically it appears that their function is to indicate the true horizon, something hard to define when looking off a high mountain range, but that could be readily determined with the expedition's surveying instruments.

The panorama hosts a multitude of inscriptions. At the bottom of the first panel it reads "Part of Sangre de Cristo Pass Panorama." At the bottom of the second panel is "Sierra Blanca," above which near the upper edge is a two-word note the first of which I cannot decipher, but the second is "Sage," possibly referring to the color to be used in some part of the

PLATE 84. Composite drawing and photograph

scene when turning the drawing into a painting. Then farther to the right on panel 2 appears "El Sangre de Cristo Creek (Valley)," above which can be seen the note "Camp." Panel 3 has "Sierra Blanca" again at the bottom. The fourth sheet reads "Wet Mountains," and then at the far right, "Sangre de Cristo Pass Panorama."

Unlike Kern's other panoramas, the first three pieces of paper were joined together and probably attached to their backing before being drawn upon, for the paper is mounted with only the tiniest overlap and Kern's pencil marks cross the first two seams with no discontinuities at all. The third seam is overlapped to a greater degree, and there are minor discontinuities between the details on either side, which suggests the fourth panel was drawn upon separately and attached later. Its scene may even have been viewed from a slightly different position than were the other three.

The viewpoint for this panorama is high up on the slope east of Sangre de Cristo Pass, but not quite to the top. I could seemingly get very close to the correct location, but I could not see the right third of the scene from my initial position, and had to finish the panorama from approximately 1/4 mile away, down and west along the ridgeline where a gap in the forest allowed me a clear view. To make the entire panorama I had to first locate the two suitable positions and mark them with

little cairns of stones. Then I set up at the first one and made the left portion of the panorama, packed up, crawled under the fence that can be seen on the right in that segment of the photograph, walked quickly toward the second cairn and set up again, then made the second part of the picture. The time this took was enough for clouds to gather to the north over the aptly named Sierra Mojada, and they can be seen in the right-hand segment, where they markedly changed the appearance of the sky. When Kern drew his view it was just two years after a fire had scorched the area, so I imagined at first that he had an open view that made it possible for him to complete the entire view from one spot. After I tried and failed to visualize the entire panorama from a single point of view, it occurred to me that the burned trunks of trees still standing in 1853 would have been as serious a visual obstacle as today's living ones. If Kern also had to change his position, it would explain why the fourth segment of the panorama was drawn separately, and then afterward was attached to the rest of it. By continuing the panorama to the right he was better able to delineate the terrain surrounding what Gunnison already felt was to be one of the signal achievements of his expedition, the road over Sangre de Cristo Pass.

Matching the photograph with the drawing, one can appreciate both the magnificence and the accuracy of Kern's

PLATE 85. Lithograph by John Mix Stanley, "Sangre de Cristo Pass Looking towards San Luis Valley"

panorama. If the joining of the fourth sheet to the left-hand group of three was indeed done after the fact because he drew it from two different places, Kern chose the same point of discontinuity that I was forced to use, and perhaps for the same reason.

From the left there is first the outline of Rough Mountain, adjacent to which is the higher and better worked out Mount Mestas; its right slope then cuts across part of the more distant West Spanish Peak. A bit farther right in a notch in the mountain range is a distant peak in Kern's drawing, but not in my picture. It may appear that the clouds have obscured it in the photograph, but that is not the case: In fact, there is no peak there. Beginning on the far right of the first sheet and continuing onto the second and third are, a multiplicity of little x's are scattered about. These are a shorthand device that Kern often used to indicate a common character, such as snow or woods, to save the effort of drawing it out everywhere; he could later use the marks as a guide to make a finished painting. Near the left end of sheet 2, in a little notch in the hills and just above and to the left of an "x" on one of them, is a tentatively drawn and barely visible summit. The photograph shows it more clearly against some clouds, and it is Mariquita Peak. Slightly to its right, higher, and much easier to see from the ridge is Trinchera Peak, but for whatever reason Kern did not place it in his drawing.

"Sierra Blanca" was the term used by members of the expedition to designate all the mountains among which they now found themselves. The highest mountain in the vicinity is Blanca Peak, of which the expedition rarely got a clear view. It was given its name because even without snow it has a white appearance above its tree line. "El Sangre de Cristo Creek (Valley) right of the first sheet and continuing through

PLATE 86. Lithograph by John Mix Stanley: "Sangre de Cristo Pass," from near the summit, looking down Gunnison's Creek"

the second and third," above which the camp of August 14-17 appears, is a view westward over the small park through which the expedition would descend to Fort Massachusetts and the San Luis Valley. At the right end of sheet 2 is a sharp peak that is outlined against the sky as it juts up over the nearby hills, along with another slightly lower one just to its right, and some smaller, more rounded mountains to the left. The highest of these is Mount Lindsey, a landmark that the men had had intermittantly in view for more than a week. Near its base was Fort Massachusetts, towards which they were traveling, and where they would stay for several days. On sheet 3 is the ridge on which Sangre de Cristo Pass lies. It is marked out in the drawing by an irregular line starting above the right end of the word "Blanca" and leading away from the observer; in the photograph a fence runs adjacent to and a bit to the left of the apex of the ridgeline. The place where I made the second part of my panorama is visible to the right of the fence, shortly before it disappears over the hillside, near some aspens that are a bit to its right. On sheet 4 near the middle is Little Sheep Mountain and to its right the higher Sheep Mountain. Below it is the inscription "Wet Mountains," which are to be seen in the distance on both sides of Sheep Mountain. The high peak to the right is the distant Greenhorn Mountain, and adjacent yet farther right is the final landmark of the scene, the conical outline of Badito Cone. Below Badito is written "Sangre de Cristo Pass Panorama."

There are two lithographs based on segments of this one large drawing. The first (Plate 85) is titled "Sangre de Cristo Pass Looking towards San Luis Valley." At the lower left it reads "Bald Peak in the distance," and on the lower right "Sierra Blanca in the distance." The view is really very broad

PLATE 87. Panoramic drawing juxtaposed with two lithographs

and centered toward the south over today's Culebra Range; only on the right is it looking down the valley of Sangre de Cristo Creek towards the San Luis Valley. "Bald Peak" may refer to Mount Mestas on the far left, or else to West Spanish Peak, also distinctly bald in the drawing, but Stanley's use of atmospheric perspective has softened its more distant presence so that its outlines are too blurred to make the baldness explicit. Elsewhere in the *Report* Beckwith describes an examination that Gunnison and a small party made of the Culebra Mountains to the south, and includes in it quotes from Gunnison's journal.

> *August* 13. (continued)—... After completing the examination of the Sangre de Cristo Pass, Captain Gunnison made an examination of the mountains to the south of the Spanish Peaks... the party ascended a high peak and looked down upon the extensive plains, over which, for a month, we had wound our way. The view was majestically beautiful, with the Huerfano, Cuchara and Apishapa at their feet, and towering mountains to the north and south, with the valley of San Luis to the west. Descending again...[they] then rode up hill for two hours...and arrived at the summit of the ridge, "where one could look almost vertically down on the heads of creeks of the Cuchara—one of which winds under Bald mountain, considerably to the south of the Spanish Peaks..." (G-B, 37-39).

"Sierra Blanca" is what Kern wrote at the bottom of the corresponding part of his sketch, but when the annotator added "in the distance" he perhaps makes too fine a distinction. All of the high mountain ranges in the area were called "Sierra Blanca" by the expedition, so this view is both from the Sierra Blanca and includes a portion of it, distance notwithstanding.

The second lithograph (Plate 86) is titled "Sangre de Cristo Pass, From near the Summit, looking down Gunnison's Creek." In this case the title is precisely correct. Gunnison's Creek (now called Pass Creek) arises near Sangre de Cristo Pass and flows generally north to join the Huerfano River. The two lithographs that were created from this one panorama are shown here (Plate 87) juxtaposed to the portion of the panoramic drawing from which each is derived.

Aside from the high quality of Stanley's renderings, one thing stands out about the presentation of the drawing: The portions of it that became lithographs were largely worked over and elaborated by Kern, while the rest remained simpler in execution. Gunnison must have anticipated that he would comprehensively and elegantly illustrate parts of this view from El Sangre de Cristo Pass in his published account, and apparently told Kern, who responded by making chosen portions of his drawing more elaborate and "artistic." Unlike the similarly well-worked-out drawing of Huerfano Butte (Plate 48), these two segments were ultimately incorporated by Beckwith into the *Report*.

The guide Massalino now observed that a route roughly along Gunnison's Creek would be a better approach to Sangre de Cristo Pass from the Huerfano Valley than the one the expedition's men had labored over so intensively, and that Beckwith would describe as "a line entirely impracticable for a railroad." He then devotes a whole page of the *Report* to detailing the better alternative that Mossalino pointed out (G-B, 37-38). On August 13 Captain Gunnison and a small party explored Massalino's route and confirmed its superior qualities. Schiel went along and described the event.

> With Mossalino as a guide and escorted by eight dragoons Captain Gunnison and I rode out in the early morning to investigate a pass that until now had only been known to hunters. Our guide assured us that it was less steep than those of the Sangre de Cristo. We found the remarks of our guide confirmed, for this pass descends constantly and gradually from the ridge of the mountain that connects it with the Sangre de Cristo pass into the Huerfano valley (Schiel, 66).

It is this route of Massalino's that the ultimate map of the expedition marks out as "Sangre de Cristo Pass," not the road that Gunnison's exhausted men cut more directly up the slopes. Today, county roads follow very much along this line, from the town of Malachite in the Huerfano Valley up to Pass Creek Pass, emerging on US 160 just a few miles from Sangre de Cristo Pass and North La Veda Pass. Creutzfeldt often expressed strong criticisms of Gunnison's personal conduct, but perhaps triggered by this episode there now begins a recurring theme in which he questions Gunnison's judgment as leader of the expedition as well. By acting decisively but prematurely, Gunnison had entered into a brute-force approach to the crossing and exhausted his men, instead of first looking to see if there was a better and easier way. Neither, apparently, did he even discuss the issue with Massalino, the guide Beckwith had just hired. Creutzfeldt noted the possibility of an easier way over the mountains the day before Gunnison conducted his examination of it.

> It becomes evident that there is a better pass farther North, which we could have taken if we had acted with more circumspection (Creutzfeldt, August 12).

PLATE 89. Photograph, following Untitled [August 15]

PLATE 88. Untitled [August 15?], 17.7 x 8.4 cm

**ERROR HAS ITS USES**

Plate 88 is without a title, either because it was trimmed off or never had one. Its appearance is deceptive because of its general resemblance to "Sierra Mohada from 2-30 Camp 40" (Plate 54). I wandered all over the Huerfano Valley looking for

PLATE 90. Composite drawing and photograph

the scene of this "Untitled," but fortunately I also spent days high up near Sangre de Cristo Pass hunting for something else that by its title should have been there but was not, a drawing titled "In Sangre de Cristo Pass" (Plate 155). The futile search for it led me ultimately to a spot high up along the ridge of the pass, from where the view in this "Untitled" scene suddenly materialized. Error occasionally has its uses: In the extended process of failing to find a scene that was mistitled and in fact not there at all, I came across another that I probably never would have located otherwise. The aspens in the left foreground of my photograph obscure some of the detail in the valley, but the rest of the match is extraordinarily good.

# 3

# The Rio Grande del Norte

*Fort Massachusetts, then up the San Luis Valley, and over the Continental Divide at Cochetopa Pass*

THE EXPEDITION NOW DESCENDED along the Sangre de Cristo Valley to Fort Massachusetts, a military outpost that had been established a few years earlier on Ute Creek in order to control Indian incursions into the San Luis Valley. (The location was ill chosen, and a few years after Gunnison's expedition visited here the garrison moved to a better site a few miles to the south and there constructed Fort Garland.) Gunnison's men began their descent from the mountains while Lieutenants Beckwith and Baker (the latter being second in command to Captain Morris of the armed escort) were sent to Taos to find a guide to replace Massalino. He was leaving them after having fulfilled his contract to bring them "to Fort Massachusetts, in the San Luis Valley of New Mexico," and Creutzfeldt was going to miss him and his companions.

> Our guide and two hunters leave us today, in consequence of which both lieutenants are sent to Taos, about 70 miles distant in order to get guides for the passes on the sources of the Rio Grande... (Creutzfeldt, August 15).
>
> We have these last 8 days always fresh meat, the huntsmen knowing the hiding places of the game. It is a pity that they left us with the guide (Creutzfeldt, August 16).

While Creutzfeldt looked back to past gustatory pleasures, Beckwith moved forward to find a replacement for Massalino, and reflected on the hard-won knowledge possessed by the mountain men.

> Our recent experience in exploring a wild mountainous country without guides, was such as to show the necessity of profiting by the practical lessons in geography gained in the school of the trapper and hunter, by that useful class of mountaineers who have spent many years of their lives in encountering the hardships and the imminent dangers hourly incident to their occupation in these fields of savage barbarity, short-lived gratitude and native grandeur, which are annually stained by the sacrifice of some of their number as victims to unbridled ferocity. Accompanied by Lieutenant Baker, I accordingly started on the $15^{th}$ instant from our camp at the head of El Sangre de Cristo valley, for Taos, New Mexico, the headquarters of many of the most reliable and experienced of these mountain men...
>
> ...Procuring what information we could of the country westward over which we were to pass, and the services of a guide, we returned in thirty hours to

PLATE 91. San Luis Valley, Williams Ranch, Sangre de Cristo Pass, (Sierra Blanca, Rocky Mountains) [August 19?] 17.8 x 13.2 cm

> our camp, (which in our absence had been moved but fifteen miles,)...arriving at noon on the $19^{th}$ of August. On the following day we were joined by the experienced and well-known guide, Antoine Leroux (G-B, 39-40).

Here at the edge of the San Luis Valley, Kern would meet once again a famous mountain man and old acquaintance. Leroux was widely traveled and greatly respected for his knowledge of the West. He had been one of the principle sources from whom Kern gleaned geographic information while in Santa Fe when he was compiling the 1851 "Map of New Mexico" with Lieutenant Parke. Later in 1851 Leroux had been the guide for Lorenzo Sitgreaves' expedition from Santa Fe to the Pacific that Kern accompanied as "draughtsman." Beckwith now engaged Leroux to guide the "Central Route" exploration, but only as far as the main branch of the Spanish Trail near the present town of Green River, Utah. Then Leroux would have to return east because of a prior commitment to conduct Lieutenant Amiel Weeks Whipple's railroad exploration along the $35^{th}$ parallel, the one to which Kern had hoped to be assigned before Secretary of War Davis attached him to Gunnison's instead. I imagine Leroux was the source for many of the names of geographic features that are on Kern's sketches made between Fort Massachusetts to the Green River in Utah, and on the maps and in the accounts of the Gunnison-Beckwith *Report*.

While waiting for Beckwith's return the expedition moved down the Sangre de Cristo Valley to Williams' Ranch, crossed over the divide to Ute Creek, and followed it upstream to Fort Massachusetts. No visible sign of the fort remains, but it was located on land that today is part of the Trinchera Ranch, a segment of which I had crossed to find Gunnison's road down from the crest of Sangre de Cristo Pass

PLATE 92. Photograph of San Luis Valley

into the Huerfano Valley. After again obtaining permission from managers Ty and Alicia Ryland, I was loaned keys for access and generously encouraged to drive, wander, search, and return as often as necessary, with the sole proviso that I stay away from hunting parties. In this truly lovely spot Gunnison and his men had remained for several days, during which time Kern created three exceptional drawings.

The multiple titles on Plate 91, "St. Louis Valley, Williams Ranch," are printed by an unknown hand and are perhaps the sum of the geographic names applied to the region, enumerated here with general, not specific, intent. It may not be possible to rely on the most explicit of them, "Williams Ranch"; rather, I believe, this drawing includes

PLATE 93. Composite drawing and photograph

part of Fort Massachusetts, perhaps the corral. Beckwith in the *Report* places "Williams' herd-grounds" on the "Sangre de Cristo," but this view is actually from along Ute Creek, a tributary to Sangre de Cristo Creek. The exact position overlooks the site where Fort Massachusetts once stood, nestled near to but not quite in the "St. Louis Valley" and

PLATE 94. Main Peaks of Sierra Blanca [August 19?], 19.6 x 11.8 cm

PLATE 95. Photograph, main peak of Sierra Blanca

within the "Sierra Blanca" that here are seen to rise behind it. Beckwith's placement of Williams' Ranch in the valley of Sangre de Cristo Creek is at the westernmost limit of the Sangre de Cristo Pass, from where this view of the mountains does not present itself.

At long last the men of the expedition had a clear view of Blanca Peak, which is the high, sharp summit about one quarter of the way in from the right that in the photograph looks dark. The flat-topped mountain in the center just left of the cloud is Hamilton Peak, and emerging behind Hamilton lower and off to the left is a slope of Little Bear Peak, the crest of which is hidden.

The paper of a second drawing from this point of view that is captioned "Main Peaks of Sierra Blanca" (Plate 94) was clearly trimmed on its left side, and there is no way to be certain of how much of the sketch is missing. The title implies that other high mountains might once have been included. If they were, they would be the same ones visible in the previous drawing, because the two are of adjacent scenes and were made from very nearly the same position. The view is looking almost due north and includes the whole of the fort, as well as a portion of the corral at the left edge. The dominant peak at the left is Mount Lindsey. On the right are two foreground trees drawn over details of the sketch, a compositional device that Kern often added as an

PLATE 96. Composite drawing and photograph

PLATE 97. Lithograph by John Mix Stanley: Fort Massachusetts, at the foot of the Sierra Blanca, San Luis Valley.

afterthought to drawings that were intended to become illustrative lithographs, as this one did.

The principal difficulty in making photographs that correspond closely with either of these sketches is that the original viewpoint was very low, probably in the flood plain of the creek. Fort Massachusetts was built of wood; most of the nearby trees were cut, both as a convenient source of material during its construction and perhaps to remove cover for possible attackers. When I visited the site the trees had returned in force, so I had to seek my views from somewhat above the river bottom and farther away. The view from Fort Massachusetts also reveals that these two sketches are of scenes so closely adjacent as to suggest they were originally conceived as a continuous panorama. To make this work I had to first alter the relative size of the sketches, but not by much; the problem then turned out to be that the point of view that was the best compromise for the pair is not really satisfactory for either individually. The two are simply views of adjoining scenes. "Main Peaks of Sierra Blanca" is the basis for a lithograph by Stanley (Plate 97) titled "Fort Massachusetts, At the foot of the Sierra Blanca. Valley of San Luis."

PLATE 98. Juxtaposition of the drawing and the lithograph

The lithograph extends the scene to the left by a small but noticeable amount, suggesting that when Stanley made his painting from the sketch it was more nearly intact than it is now, and that its left edge was later trimmed or torn. The right edge was cut very close, but does not seem to be missing anything. Stanley makes an unjustified inference from the drawing by extending the slope of the foothill in the center diagonally down in front of Mount Lindsey when it actually joins a ridge that ascents toward Lindsay's summit; he also may have distorted the ground plan of the fort, but this is hard to interpret from Kern's sketch. Otherwise the lithograph is a remarkably fine rendering of the landscape in the drawing. Startlingly different, though, are the wooden walls of Fort Massachusetts. Kern drew them in a somewhat irregular, romantic manner that reflects the logs of which they were constructed. Stanley has transformed this rustic, bucolic fort into a clean, neat, and regular military structure that looks more nearly as if it were made of stone or brick.

Creutzfeldt described the arrival and stay in the vicinity of Fort Massachusetts, where the visitors camped some distance downstream on Ute Creek:

> The [Sangre de Cristo] creek, the valley of which becomes soon enlarged, is followed today for about 7 miles, then crossed and our way taken towards North to the Yutah Creek, where we encamp, 3 m. below Fort Massachusetts. The wagons make about 12 m... The woods here have been dreadfully devastated by a large fire, but some places remained untouched and some grow verdant again...
>
> Different arrangements having to be made here and since the guide has not yet arrived, we remain here having good grass and water. The creek is much

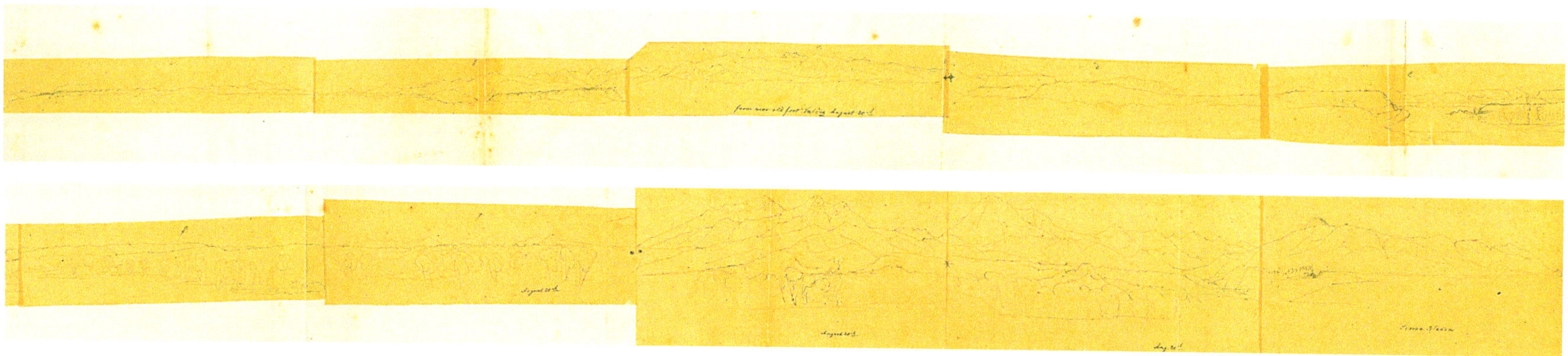

PLATE 99. From near old Fort Valdez, August 20; Sierra Blanca:. 193.3 x 11.7 cm, made up of ten sheets of paper each between 19 and 20 cm wide, and labeled progressively from left to right: a, b, c, d, e, f, g, h, i and k.

PLATE 100. Panoramic photograph

ramified here and approximately in a width of ¼ m. overgrown with willows, elders and especially *Pop laurifol* [probably cottonwood]... The situation of the Fort is so hidden, that one could stumble over it before seeing it and from 2 sides so enclosed by the White Mountains [Sierra Blanca], that the enemy

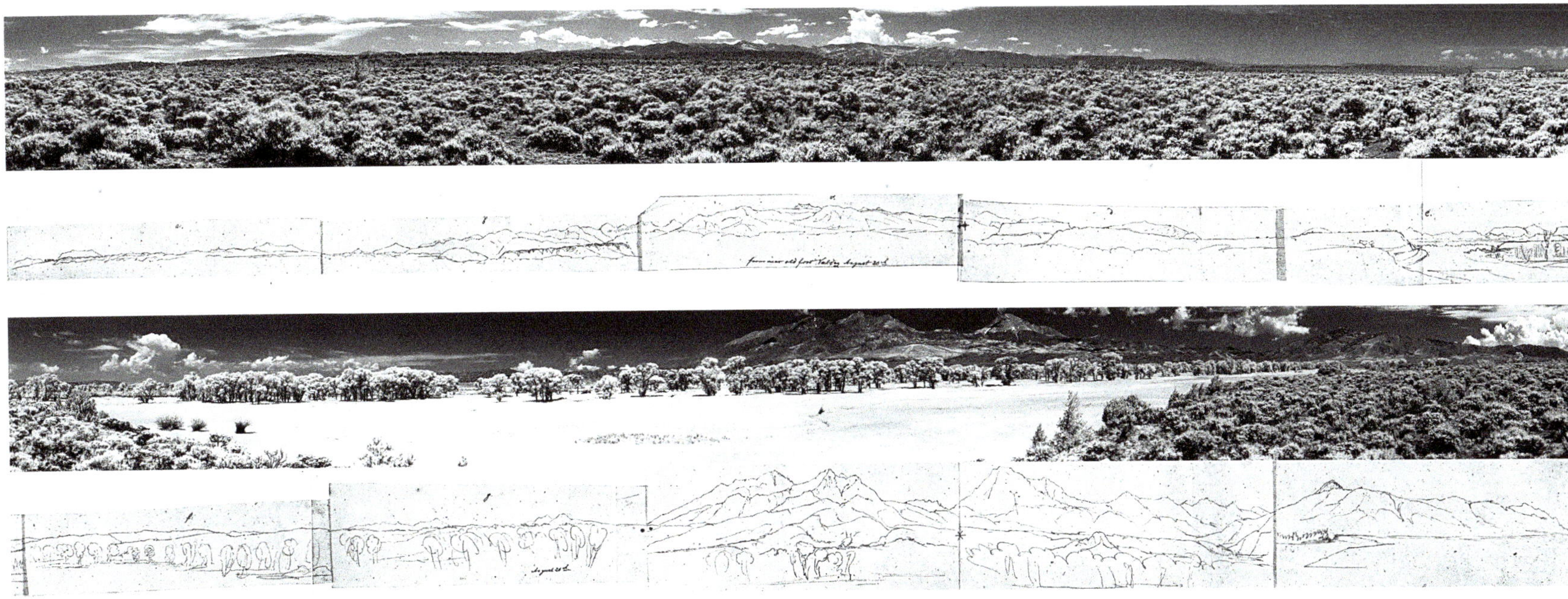

PLATE 101. Composite drawing and photograph

> would [be] able to destroy all within without great exertion (Creutzfeldt, August 19-20).

Schiel took note of the fort in similar terms:

> Leaving the Sangre de Cristo Valley by way of a low mountain ridge we came to a broad plain connecting with the San Luis Valley at the Sierra Blanca. A march of eleven miles brought us to Fort Massachusetts at the foot of a snow covered peak of the Sierra and so concealed that you cannot see it until you stand directly before it (Schiel, 71).

The foldout panoramic drawing "From near old fort Valdez," (Plate 99) was made some distance downstream from Fort Massachusetts close to where the expedition camped during its stay, and encompasses a full 360° view. The evidence from the nine seams that join the panorama together is ambiguous. Some of them seem to have been mated before drawing; some were marked to indicate the desired alignment, then mounted afterwards; some appear to have been trimmed so as to lose a bit of detail before being attached to their fellows; some appear to have various of their details extended in a continuous line across to the adjacent sheet after mounting, while other lines stop at the same seam. On many of the sheets are horizontal lines, sometimes at the very top and sometimes at the bottom, with lengths varying from short to reaching the entire width of the paper. In conjunction with the nearly identical long dimension of all the sheets, it appears that the sketches were done on a single tall piece of paper about 8 inches in width, then cut apart with those lines serving as cutting guides. That all of the panels are of the same tint also suggests the drawing was initially on a single sheet; for the shades of yellow found among the pieces of paper Kern used are otherwise highly variable.

On its top each sheet is labled alphabetically from left to right, "a" to "k," with "j" omitted. To aid in composing this rather awkward illustration I have digitally trimmed the tops of the last three sheets, (thereby removing their identifying letters,) because they are so much taller than the others; but there is no question of where they fit in. The date of August 20 appears repeatedly, perhaps to insure against misplacing any of the panels, and "Sierra Blanca" is written on the last sheet. None if this is particularly puzzling, but the inscription on sheet "c," reading "from near old fort Valdez August 20th," is a total mystery. It may simply be a reference to the camp that the men of the expedition made nearby, for I can find no other references to a fort of this name in the region. The Spanish of New Mexico never established a presence this far to the north, and during the Mexican period only herders and hunters occasionally came here in the summer.

Kern's panoramic sketch displays a good deal of elasticity on its left when compared with my photograph, but the important landmarks can be identified by shape. On the left side of sheet "e" is a dome-shaped silhouette against the sky; almost due south, that distant, almost perfectly rounded arc is Ute Mountain near Costilla, New Mexico, which Lieutenant Beckwith passed on his way to Taos to find a guide. Placing its distinctive contour above a nearer hill that is readily recognizable from the sketch defined the permissible limits of east-west motion in locating the vantage point. The dramatic pair of high peaks in panel "h" (the first of the taller sheets,) are Little Bear Peak on the left, with some vertical lines just below its summit in the drawing, that turned out to be a snow-filled couloir in the photograph, and Hamilton Peak on the right, separated by a high ridge from an adjacent but lower summit. Peeking up over that ridge is Blanca Peak, the presence of which Kern indicated with just a tiny triangular shape, and which is so dark in my photograph that it merges with the sky and is barely visible. The alignments of these high mountains to the northwest were also useful in pinning down Kern's position, which was on a low embankment above the east side of Ute Creek. Finally, on the left end of sheet "i" (the second of the taller sheets,) is the lofty contour of Mount Lindsey, which had been intermittently visible to the men of the expedition for weeks.

The next morning, August 21, Gunnison wrote a letter to his wife. Antoine Leroux, the guide whom Lieutenant Beckwith recruited in Taos, had arrived with some companions. Gunnison seemed already to be at odds with him, although his complaint may relate as well to experiences with the earlier guide, Massalino. Gunnison's relationship with Leroux became ever more prickly over the next month despite the incalculably valuable services the guide provided to the expedition.

> Sunday morn —Aug. 21 [1853]
> Since writing the above [an extensive disapproval of the morals of New Mexicans] I have had an old trapper here to confuse me about the road onwards. These fellows were on a different business in early times & never dreamed of road making in such terribly rocky & <u>chasmy</u> places—& their description[s] are very confused...
>
> It's no use to try to write with forty men to pester me...
>
> Our real difficulties are ahead no doubt. No wagons have ever been farther than Grand River I am now credibly informed. If I get through it will be a triumph—but I must try at least & try I shall (Gunnison Archives, Huntington Library).

Two days later the expedition finally left Fort Massachusetts, with Leroux to guide them.

> *August* 23.—We were detained in making necessary repairs, and in obtaining supplies at Fort Massachusetts, until this morning, when we took leave...and, following down Utah creek for three miles and a half, crossed it, and passed along the base of the gravelly hills which lie directly at the foot of the Sierra Blanca, southwest and opposite the sharpest peak of which we encamped, at White Mountain spring, seven miles from Utah creek... (G-B, 41).

By 2:00 p.m. the men had made their "Camp 45, White Mountain spring," giving Kern plenty of time before dark to sketch "the sharpest peak" (Plate 102). The many lines of the drawing that continue to the edges demonstrate that the paper has been trimmed or torn so that an indeterminate amount of material is now lost from both sides. The outlines of Blanca and its adjoining peaks are visible for a great distance from along US 160, where at one point a sign by the road with an arrow on it points out "Blanca Peak." On the plain at the foot of the mountain a grid of roads has been bladed, graveled, named, and marked with street signs in preparation for development, all of which can be accessed by driving north from the town of Blanca, Colorado. From this close to the mountains the dominant summit and sharpest peak is actually Little Bear, which is the high central feature of the scene. Just to the right of Little Bear Peak is the more distant and lower-seeming crest of Blanca Peak; it appears as a tiny protuberance against the sky with its lower slopes more easily visible farther to the right, from where a ridge connects it to the summit of Hamilton Peak.

PLATE 102. Sierra Blanca [August 23], 22.4 x 14.4 cm

> We set out today under the leadership of La Roux... we cross some dry creeks and encamp near the foot of the mountains, where a green spot with good pasture is intersected by a rivulet; on its banks, willows are thinly growing but they supply us with fuel. The Rio Gr. is in sight but may be distant 25-30 miles yet (Creutzfeldt, August 23).

Stretching in front of the foothills and roughly parallel to the plane of the photograph is an elongated low area that suggests a marginal wetland fed by intermittent springs. This was probably Creutzfeldt's "good pasture" in 1853. My vantage point was on MM 13th Street, in the sparsely populated development on the plain, and just west of Spruce Avenue.

PLATE 103. Photograph, Sierra Blanca

PLATE 104. Composite drawing and photograph

The third and last of Kern's large, fold-out panoramic drawings is titled "San Juan Mountains, Source of the Rio del Norte" (Plate 105). All the sheets in it are 23 cm wide except the last one, which is 20 cm. The eight pieces are marked in order: "1. a." through "1. h." They appear to have been completely mounted before being drawn upon as one long sketch. Near the left and right edges of several of the sheets are short horizontal marks at the bottom that align with similar marks on adjacent pieces of paper. Their purpose is unclear, but perhaps they were used as guides to maintain a straight and level reference in the drawing. Toward the right on sheet d. some tiny lettering is visible against the low, distant hills. Because the Conejos River flows through the region southwest of the vantage point it might be "Conejo," but this is not a very convincing reading. The only appropriately positioned stream marked on the expedition's map is named "Trenchara Cr."

PLATE 105. San Juan Mountains, Source of the Rio del Norte [August 23] 181.3 x 14.6 cm

PLATE 106. Panoramic photograph of distant San Juan Mountains

PLATE 107. Composite drawing and photograph

and is today spelled Trinchera, but it does join the Conejos River, which in turn feeds into the Rio Grande del Norte. There is some small consolation in the thought that anything written so illegibly on a drawing could not have been of great significance to Kern.

This view contains the same distant alignment clue, Ute Mountain, that appears in the panorama, "From near Old Fort Valdez" (Plate 99). With its characteristic dome-like appearance from the north, Ute Mountain is visible behind some distinctive nearby hills, and can be seen on panel "c." about ¼ of the way in from the right. Then, looking east (panel a.), there is a near hill against some more distant mountains that helps to define a line at 90° from the first; the road on which my van is parked is aligned east to west. The network of roads here simplified my search, and I was both surprised and pleased that when I finally located the correct spot for this panorama, it was in almost the same spot from where Kern had viewed Little Bear Peak for the previous drawing, "Sierra Blanca" (Plate 102). His panoramic rendering includes very nearly a complete 360° view that led me to wonder if one of its panels had been somehow lost, but neither end of the drawing is broken off in a way that would confirm this. Nonetheless I made a complete 360° photograph to embrace the part that may be missing, which includes Hamilton Peak and its slopes descending to the right. At the base of the San Juan Mountains far to the west Kern indicates the trees along the course of the Rio Grande by the nuance of a roughened line; they are present in the photograph as well, though barely visible.

PLATE 108. Peaks of the Sierra Blanca, 20.1 x 12.4 cm

Plate 108, "Peaks of the Sierra Blanca from near Fort Massachusetts," is a complete puzzle. The members of the expedition applied the term "Sierra Blanca" to a wide geographic area, including the mountains bordering the south side of the Huerfano Valley from Silver Mountain to the Blanca Peak complex (the base of which they had just rounded before turning north); those on the east side of the

PLATE 109. Lithograph by John Mix Stanley, "Peaks of the Sierra Blanca from near Fort Massachusetts"

PLATE 110. Composite of drawing and lithograph

San Luis Valley reaching southwards to Taos; and similarly northward at least as far as Poncha Pass and including "Les Trois Tetons." Perhaps they were also including the Sierra Mojada or Greenhorns north of the Huerfano Valley and even the free-standing Spanish Peaks to the southeast, so the area over which the expedition viewed some of these "Peaks of the Sierra Blanca" was extremely broad. The only thing to help limit a search was that this drawing became one of the illustrative lithographs in the final *Report*, titled "Peaks of the Sierra Blanca from near Fort Massachusetts," (Plate 109) so one would think the subject was of some importance. If we can rely on the lithograph to be correctly titled (often a

PLATE 111. Composite of Plate 102, "Sierra Blanca" (above), and Plate 108, "Peaks of the Sierra Blanca" (below)

dubious proposition, as will be seen in some later examples), the sketch was not made from the more northern reaches of the San Luis Valley, thus narrowing my search area.

For his book on Richard Kern, David Weber had only Stanley's lithograph of this scene, but from it sensed that something was wrong; he came to think that this picture had been redrawn from an earlier painting:

> From near Fort Massachusetts, Kern also redrew a scene he had painted in 1849—the *Peaks of the Sierra Blanca* looking much craggier than he had delineated them in his earlier work (Weber, 229).

The supposition that Kern redrew something of his own is doubtful because there was no reason for him to have brought earlier work along on this expedition, where his experience must have told him that he could expect to find plenty of ruggedly dramatic mountains to use as exemplars.

> If Richard Kern saw any contradiction between the imperatives of accurate scientific recording and the artistic impulse, or between the scientist's realism and the artist's idealism, his remaining letters and diaries do not reveal his concern. Indeed, he may

> have felt no tension as a result of these inherent dilemmas...
>
> By altering details to improve composition or perspective, yet retaining verisimilitude, Kern often managed to have it both ways... In *Peaks of the Sierra Blanca*, however, Kern, or John Mix Stanley, who reworked his sketch, went too far... In this view, trees on a pond lean improbably in opposite directions (Weber, 276).

Weber articulated what it was about this picture that made him uncomfortable. Now that we have the sketch it is first of all possible to say that the excesses of this illustration did not originate elsewhere but were Kern's alone, including the trees at odd angles and the exaggeratedly rugged mountains. The only alteration by Stanley is the addition of a pair of hazy, distant peaks to the left, for which there is but the barest hint in the drawing. Inspection of the sketch reveals that the well worked-out trees on the far left were part of Kern's initial representation, because where they cut across particulars of the scene the background lines stop at the trees. Either the trees were drawn first, or else Kern left gaps in the background to provide space for the trees to occupy without conflict. (Although seemingly illogical, this technique of drawing the distant objects first and leaving gaps to accommodate nearer objects can often be detected in Kern's works.) The rest of the foliage has been drawn over the background details and so suggest a subsequent addition, something that occurs in drawings Kern possibly intended for later use as lithographs. Stanley's transcription of the foreground is here quite blameless, including the trees leaning so far in opposite directions that they create the oddly disturbing effect Weber noted. The real wonderland, though, is in the mountain; after repeatedly studying the sketch and spending days looking for the scene, I am convinced it does not exist! There are not so many places where the expedition was near Fort Massachusetts and from where Kern could have made this view. Their path here was along open ground from which the surrounding mountains are readily seen; nowhere among them can a convincing match be found. For what conceivable purpose was this work even created, when Kern had exquisite views of the Sierra Blanca before him, including one (Plate 102) that bears a great deal of formal similarity to this exaggerated sketch, but that cannot be made to match it in any of its significant details? The two sketches are juxtaposed in Plate 111. It is difficult to understand why Kern would have taken time off from his myriad duties to concoct this fantastically rugged but imaginary scene, when he had perfectly

PLATE 112. Sierra Blanca [August 23] 19.3 x 11.9 cm

PLATE 113. Photograph, Sierra Blanca

good real ones at hand! I can only imagine that Kern was asked to create an especially rugged view of the mountains in the vicinity as an illustration that would emphasize the magnitude of Gunnison's achievement in cutting a road over and through such difficult terrain. I continue to believe that "Peaks of the Sierra Blanca" is a drawing of a subject that does not exist.

From here the new guide, Antoine Leroux, led the expedition along the north branch of the Spanish Trail (today called the Old Spanish Trail) that went from Santa Fe to Taos, north into the San Luis Valley, over the Continental Divide at Cochetopa Pass, down the Gunnison River, and through the deserts of Utah, where it would join the main branch of the trail near the town of Green River, Utah, and ultimately reach Los Angeles. Much of what is known today about the course of this trail is derived from the surveys of the Gunnison expedition, which was the first to produce detailed maps of and commentary on the region through which it passed. The expedition did not always follow the Spanish Trail even though it seemed to be the easiest and most visible route through the wilderness, but since its usual traffic consisted of men (both mounted and on foot), enslaved Indians, herds

PLATE 114. Composite drawing and photograph

of animals, and goods carried by pack mules, it was not everywhere a road suitable for wagons. This seems to be the initial source of friction between Gunnison and Leroux, who Gunnison felt did not fully understand the problem.

Plate 112 "Sierra Blanca" is another drawing that contains misleading elements. On the right are some lines of uncertain significance that imply a higher mountain or other object, but which does not seem to be integrated with the rest of the sketch. Not knowing if these jottings are part of the whole or some irrelevant superfluity, I again spent days looking for something that approximated the entire sketch. Fortunately I was able to combine the entirely fruitless search for the last scene with the initially fruitless search for this one, and at some point I decided that its intended subject excluded the details on the right. I cannot say what the right-hand lines represent, but I imagine that the piece of paper was used to start a sketch that was quickly abandoned, then the same sheet taken up and a different, more nearly finished drawing placed on it while ignoring the relatively meaningless beginnings of the earlier outline. The opposite, that the artist accidentally took up a fairly well-finished sketch with its title and drew upon it, before he realized that the page was otherwise occupied, seems less likely. Disregarding the right side of the drawing, I then was able to find the scene.

The vantage point is east of Colorado 150 just north of LN6, looking to the north with the Great Sand Dunes in the foreground. Crestone Needle is the isolated peak on the left of the sketch, and the closer rugged summit in its center is Cleveland Peak with its associated ridges. Although the Great Sand Dunes are in the foreground of my photograph, Kern did not represent them in his enigmatic sketch, but he did take care with the line descending to the left from Cleveland Peak by roughening it with small irregularities that suggest trees in silhouette, much as he did in the panorama of the San Juan

Mountains (Plate 105) to indicate the tree line along the distant Rio Grande del Norte. Lines in Kern's sketches are often more than just lines, for, like this one, they may carry subtleties that indicate some property of the view. Absent a key to Kern's personal code, it is only by minutely comparing the drawings to the actual scenes that these associations can sometimes be discovered. Schiel describes this view, or one very similar.

> The slopes of the Sierra Blanca are covered with cedars and *Pinus*, which, however, are dwarfed and only suitable for fire wood. From this side also the mountains of 4000 feet altitude show sharp ridges but more often they have the shape of needles (Schiel, 72).

The expedition continued up the east side of the San Luis Valley to the mouth of Robideau's Pass (today Mosca Pass), where the headquarters of the Great Sand Dunes National Park is now located. Antoine Robidoux was a trader based in New Mexico who regularly brought carts loaded with goods over this pass, which was initially named for him. He was also a fellow Taos resident and colleague of Antoine Leroux. The slightly misspelled Robideau's Pass connects the San Luis Valley to the Huerfano River Valley, and was one of the possible alternatives to Gunnison's choice of Sangre de Cristo Pass for railroad access to the San Luis Valley from the Great Plains. Kern, Creutzfeldt, and Taplin had gone through it in the winter of 1848 with Frémont's fourth expedition. What had then been a narrow but fairly easy-to-negotiate gap in the mountain chain was now found to be heavily obstructed as the result of debris from a recent flash flood. It was nonetheless necessary for Gunnison to look it over.

> *August* 24.—Following the base of the Sierra Blanca on our right, with the broad valley of San Luis on our left, we encamped, after traveling fourteen miles, on a small stream from the mountain, which soon sinks in the plain. The grass along our path was scattered, and we experienced considerable difficulty in driving over the thick masses of sage which cover almost the entire surface of this immense valley. We were here nearly opposite to Roubideau's or Musca Pass. Captain Gunnison immediately proceeded to examine it. It was found impracticable to ascend it with horses, in consequence of one of those great mountain torrents, to which all mountain countries are subject, having swept down it, depositing trees and rocks in every direction, and tearing the bed of the creek, over which two light wagons crossing from

the Green horn settlement to Taos had descended but a few days before, into holes and gullies ten and twelve feet in depth... *Our guide informs us* that to the west of our trail, along the banks of the Rio del Norte to where it enters a plain through a cañon from the San Juan mountains, bearing west from our present camp, and thence above on its tributaries, the valley of San Luis, which in this part is known to many as the valley of San Juan, is rich and fertile, covered with extensive meadows of grass, and abounding in game and wild horses. The narrow line of timber, thirty-five miles distant upon the Rio del Norte, is plainly seen from our trail; but it is represented to be difficult to cross the valley with wagons, on account of the marshes along the river and the miry banks of the sunken creeks, and we have therefore followed the base of the Sierra Blanca, which extends from the Sangre de Cristo to Gunnison's [today Poncha] Pass. To the north of this range, but partially connected with it, a broken range of mountains extends towards the Arkansas river, called the Sierra Mojada, or Wet mountains, from the constant rains which fall upon it. The Indian name of the range on the west of the San Luis valley is Sahwatch, but it is more generally known by the Spanish name of San Juan. The San Luis valley is from 40 to 70 miles in width, and still more in length, and so level that trees are seen in any direction, growing on the streams, as far as the eye can discern them (G-B, 41-42).

Creutzfeldt twice made a note of where they were, because it was at this spot in 1848 that his winter sufferings with Frémont really began.

We are marching on the foot of the mountains in N.W. direction the valley up. The Captain, Guide, Kern and the consorts go ahead of us to examine the Roubadeaux pass believing to find it in a distance of 6 mi. But after a march of 14 miles we find their wagons, where the pass is in sight but probably still 6-8 m. distant; they have gone there on mules. We encamp next to the wagons... We are near the spot, where we were encamped 5 years ago in a snow and cold. The sand hills blown together by the wind, seem to have multiplied, extending now for miles on the foot of the high, sharp, conical and pyramidical mountains, glittering now and then with snow... (Creutzfeldt, August 24).

The officers and I leave the camp to day, to make better observations in the Rubd. Pass, since the day before it became quite dark, before we reached the highest point. Arriving at the pass, we follow the path winding itself for about 2 miles through defiles, deeply cut in by the water and so barricaded by logs and tumbled down rocks, that the march can only be continued on foot and this with difficulty... At the outlet of the pass I remember very well our camp 5 years ago, and the strange sand hills North of the creek, which we circled to examine in high snow the Williams [today Medano or Sandhill] pass, before we returned to the Valley. The pass is seen here coming in between high mountainsides and our Capt. does visit it not far from Rob. P. What they saw there I do not know (Creutzfeldt, August 25).

*From Roubideau's Pass, via the Coochetopa Pass and Grand River valley, [today the Gunnison River Valley] to the Nah-un-kah-rea or Blue [today the Colorado] river.—August 25 to September 20, 1853* (G-B, 43).

*August* 25.—The examination of Roubideau's Pass being completed this morning, the main body of the party proceeded up the valley, under the command of Lieutenant Baker, while Captain Gunnison, Captain Morris and myself, after leaving this pass, rode to Williams' Pass, the approach to which from the San Luis valley is through a grove of pitch-pine, behind most gigantic sand-hills, rising above the plain to half the height (apparently, at least, 700 or 800 feet,) of the adjacent mountain, and shaped by the winds into beautiful and fanciful forms with waving outlines, for within certain limits this sand drifts about like snow. These immense hills are from eight to ten miles in length, lying along the base of the mountains, and four or five in width, and therefore constitute a great barrier to the western approach to Williams' Pass, directly before which they stand. The stream which flows from it is turned immediately southward, and soon sinks in the sand plain. These hills are so steep and smooth on the side towards this creek, that the smallest pebbles started at their summits roll uninterruptedly into the creek, leaving their paths distinctly marked from the summits to the bases. High up on the sides are seen, at half a dozen points, single bushes of artemisia—the only vegetation seen upon them, and the only change

> discoverable since they were visited by Captain Pike, fifty years ago, when they were entirely destitute of vegetation, and "appeared exactly like the sea in a storm, except in color" (G-B, 43).

Except for further changes in vegetation, Beckwith's description of what is today part of the Great Sand Dunes National Park conforms faithfully to their appearance today; the visually evocative quality of his prose certainly deserves high praise, especially since there is no illustration of the dunes by Kern in the Newberry album. If *artemisia* were present on the sand in 1853 they seem to have disappeared again, or else what Beckwith saw was so distant that he misidentified the species. The expedition detoured around the dunes and then continued north, staying close to the foothills of the Sierra Blanca to avoid the marshes in the middle of the San Luis Valley.

> *August* 26.—... We encamped on Chatillon's [today Cottonwood] creek... A few scattered cotton-woods are the only trees upon these streams, on which willow bushes also flourish. The mountain sides and ravines are dark with low-branching cedar and pine; but they are generally of too small a size to be of any use except for fuel.

> *August* 27.—In our course to-day we approached nearer the base of the mountains on the eastern line of the valley, the soil being still sandy, but much less so than for the last two days. The sage, however, being no less luxuriant, forced us constantly to wind about to avoid the thickest patches. A few small spots of prairie-grass were passed, and marsh-grass grew luxuriantly for a few hundred yards on either side of two small creeks which we crossed, one of which, Trois Tetons [today Crestone Creek], deriving its name from the peaks whence it descends, was so miry that it turned us a mile directly towards the mountains before we could effect a crossing. To our left we could see fine prairie-grass fields, directly in the course to the Coochetopa Pass, for which we were traveling around the valley; but the guide warned us of marshes, and the attempt was not made to cross them. Thirteen miles from camp we reached a fine meadow of bottom-grass a mile in width, extending from the base of the mountains far out into the plain, through the center of which winds a fine stream of mountain water, named, after our guide, Leroux creek... The sharp edges and needle forms of the summits of the Sierra Blanca, rising

> 3,000 feet above the valley, attract much admiration at our camp tonight; and the promising opening in the Sierra San Juan, to the southwest, which allured Colonel Frémont to the disaster of 1848-'49, attracts its full share of attention and comment, some of the gentlemen of our party having participated in that misfortune (G-B, 44).

The mountains to the east of the camp that are described here are not mentioned in Beckwith's private *Journal*, and the day's camp was too close to the foothills for the men to discern their highest pinnacles. Kern and the scientific corps of the expedition probably did not measure their altitudes, which could have to have been done by triangulation from out on the floor of the valley, and which would have entailed a considerable amount of time and trouble. Beckwith's estimate of "3,000 feet above the valley" for the loftiest of them is a number picked literally out of the air for the purpose of the narrative, but it seriously underestimates the actuality; at about 14,300 feet Crestone was the tallest nearby peak, invisibly towering some 6,700 feet over the camp.

Creutzfeldt commented on the marshes and again on the hardships he suffered with Frémont when his fourth expedition wound up trapped in the snowy San Juan Mountains visible to the southwest.

> We having been obliged to go round some places which are marshy and for wagons unpracticable. The valley is now in the North entirely bounded by mountains, which seem to be progressively flattened in the N. N. W. direction towards the sources of the Arkansas. In N. W. direction is the Quichitipas pass we are about to surmount and more to the W. are the memorable St. John Mountains of malignant memory (Creutzfeldt, August 27).

The pass Creutzfeldt phoneticizes as "Quichitipas" is today spelled Cochetopa, and leads from the San Luis Valley over the Continental Divide and down to the valley of the Grand (now Gunnison) River. The variants in spelling arise because it is a phonetic rendering of a Utah Indian word meaning "Buffalo Gate"; when Frémont missed this pass in the winter of 1848, his fourth expedition ended in disaster. Leroux Creek, where the expedition stopped on the afternoon of August 27 and stayed two nights, is today Rito Alto Creek. There was once a town on it named Rito Alto, of which there remains only a church and a few houses.

On the afternoon of August 27 Kern made a broad panorama of the Sierra Blanca that comes to us in a somewhat disconnected form as a six-part panoramic sketch on four pieces of paper (Plate 115), mounted on three widely separated pages of the album. I have edited them with Photoshop® into a single picture.

The top two sheets are mounted end to end— the left one measures 14.7 x 3.7 cm, and the right one 14.6 x 4.2 cm. They were probably drawn one above the other on a single sheet and then cut apart, because at the very top of the right sheet is a line to indicate where that should be done, just as in the earlier panorama "From near Old Fort Valdez" (Plate 99). The third sheet is 19.3 x 11.3 cm; the fourth sheet 19.3 x 11.6 cm. Some of the edges show evidence of having been trimmed in a way that removes parts of the drawing, causing discontinuities to appear when they are assembled in order and compared with the scene.

PLATE 115. Panoramic view of the Sierra Blanca, August 27

The sequence of drawings is numbered from right to left. As assembled (Plate 116), the panel to the far right (the bottom half of the fourth sheet) is labeled "Pan. V. [View] Sierra Blanca Aug. $27^{th}$ No/1" where the "7" appears to have originally been a "2" that was later overwritten. Above at its far right a note indicates the position of "Roubideaux Pass." The third panel from the right (the bottom half of the third sheet) has the slightly less abbreviated title of "Pan. View Sierra Blanca Aug. 27. No/2," as well as the notes "gate" written in two places on the sketch to mark the canyons from which the most prominent streams originate. The fifth panel from the right is marked on its bottom "No/3. Aug. 27th," while at the top it says "2. b.," and analogously, in the panel farthest to the left "No/ 4 Aug. $27^{th}$" can be read on its bottom, while "2. a."

PLATE 116. Drawings digitally cut apart and reassembled as a continuous panorama

PLATE 117. Photograph, panoramic view of the Sierra Blanca

PLATE 118. Composite drawings and photograph

is on its top. Apparently there were two competing systems of numbering, one left to right but incomplete, and the other right to left. The view represented by this set of drawings from the bottom of the San Luis Valley is truly splendid.

When trying to accommodate the drawing to the photograph I found that the sections of the sketch are not scaled to match each other, and that small portions of the scene are missing between some of the panels. To make a reasonable presentation where the features of the mountains are more or less aligned vertically between drawing and photograph, I adjusted the size of each segment individually and juxtaposed them without concerning myself with making their continuity carry over at the edges, or worrying about the missing portions. The two smaller panels on the left that were already mounted end to end in the album appear to show some redundancy where they join. That was confirmed by viewing the actual scene, so I digitally slid the drawings one over the other to make them appear to be continuous.

The whole view extends almost 180° from the northwest to the southeast; at the far left are some of the foothills of the Sahwatch (today Saguache) Mountains bordering the west side of the San Luis Valley. The steeply sloping mountain outlined on the left of the second panel is Hayden Peak; the more distant one on the right of that panel is Antora Peak.

Continuing to the right, and missing in the drawings, is a gap in the nearer mountains where the view is northward to Poncha Pass and beyond, a place that Captain Gunnison and a small party of companions were to explore a few days later. In the third panel there are a few trees that suggest the line of them that follow the creek toward its origins in the mountains. They mark Beckwith's "fine meadow of bottom-grass a mile in width, extending from the base of the mountains far out into the plain, through the center of which winds a fine stream of mountain water, named, after our guide, Leroux creek." Continuing right to the fourth panel and looking to the northeast is Gibson Peak, the highest-appearing mountain in the view, and from the foothills of which Leroux Creek originates. On the right in the fifth panel, the tall mountain that seems flat on top is a combined view of Challenger Point and Kit Carson Mountain just behind it. Slightly to the right and lower than Kit Carson is what looks like an attached flat step, but is actually a combination of Crestone Needle with Crestone Peak on its right; so although not identified as such in this drawing, these prominent peaks are collectively "Les Trois Tetons," from which today's name "Crestone" may be derived. Where the mountains slope down to the right in the sixth panel are the Great Sand Dunes, behind which is the entrance to "Robideaux Pass." Farthest to the right there is a rise hinting at more of the Sierra Blanca to the south, which, if it had been continued in the drawing, would show Mount Lindsey and Blanca Peak in the distance.

While wandering over the east side of the San Luis Valley looking for the viewpoint of this scene I met Marty Shellabarger, a rancher who leases BLM land extending east to the foot of the mountains. I showed him the drawings, and as we looked at the western face of the Sangre de Cristos he suggested that the best access point would be from near the Rito Alto Church. He gave me permission to wander as I wished over his range, and his phone number in case of trouble. He suggested that if I walked southeast from the church I would find a bridge and so could avoid having to ford the stream. From his grandfather, Marty had heard a story told by his great-grandfather, who came to the area in the 1870s: along Leroux Creek near the mountains to the east of where the old church is now he had seen steel ax marks on the stumps of felled trees. Both the Gunnison expedition and Frémont's fifth expedition came this way in 1853, and both remained in a camp on the east side of the valley for more than a day, Frémont near Crestone Creek, where his expedition hunted deer and dried the meat as future provisions, and Gunnison along what is now Rito Alto Creek. It seems probable that Marty's great-grandfather came across traces left by the axes of Gunnison's men as they cut firewood for the two days they spent in camp here. Similar evidence of the use of steel axes has been found on stumps on the other side of the valley, made there by Frémont's fourth expedition of 1848 (Richmond, 1990).

When I first came looking for this view I had not associated the two smaller parts of the drawing, marked "2. a." and "2. b.," with the rest of the scene. It wasn't until Bonnie Hardwick correctly read the numbers at the bottoms of the sketches and pointed out their connection that I realized I was dealing with a larger panorama. I then had to go back to photograph the whole scene again from a single point of view. Even though the totality of the subject was in plain sight, the search for the place that satisfied the requirements of the entire panorama was among the most time-consuming and exhausting of the entire project. Overlooking the level plain from which Kern worked, the summit of Gibson Peak is only five miles distant, Crestone Peak to the southeast is thirteen miles, and the mountains tapering away to the left near Poncha Pass finally disappear at more than 20 miles. It is possible to hike for great distances on the plains near Rito Alto and see only a minor effect on the alignment of distant features. The dense sagebrush was another source of trouble, for except where there were cattle paths it was impossible to

PLATE 119. Untitled sketch [looking northwest through Gunnison's Pass, August 28?] 17.2 x 9.0 cm

PLATE 120. Photograph looking northwest through Gunnison's Pass

move in a straight line in any direction. Beckwith's complaint, that "The sage...forced us constantly to wind about to avoid the thickest patches." holds true today. It is one of the toughest

PLATE 121. Composite drawing and photograph

PLATE 122. Panorama, Rocky Mountains Plate 1 and Plate 2 [August 28?]

and most resilient plants I have ever encountered, a considerable obstacle to foot travel. Walking straight through or over even the smaller specimens is practically impossible, so it is always necessary to meander among the clumps; covering a linear mile requires walking circuitously over perhaps two or three, all the while paying careful attention to where to place each footfall. A location found with great effort, and showing perfect alignment for some details, might be clearly wrong for others. Often I had associated a feature in the drawing with something I could see clearly in the mountains when Kern was really depicting something else, usually the "next bump" over. My final choice is a pretty good compromise overall, but a careful inspection reveals many ambiguities and inadequacies; I wonder now if Kern sketched parts of the scene from slightly different locations, and I am certain that the drawings are in some respects unfinished. Were the two leftmost panels done either beforehand or afterwards, and then only later renumbered to connect them to the main view?

In my photograph of the "Panoramic View of the Sierra Blanca" (Plates 117, 118) the gap between the two left panels and the rest of the scene is obscured by trees, as it would have been for Kern as well. In the next drawing (untitled sketch, Plate 119) Kern filled in the missing segment by moving to a different spot, which provided a clear view farther up the valley. It fills the gap in the previous panorama (Plate 115, 116) between the Saguache Mountains on the left and the Sierra

PLATE 123. Panoramic drawing;

PLATE 124. Panoramic photograph

PLATE 125. Composite drawing and photograph

Blanca on the right, at the low point where the left-hand pair of drawings joins onto the rest of the view. It was made from about a mile farther west than was the panorama, where the trees that line Rito Alto Creek cannot obscure the view. It looks towards a connection with the Arkansas River Valley through a pass at the north end of the San Luis Valley, one that Beckwith renamed "Gunnison's Pass," but that has reverted to its older appellation, Puncha, or Poncha. Probably the sketch was made on August 28 because the day before was characterized both by "rain" and "dark clouds" that would have made it difficult to see beyond the pass to the more distant mountains, and the 28$^{th}$ was mostly clear. The highest sharp peak centered in the sketch is Mount Shavano, at a distance of more than forty miles. The next highest pointed peak to its right is Mount Antero, while the last spiky peak near the right side and yet farther away is Mount Princeton.

Plate 122 is a broad six-part view "Panorama Rocky Mts" on two pieces of paper. The first one is 19.4 x 11.7 cm; the second is 19.4 x 14.6 cm. At the bottom of the first sheet is "Panorama Rocky Mts No/1," and on the second "Panorama Rocky Mts No/2—." In what by now must seem a familiar procedure, I have cut and pasted the drawings into a linear sequence.

The site from which I believe Kern drew his panorama is on private land, inaccessible, and even if I had entered it the view to the west would have been obscured by irrigation canal embankments, buildings, and trees. With landscape details that are so far away it makes comparatively little difference if the point of view is located a bit imprecisely, so I took the easy way and made my picture from along a road about a mile to the north. Intensive agriculture creates a perpetual haze that covers the valley and makes the more distant subjects in the left half of the photograph lower in contrast, just as the left half of Kern's panorama is comparatively lacking in detail. There were clouds and rain that day over Poncha Pass, which is at the right end of the panorama. Fortunately they did not quite obscure the view through the pass to the north, and in combination with the very similar previous view (Plate 119) it is possible to obtain a good idea of the appearance of the remote mountains found there.

In the second panel from the left there is a low spot in the distance where the Rio Grande del Norte exits the San Juan Mountains into the San Luis Valley. Adjacent to it are some rough cliffs that Kern has shown schematically by an angular outline on the horizon and some additional pencil strokes. (A day or two later Kern made a separate sketch (Plate 129) of this far-off segment of the San Juan Mountains, and titled it "Entrance to Del Norte.") In the fourth panel of the panorama the highest mountain is Saguache Peak, which in my photograph of June 20, 2004, looks as if it has been dusted with fresh snow—believable, but an artifact caused by high contrast lighting and the use of infrared film. The San Luis Valley and its surrounding mountains enjoy a reputation for weather conditions that are among the most unpredictable and rapidly variable on earth, and summer snow is quite possible here. The fifth panel from the left contains the high, sharp crest of Hayden Peak. The last panel is a view through Poncha Pass very similar to that in the previous drawing (Plate 119), and shows the same high peaks: from left to right, Mounts Shavano, Antero, and Princeton.

On August 29 the expedition broke camp on Leroux Creek and began crossing the San Luis Valley at its north end, with a march of six miles. While the men moved over that short distance to Camp 50, Gunnison and several others left to explore Poncha Pass and its connection to the Arkansas River to see if it was a practicable route by which a railroad might enter the San Luis Valley. They did not return until late the next day.

> *August* 29.—Our course bore strongly to the west to-day in nearly a direct line for the entrance to the Coochetopa pass—keeping, however, somewhat to the north to secure a good crossing at Homans' creek, on which we are encamped—there being large marshes further to the south, and the dams of the beaver, which are numerous, flowing the water back to some extent (G-B, 44).

> *August* 31.—... On the morning of the 29th instant Captain Gunnison, and Mr. Homans, accompanied by a guide and four or five men, left the main body of the party and continued up the San Luis valley for fourteen miles to its head, where a small park, into which several small streams flow and unite, forming a single creek, is nearly separated from the main valley by low hills extending from the mountains on either side, into the plain. To this park, which is ten miles in width by fourteen in length, as well as to the creek flowing from it, Captain Gunnison gave the name of his assistant, Mr. Homans, who located them. As a testimony of respect to the memory of the officer who explored it, I have given his name to this pass (G-B, 46).

Like Gunnison's Pass, Homans' name on the park and the creek has not survived into modern usage; the park is now an unnamed portion of the San Luis Valley, and Homans' Creek is today the San Luis Creek.

PLATE 126. Entrance to Cochetopa Pass [August 30?] 19.4 x 9.1 cm

PLATE 127. Photograph, entrance to Cochetopa Pass

PLATE 128. Composite drawing and photograph

The efforts of the expedition were now concentrated on making an approach to the Continental Divide, and Creutzfeldt noted that Leroux was away scouting the route.

> La Roux, his men and some soldiers are ahead of us, trying to find the better wagon road in the mountains, now only 8-10 m. distant (Creutzfeldt, August 29).

In a few days Gunnison would have to choose between two approaches to the divide that would be presented to him by his guide.

> *August* 30.—Leaving camp we reached Sahwatch spring and butte, by a very direct course across the valley, in ten miles and a half. This spring of pure cold water bursts from the base of the granitic butte which is immediately west of it, but detached from the Sahwatch mountains, to which it properly pertains... This butte is not high, but its isolation makes

PLATE 129. Entrance to Del Norte [August 30?] 14.1 x 4.9 cm

PLATE 130. Photograph, entrance to Del Norte

PLATE 131. Composite drawing and photograph

> it a prominent feature, standing as it does at the puerta or gate of the Coochetopa Pass. It is formed of coarse, gray granite rocks. The spring sends out a fine little stream, winding south and east along grassy fields until it joins the Sahwatch creek, which we reached five miles from the butte in the broad opening leading to the Coochetopa Pass. This stream, which is said to sink before reaching the Rio Grande, flows past our camp over a pebbly bed... Its valley at this point is five or seven miles in width, growing narrow towards the west; and there are several isolated buttes standing in it, but none of them of considerable height. A few cotton-wood trees and a margin of willow bushes line the stream (G-B, 45).

The men of the expedition marched almost straight west from their camp on Homans' (today San Luis) Creek and came to Beckwith's "Sahwatch butte" (today justifiably called Rattlesnake Hill), where they found a spring. The site from which Kern drew "Entrance to Coochutoke [Cochetopa] Pass" (Plate 126) is a few miles west of their camp, so dating it to August 30 is almost certain, and it must have been made in the morning. The view is to the west along the path upon which the expedition was to continue that day. Saguache Butte is the nearest low, rounded form cut by the left edge of the illustration. Among the features in the distant foothills of the Saguache Mountains was the gap through which the expedition would enter Cochetopa Pass and climb to its crest on the Continental Divide.

The "Entrance to Del Norte" (Plate 129) is where the Rio Grande gushes out of the San Juan Mountains into the San Luis Valley. The title is not in Kern's hand, and although we might not use the same description today, "Entrance to Del

PLATE 132. August 30, Saguache Mountains? 20.7 x 17.9 cm

PLATE 133. Assembled panoramic drawing

PLATE 134. Panoramic photograph Saguache Mountains

Norte" seems unambiguously evocative of its subject. The source of the Rio Grande was considered to be the entire San Luis Valley and the streams that enter it from its surrounding mountains, but the largest continuous flow comes out of the San Juan Mountains to the west near the present-day town of Del Norte, and the opening in the mountain range through which it flows is the subject of the sketch.

The formations are more than forty miles distant, and the atmospheric haze, combined with heat waves near the ground, prevented a clear photograph. The exact point of view Kern used is impossible to determine from such a distance, so I took my photograph from the same place as the previous one, "Entrance to Cochetopa Pass" (Plate 126), to place the viewpoint along the path of the expedition as it crossed the San Luis Valley. The moisture that arises from the river as it emerges onto the plain almost always obscures this part of the San Juan Mountains with clouds, even on an otherwise clear day.

The match is only fair, although some of the elements in both drawing and photograph correspond to each other. I do wonder if the ever-present clouds over the river's entrance mean that Kern could not see the subject of his sketch any more clearly than I did.

"August 30th, Sah-watch Mts?" (Plate 132) was made later in the day than "Entrance to Cochetopa Pass" (Plate 126), because its viewpoint is some eight miles farther to the west. At 12:30 in the afternoon the expedition reached Saguache Butte (where its spring no longer flows), then by 3:00 p.m. arrived at "Camp 51, Sahwatch creek," which is southwest of there. Saguache Butte (Rattlesnake Hill) was just a lesser detail in "Entrance to Cochetopa Pass" (Plate 126), but here it is a major presence in the upper left of the sketch, one that is again a multiple-segment panorama on a single sheet of paper. This highly characteristic landmark made the search for a vantage straightforward enough, but there were a few obstacles, both

PLATE 135. Composite drawing and photograph, adjusted in size

manmade and natural. A meandering path from the east goes in the right direction, and in both its irregularity and its conformance to the terrain suggested an antique origin, or at least from a time before the advent of surveyors and bulldozers. My attempt to walk in from the east was stymied, however, by the usual triumvirate of fence, closed gate, and No Trespassing sign. Changing my direction of approach, I located the other end of the primitive road where it joined US 285 just east of Rattlesnake Hill and walked south-eastward along what proved to be the same path, since here was an unlocked gate with no forbidding signs. All went well, but the path was plainly in long disuse and in places overgrown with brush that was very difficult to penetrate. When I finally got beyond a broad field of vegetable barbwire I met a ranch hand who assured me that nobody would have minded if I had jumped the other gate and gone in the easy way, but after this unnecessary struggle I was rewarded with a view of Rattlesnake Hill where some details came into precise alignment, although others seemed at first look to be impossibly confused. It then became apparent that the sequence of the sketches were not in a regular order; the middle drawing belongs to the left, the top part is the middle of the scene, and the bottom belongs on the right. I later cut the drawing with Photoshop® and assembled it in the proper order. When I then compared it with my photograph I saw that each segment of the panorama was drawn to a different scale.

Rattlesnake Hill (Beckwith's Sahwatch butte) is now to the left in the central panel; at its base is some cursive writing, hard to decipher, that I think says "dark." I can only imagine that Kern at first intended to draw only this landmark bluff and its neighboring cliffs, but when it became clear that the expedition would travel toward the left of the butte he added the distant hills at a scale that filled the width of the paper, then finished on the bottom of the sheet with the highest of the cliffs to the right.

The scene made a magnificent photograph (Plate 134), with the barricade of vegetation on the road I traveled visible in the mid distance. For the composite (Plate 135) I have adjusted the sizes of the drawings to match the horizontal scale of the photograph. In front of the left portion of the butte Kern has schematically marked out the spring and stream that issued from its base, but now it is dry, and there is little of it to be seen in my photograph. On the plain to the left and in front of the distant hills is a line of trees along the Saguache River, next to which the expedition would make its camp that evening. From there it was a simple matter to go upstream in the direction of Cochetopa Pass. Creutzfeldt noted the progress made that day.

> Over alternate Sand and meadow land with the same products as yesterday we make a journey of 15 m. and enter on the foot of rocky mountains and isolated Butes the narrow pass-like valley or the opening of the Quitchitopas and encamp (where the valley may have

PLATE 136. Saguache Creek, in Cochetopa Pass (August 31, 1853) 27.3 x 12.6 cm

PLATE 137. Sheet with three drawings, the topmost titled: "Coo-che-to-pa Pass —(San Juan Mts) —East end—" [August 31?] 20.3 x 14.8 cm

> a breadth of 8-10 m.) on one of the principal branches of the Rio Grande... (Creutzfeldt, August 30).

Beckwith took note of the approach to Cochetopa Pass as well.

> *August* 30.—...We here leave the immense valley of San Luis, which is one of the finest in New Mexico...
>
> *August* 31.—Five miles from camp the valley narrowed to a few hundred yards in width, and continued so for most of the day's travel of twelve miles... When ten miles from our morning camp the sand-hills in front of Williams' Pass lay plainly in sight, directly down the valley... The hills and mountains enclosing this thus far beautiful valley, vary in height from two or three hundred to twelve or fifteen hundred feet, covered with a scanty growth of small pine. No mountain pass ever opened more favorably for a railroad than this (G-B, 45).

Plate 136, inscribed "Sah-watch Cr. in Coo-che-to-pa Pass," shows a river bottom flanked on both sides by steep cliffs. The trees on the foreground bank were added later, for they have been drawn over details of the more distant view. Plate 137 shows a second drawing, inscribed "Coo-che-to-pa

PLATE 138. Juxtaposed drawings

Pass— (San Juan Mts/-East end-"that is apparently of the same scene though very different in its rendering. It is the top sketch in a set of three resident on one sheet (Plate 137). The three views relate to the expedition's traverse of the Cochetopa Pass in a sequence starting at the top of the page. The previous drawing (Plate 136) and the uppermost one here seem at first to depict entirely different subjects, but I have come to the conclusion that they are of the same scene and probably from the same point of view. The two are juxtaposed in Plate 138.

I imagine that the idea of creating a sequential set of drawings on one piece of paper emerged after the expedition

PLATE 139. Photograph of Saguache Creek, in Cochetopa Pass

PLATE 140. Composite drawings and photograph

left the site where the first sketch was made, and so Plate 136 was imprecisely copied onto the top of a separate sheet as "Coo-che-to-pa Pass — (San Juan Mts) — East end." The two views below it were added later as each was encountered The viewpoint I chose for my photograph (Plate 139) yields a fair approximation to both sketches (Plate 140). Because the Saguache River Valley is very narrow, and the paved Colorado Highway 114 stretches along its length, I could readily survey its entire extent and did not find a better match. The grove of cottonwoods described by Beckwith extends all along the river here and prevented me from taking up a possibly better position; Kern seems to have been low on the bank and more to the left, perhaps in front of most of the foliage. After making this photograph I thought it might help to come back in the winter when the leaves would be down, and perhaps try to get closer in as well. Gary and Alice Hill, who own the land,

PLATE 141. Near summit of Cochetopa Pass, August 31. Top drawing on a sheet 20.8 x 14.7 c

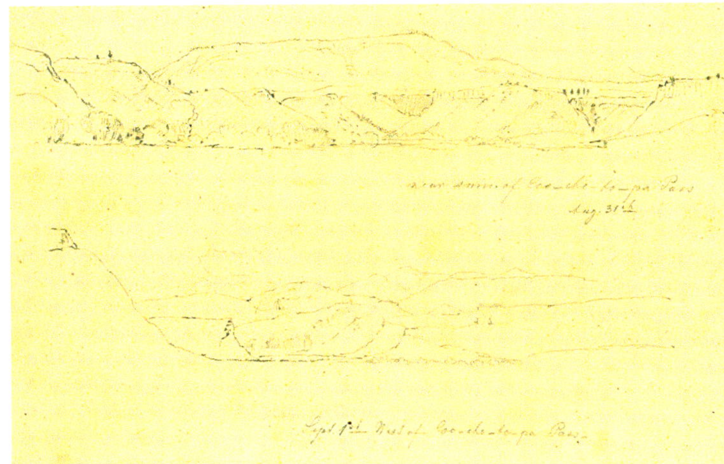

PLATE 142. The entire sheet with both drawings; the title of the bottom sketch is "Sept. 1st West of Coo-che-to-pa Pass

gave me permission to go onto it whenever I wanted, but my pictures were no better, for the bare branches were still dense enough to hide important details that are clearly present in the scene, and to which Kern gave careful attention.

Plate 141, "Near summit of Cochetopa Pass, August 31 (G-B, 100)," is one of two sketches that make up Plate 142 and looks like another attempt to create a sketch narrative of Gunnison's traverse of Cochetopa Pass, but the titles on it, both top and bottom, contain errors that suggest again the principal reason for many of the mistakes in Kern's annotations: Titles were not always added when scenes were drawn, but sometimes days or weeks later. The expedition was not really "near summit of Coo-che-to-pa Pass," although the date of "Aug. 31st" is correct for the drawing; perhaps Kern mistakenly thought they were approaching the summit, but they didn't reach it until two days later, on September 2. The bottom sketch, "Sept 1st West of Coo-che-to-pa Pass" (see Plate 161), *is* from very near the summit of Cochetopa Pass; it is however dated a day too early and was made, as it turns out, from a place and of a scene that are both *east*, not west, of the pass. The upper drawing, that we are considering here, was made on the same day as the last two (Plate 138), but just a little way farther up the valley, and a few miles before the expedition made its "Camp 52, approach to Coochetopa Pass" of August 31. The land here also belongs to Gary and Alice Hill, and I had permission to wander over it, but the best viewpoint was from an embankment next to the

PLATE 143. Photograph near summit of Cochetopa Pass

PLATE 144. Composite drawing and photograph

highway and just high enough that the corrals did not block essential details.

The highly detailed drawing closely matches the photograph, but on the left side it demonstrates a tendency of Kern's to laterally compress details at the edges in relation to central features, which was here a source of confusion when trying to locate the best vantage point. Saguache Creek is defined by a line of trees in front of the adjoining hills, closer on the left, and becoming more distant on the right.

The caption on Plate 145 reads "Coo-che-to-pa Pass—leaving Sawatch Creek." This is correct, for the expedition was in fact leaving Saguache Creek, but that stream was behind Kern when he drew this; the view is up East Pass Creek. Here Gunnison had to choose between two possible routes over the Continental Divide, one leading to the more southerly Carnero Pass, and the other ascending along East Pass Creek to Cochetopa Pass. Leroux had gone ahead to scout these possibilities, and Gunnison chose the Cochetopa. Today the names of these passes have migrated: Carnero Pass has been renamed Cochetopa Pass by the Forest Service on maps and a historical marker at its crest, while what was originally Cochetopa Pass came to be called North Pass by the Colorado Highway Department when it ran State Highway 114 through here, later amended by way of compromise to North Cochetopa Pass.

Kern represents the rounded hill on the right with

exaggeratedly steep, high cliffs that it does not really possess. This scene is one of the first that I located. I was aided in discovery by Pat Richmond, the author of a wonderful book on Frémont's fourth expedition in the San Luis Valley and La Garita Wilderness, *Trail to Disaster* (1990). She accompanied me on a very productive daylong reconnaissance from the lower San Luis Valley to the town of Gunnison, to see if we could find any of Kern's subjects. We stopped first at the Forest Service headquarters in Saguache to show the rangers this drawing, and they immediately told us where it was. They knew it well because at the bottom of the right-hand hill there is now a Forest Service building, and in front of it are trees along East Pass Creek, which flows down through the gap in the center of the picture before turning to the right.

> *September* 1.—... We continued on the southern course, on which we encamped last evening, for about two miles, and then turned west, following the Sahwatch creek for six miles, where we crossed it for the last time, and left the main Indian trail which still follows that creek, which rises considerably to the south. This main trail is said to lead through thick forests of timber, through which it would require much labor to open a wagon road to Carnero Pass, equal if not superior to that of our route. We pursued for three miles a fine branch of the Sahwatch, coming in from the north, when we left it, and, turning west, followed a branch of this creek, and after a march of fifteen miles, encamped where a low opening in the mountains afforded a small supply of grass, and enabled us to enter and encamp with our train. The valley of the Sahwatch to-day continued narrow, as at our camp last evening, and travelling in it very fine, at this dry season. The valley of the next branch was still narrower, varying from 130 yards to 150 feet, and the travelling equally fine; and in the succeeding valley, often narrowed until the huge, fallen rocks from either side had passed each other and lay scattered over the bottom, the road was still good, although we had constantly to wind around these rocks, and to cross and re-cross the creek... The pines are confined to the mountain tops and sides, and but few are of respectable size. Surrounding our camp they are small but numerous, extending from our camp-fires quite to the mountain tops (G-B, 46-47).

The choice of the approach to Cochetopa Pass was of such geographical importance that the *Report* illustrated the

PLATE 145. Cochetopa Pass —Leaving Saguache Creek [September 1]
17.5 x 7.1 cm

PLATE 146. Photograph of Cochetopa Pass

expedition's position with two lithographs; the first one (Plate 148), derived from this drawing, is "COO-CHE-TO-PA PASS View looking up Sahwatch Creek Septbr[t] 1[st]." Once again Stanley's skills are on display in this very high quality reproduction of Kern's drawing (Plate 149). Both sketch and the derived lithograph seem to indicate by a line of shrubs that a creek enters from the left instead of coming down towards the observer through the center, which is the actual case.

PLATE 147. Composite drawing and photograph

Unfortunately, whoever decided on the caption of the lithograph changed "leaving Sawatch Creek" on the drawing that correctly described whast was happening here, into "View looking up Sahwatch Creek," which it is not; the view is looking straight up East Pass Creek, along which the expedition would approach Cochetopa Pass.

After traveling a short distance up Beckwith's "fine branch of the Sahwatch, coming in from the north," the expedition "left it, and, turning west, followed a branch of this creek," to continue their climb. Shortly after that Kern made another drawing (Plate 150), the title of which, "In Coo-che-to-pa Pass, leaving Sah-watch Cr.," is practically identical to that previous (Plate 145).

PLATE 148. Lithograph by John Mix Stanley, Cochetopa Pass, view looking up Saguache Creek, September 1

PLATE 149. Composite drawing and lithograph

At first glance, the view in the photograph, Plate 151, seemed to be the proper place. I had climbed to a cliff along the expedition's route, and when I looked off it was rewarded with an "aha!" moment of immediate recognition. The scene corresponds closely to the title on the drawing. It is a short distance from a branch of the Saguache Creek that comes in from the north (today Spanish Creek), and the view is looking northwest up a yet smaller branch (today East Pass Creek) that flows down from Cochetopa Pass. The problems began when I tried to align details of the scene by shifting my position. The cliff is crumbling, so there were only two safe vantage points separated by some 200 feet, and neither seemed to offer an ideal correspondence. My photograph is perhaps the best possible, but when juxtaposed with the sketch it leaves a bit to be desired. While I was mired in puzzlement over this scene and contemplating what to do next, Mark Swinney, a range resource manager from the BLM, came by. I showed him the sketch, and told him I

PLATE 150. In Cochetopa Pass, leaving Saguache Creek [September 1] 18.5 x 9.6 cm

PLATE 152. Composite drawing and photograph

PLATE 151. Photograph in Cochetopa Pass

was contemplating a hike up the canyon before us to see if I could find a better point of view. He was familiar with the area and assured me that if I did I would find nothing along East Pass Creek that would be an improvement. After he left I hiked far enough along this beautiful valley to observe how the cliffs gave way to rounded hills, and its character then changed completely. Mark was right. I now believe that the sketch was done quickly, somewhat carelessly, and is unfinished. The softly contoured mountains in the distance have been omitted, and the distant and vaguely outlined "peak" in the center of the drawing probably represents some cliffs on or in front of them that are barely visible in the photograph.

As with the previous drawing, "Leaving Sawatch Creek" and its lithograph (Plate 149), the importance of Gunnison's approach to Cochetopa Pass might have been made plain by another lithograph in the *Report,* to illustrate the spot. Such a lithograph was indeed produced by Stanley with his usual

PLATE 153. Lithograph by John Mix Stanley, Head of the first canyon of the Grand River below the mouth of Cochetopa Creek, September 7

PLATE 154. Composite drawing and lithograph

skill (Plate 153), but ultimately it was put to an entirely different use. The lithograph's title, "Head of the First Canyon of Grand River below the Mouth of Coo-che-to-pa Creek, Sept. 7," is incorrect, for the mouth of Cochetopa (now Tomichi) Creek was not reached until after some 70 miles of additional travel, and September 7 is six days later than when Kern made the sketch on which the lithograph is based. The published illustration is also is placed in the *Report* adjacent to the page on which is the narrative for September 7. Why, with the correctly labeled drawing (though admittedly undated) in hand, was a grossly inaccurate title and date introduced on the lithograph and then buttressed by a correspondingly incorrect placement of it in the text?

The expedition went straight up the valley in the picture (East Pass Creek) and made "Camp 53, foot of Coochetopa Pass" (G-B, 100) on the site where today is the Forest Service's Buffalo Gate, or Buffalo Pass, Campground. Beckwith describes how the canyon narrowed and deepened as they approached their campsite.

PLATE 155. In Sangre de Cristo Pass [in Cochetopa Pass, September 2]: 20.3 x 15.2 cm

PLATE 156. Lithograph of Cochetopa Pass, from a drawing by Gwinn Harris Heap

September 1.—(continued)... The precipitous escarpments of the narrow ravines are...in formations of from twenty to sixty and eighty feet in thickness. The crests of these bluffs are covered with earth a few feet in thickness, some terminating in larger or smaller plains of table-land, while others are rounded off into points and ridges (G-B, 47).

Among the drawings in the album of scenes that were found only with great difficulty, "In Sangre de Cristo Pass" (Plate 155), was perhaps the most challenging of all. I spent days examining the vicinity of Sangre de Cristo Pass, during which time I unexpectedly discovered an unlabeled scene that looked very much as if it came from somewhere else (Plate 88). But nowhere in my search did this view appear before me. Later at home I was looking over the as-yet-unlocated drawings (something I would do at irregular intervals, especially during bad weather) when I suddenly realized I had seen the cliff in this

PLATE 157. Engraving based on a daguerreotype by Solomon Nunes Carvalho, Cochetopa Pass

PLATE 158. Daguerreotype made in Cochetopa Pass

drawing before, and was immediately able to figure out where. It is about two miles up East Pass Creek from Buffalo Gate Campground, which was the site of the expedition's September 1 camp. The earliest illustration of this distinctive cliff of which I am aware is a tinted lithograph after a drawing by Gwinn Harris Heap. In the summer of 1853 he passed by it with his cousin Edward Fitzgerald Beale on their way to California, and also noted in his journal that he had seen this "remarkable" formation while on his way over Cochetopa Pass (Plate 156).

> We resumed our journey at 5.30 A. M.... Eight miles brought us to a remarkable cliff, about one hundred feet in height, which beetled over the trail on our left... (Heap, 39).

PLATE 159. Photograph taken in Cochetopa Pass of the subject in Plate 155, which was mislabeled “Sangre de Cristo Pass”

PLATE 160. Composite drawing and photograph

Then there was a steel engraving intended for John Charles Frémont’s never-written account of his fifth expedition, based on a daguerreotype by Solomon Nunes Carvalho and found in the *Prospectus* for Frémont’s *Memoirs* (1886). I have reversed it to appear in the the same orientation as the actual scene (Plate 157). My daguerreotype of the cliff shows the left—to-right reversal that is characteristic of this process (Plate 158), (Shlaer, 106-107). To find the scene start at Buffalo Gate Campground, then walk westward about two miles along the old road by the stream at the bottom of the canyon, and this cliff comes into view. The canyon sides are fairly steep, and there is no other route the expedition could reasonably have taken. The expedition then continued up along East Pass Creek and climbed out of its canyon on a slope to the right, finding the crest of (North) Cochetopa Pass where Colorado 114 crosses it today.

> *September* 2.—Captain Morris and myself went forward with working parties, to make practicable crossings for the wagons at the various points where, from the widening of the streams and narrowness of the pass, it should be necessary, and to cut out the timber which at various points quite filled the pass as it covered the ridges, which at this point divide the waters of the continent: those of the eastern slope flowing by the channels up which we have traveled for several days, to the Rio Grande del Norte, and thence to the Gulf of Mexico; while those from the western slope flow into the Rio Grande, or Grand [today's Gunnison] river, one of the main branches of the Colorado of the West, reaching the Pacific through the Gulf of California (G-B, 47).

In photographing here I encountered the same impediment as I had a few years before, when I made a winter daguerreotype of the cliff: The woods are now so densely grown that I could not back up far enough to replicate the perspective in the drawing. Because I was too close to the cliff, the distant, rounded hill in the middle of the picture appears smaller than it should, but in other respects this photograph is a fine evocation of the scene. This is strong evidence that the area here is more densely wooded than it was in 1853. This distinctive overhang, "which beetled over the trail," stands here in isolation and guards the path, but curiously Beckwith mentions it neither in the *Report* nor in his *Journal*, Creutzfeldt passes it by without a word, and even the geologist Schiel takes no note of it; yet artists on each of the three expeditions that came by here in 1853 found in it a worthy subject for illustration. Kern must have made his drawing of it on the morning of September 2, for despite the heavy growth of aspens along the stream the expedition reached the crest of the pass that day at 1:15 p.m., where its members could look northwest into a drainage whose waters ultimately reached the Pacific Ocean. Exhausted by their labors, they soon stopped for the day at "Camp 54, west of pass" about a mile and a half farther on.

The puzzle about the drawing "In Sangre de Cristo Pass" (Plate 155) is how it came to be mislabeled; the caption is in Kern's handwriting. According to the expedition's odometers they were 125 miles beyond Sangre de Cristo Pass, which had been crossed some two week previous. Here the party was heavily occupied clearing trees and brush from its path. Kern's drawing looks hurried in execution, and perhaps that is why it was left untitled at first. I imagine that much later he either noticed the oversight or had it brought to his attention, and then quickly added what he thought was a suitable legend.

PLATE 161. September 1, west of Cochetopa Pass [September 2, East of...] Bottom drawing of two on a sheet 20.8 x 14.7 cm
VIEW PLATES 161-163: www.Kernsketches.com/plate/161

The expedition would have to have been far enough beyond Cochetopa Pass that his memory of this distinctive rock face had become vague enough to be confused with Sangre de Cristo Pass, and we must again wonder how often drawings were left unlabeled and how long it might typically have been before these omissions were corrected, by either Kern or someone else in the company. Such delays go far toward explaining the contradictions and textual inaccuracies that all too frequently appear on the sketches, and of which the next drawing is a good example.

> *September 2.*—... We found little difficulty on the banks of the creek, but were detained some hours by the dense growth of quaking-asp, from the size of saplings to a foot in diameter, among which, fallen in every direction, was an equally large growth of dead aspens. At 11 o'clock, however, we were progressing rapidly towards the summit of the pass, which we soon reached, and, as we enjoyed the prospect before us, a slight thunder-shower was not a disagreeable accompaniment. The elevation of the pass is not enough to give an extensive view, but the numerous small, grassy valleys, and pine and aspen groves of the mountain sides to the west, afforded us a pleasant prospect, the more so as it gave hope of an easy prosecution of our future labors, at least for a time...
>
> The width of this pass at the summit does not exceed six hundred yards, but the slopes to the low peaks rising above it are not abrupt. The ascent from the valley of San Luis, by which we reached the summit, was very gradual, increasing with considerable uniformity until we approached it within a short distance, where the ravine of the stream was narrow and thickly timbered; and we left it with the wagons, making an abrupt ascent to the right to the level of the summit... (G-B, 47).

We pass to-day the water shed and encamp about 1 m. on the other side, where the waters flow to the Pacific ocean, having made 5 m. in all… The cutting down of trees and brushes did detain us to day we could not make a longer journey… Weather till now clear and hot, then thunderstorms in all directions (Creutzfeldt, September 2).

From the Saguache Butte up to the elevation of the Cochetopa Pass is not more than thirty English miles but it took us four strenuous days to reach this summit. Now trees would have to be chopped down in order to make way for the wagons, for the mountain has aspen trees up to its very top… Towards noon of the second of September we reached the summit of the pass over which a light thunderstorm was breeding as though in celebration of the occasion (Schiel, 76).

Despite its caption "Sept. 1st West of Coo-che-to-pa Pass," this scene (Plate 161) was drawn from east of the pass, though not far from its apex. Beckwith, Creutzfeldt and Schiel all noted that the approach to the crest from the east was through a narrow canyon heavily wooded with aspen, but today it is dense with conifers. Once again it seems that the condition of a forest is now quite different and perhaps better than in 1853.

PLATE 162. Photograph west of Cochetopa Pass

My photograph (Plate 162) shows that many of the sharp geological features and contours of slopes in the view are today hidden by trees. The sketch also appears to be incomplete since the distant mountains on the horizon are not represented; weather conditions might have made them invisible, for on that day both Beckwith and Creutzfeldt noted the occurrence of thunderstorms. Today the only accessible places near the crest of Cochetopa Pass from which to see eastward over the trees are pull-offs next to Colorado Highway 114; the one I used is near where the trail Beckwith describes makes "an abrupt ascent to the right" to join the modern highway. The dramatic cliff of the last illustration (Plate 155) is deep in the canyon, where it rises above the trees and is clearly visible

PLATE 163. Composite drawing and photograph

in the photograph; it is present in the drawing as close-set vertical lines, about one third of the way in from the left. Farther to the right along the bottom Kern depicted a line of what were probably aspens extending along East Pass Creek, but from the point of view available for my photograph, nearby trees obscure the creek bed. Both the date and the notation "West" on the sketch are inaccurate; September 1 should be September 2, and "West" should be "East." When he drew this view the pass had not yet been crossed, and Kern must have known that he was looking somewhat south of east, and that he was close to but not yet over the pass. Like the previous drawing (Plate 155), the caption of this sketch must have been added later when Kern might have become uncertain, or, even worse, indifferent about the correct date and place. Kern's usual working style appears to have been to sketch rapidly, and in his haste not always provide a legend;

now and then he might take up or be given unlabeled drawings to identify and did so from memory, sometimes correctly and sometimes not. It suggests that his cartographic work was far more important, and no doubt far more demanding, than taking down merely illustrative views. How else to explain that the date and the place on this drawing are incompatible? Individually they are each faulty, and if taken literally they "move" the viewpoint in opposite directions. Thinking that one part of the inscription had to be correct and not imagining that it simultaneously contained two conflicting errors, I was misled into searching a much broader area than would otherwise have been necessary.

# 4

# Down the Grand River

*From Cochetopa Pass to the Grand River and into its Rugged Canyons; Smoke Signals of the Utah Indians; the Gorge of Lake Fork*

THE NEXT DAY THE EXPEDITION descended from Cochetopa Pass along what is today West Pass Creek; Beckwith referred to it simply as "Pass creek."

> September 3.—We proceeded down the valley of Pass creek in a westerly course... Four miles from camp we passed a broad valley extending several miles to the south towards the Sierra San Juan, whose northern slopes are still covered with large fields of snow (G-B, 48).

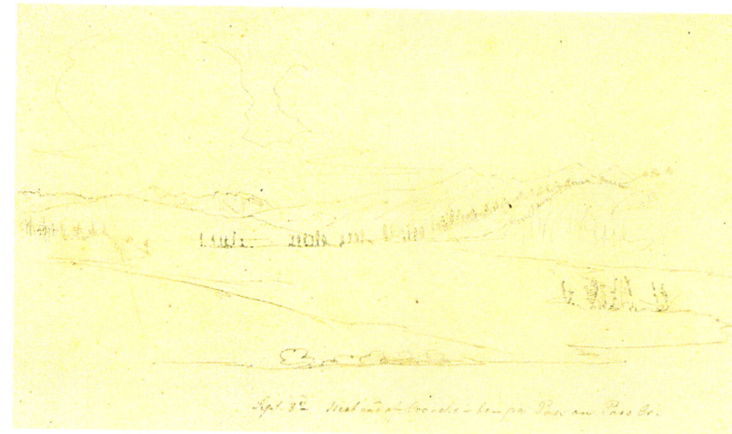

PLATE 164. September 3: West end of Cochetopa Pass on Pass Creek 19.8 x 12.9 cm

Plate 164, captioned "Sept. 3rd West end of Coo-che-to-pa Pass on Pass Cr." is a view to the southwest over the valley that Beckwith describes above, and the photograph of it was made from just west of the intersection of 17-GG with Colorado Highway 114. Towards the left in the sketch but nearer the center of the photograph are a series of distant mountains along the Continental Divide, in today's La Garita Wilderness. Farthest to the left the most elevated peak reaches to some 13,900 feet of altitude, but because it is part of a long, high ridge it does not seem to have a name. On the horizon to the right of center is a closer group of mountains; from left to right the first high peak is Organ Mountain, with two lower summits outlined on its slopes, followed by the more rounded silhouette of San Luis Peak, then farthest to the right in the drawing is Baldy Alto. Peeking out on the far right of the photograph is Stewart Peak, but Kern did not extend his sketch far enough to include it. The snow that Beckwith noted would have been visible on all of these mountains. The nearby wooded slope rising to the right is part of Cochetopa Dome, and on it there are some irregular, tentatively drawn vertical lines, not in Kern's style. The cursive note "Pines" is written over some of them, perhaps by the same hand that produced the lines. Today the incline is still covered with pines, and the other clumps of evergreen trees in Kern's sketch have maintained their clearly recognizable groupings into the present.

PLATE 165. Photograph on Pass Creek

PLATE 166. Composite drawing and photograph

Beckwith's September 3 entry continues from here and tells of the easy route the expedition had on gentle terrain while descending along Pass Creek, until its canyon became impassably narrow.

> Opposite this valley that of Pass creek widens considerably, and we passed easily down it for six miles further to where another valley sweeps off to the south, through which a fine creek descends, and, uniting with that of our path, enters a broken cañon. The valley from this point extends to the south towards the snowy peaks of the Sierra San Juan... (G-B, 48).

Creutzfeldt was delighted that the terrain now offered easier travel but did not enjoy the sight of the San Juan Mountains, because they evoked terrible memories of suffering on Frémont's failed expedition of 1848. Gunnison had just traversed Cochetopa Pass with ease, whereas Frémont missed it by going too far south and caused his men to become trapped among the frozen high summits of La Garita. The event continued to haunt Creutzfeldt.

> Without any further difficulties we are going down the small brook to-day; after a journey of 8-10 m. it

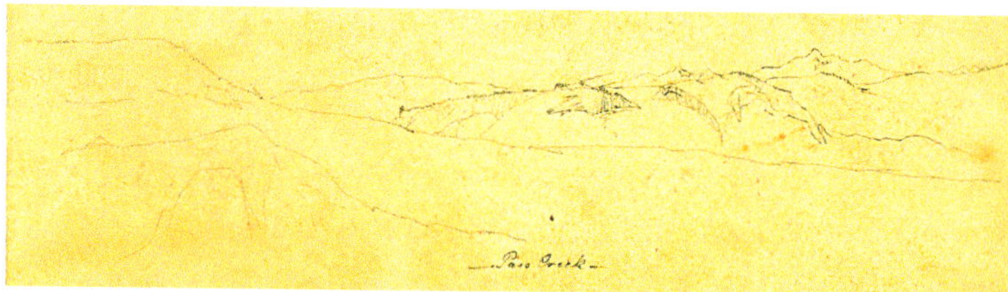

PLATE 167. Pass Creek [September 3] Second drawing of three on a sheet 20.4 x 14.8 cm

PLATE 168. Photograph, Pass Creek

PLATE 169. Composite drawing and photograph

> flows in a larger one and the country becomes several miles wide... The mountains of the St. John range are distinctly visible and awake in me with their snowy summits not very agreeable memories. They are piled up higher and higher, one after the other and do not leave any hope to find a pass in them... (Creutzfeldt, September 3).

Pass Creek (Plate 167) is the middle sketch on a sheet containing three drawings that appear to have been put in a deliberate sequence. The first of these was "Coo-chu-to-pa Pass — (San Juan Mts) - East end—" (Plate 137). This view is Beckwith's "six miles further...where another valley sweeps off to the south, through which a fine creek descends," and is about ten miles down from the crest of Cochetopa Pass. On the left descending from the top of the picture is the slope of Cochetopa Dome, the other side of which was visible in the prior illustration (Plate 164). Against the sky where this slope intersects a more distant hill, the photograph shows just a sliver of a wooded rise, one that Kern began to sketch but did not finish. Pass Creek (today West Pass Creek), flows in front of Cochetopa Dome; it is not represented in the drawing. Beckwith's "fine creek" is today Cochetopa Creek; it flows around the far side of Cochetopa Dome and in front of the distant rolling hills, then is joined by West Pass Creek out of the picture to the right. Today the conjoined streams keep the name "Cochetopa Creek," and run north into Cochetopa Canyon; Beckwith, however, assigns Cochetopa Creek to an entirely different stream, which is today Tomichi Creek. The high peak on the right of the sketch is Organ Mountain, which Kern shows as the highest on the horizon, well above the hill in front of it; three peaks that are to the left of it but lower are also prominently outlined, although they are barely visible in the photograph. Despite the title, Pass Creek is not actually in the drawing and can be discovered in the photograph, which was taken from along Highway 114, only if you know where to look. The straight segment of a road in the center crosses it where its nearer end just disappears from view. Possibly this is a simplified copy drawing made from a sketch that is not now in the album, or the title may simply refer to the viewpoint, which is above (the Valley of) Pass Creek.

Soon the expedition was compelled to leave this valley and take a less direct but easier route down to the Grand River.

> This creek here inclines more to the north, and enters a small cañon which sends out several side branches, and we were forced, in turning it, to cross a ridge to the N. N. E. to another branch of the Coochetopa creek. This ridge was rough and thickly covered with several varieties of artemisia—the sage so large and stiff that our animals were very reluctant to pass through it (G-B, 49).

About two miles downstream from where "Pass Creek" (Plate 167) was drawn, the merged streams enter Beckwith's "small cañon" and flow almost straight north between the vertical cliffs in what is today Cochetopa Canyon. The expedition did not continue downstream because the narrow, heavily overgrown chasm would have been impassable to wagons, although, thanks to the wonders of dynamite and bulldozers, Colorado Highway 114's pavement snakes down it today. This is as far from the summit of Cochetopa Pass as

PLATE 170. West of summit in Cochetopa Pass [?] 21.5 x 7.4 cm

PLATE 171. Photograph, west of summit in Cochetopa Pass

the men went before they climbed out of the valley they had followed downward and turned northeast to go roughly along the course of today's 14-PP RD. I had imagined that Kern explored the beginnings of that hopelessly rugged part of the canyon before following the expedition out of it, because the sheer cliffs in Plate 170, "West of Summit in Coo-che-to-pa Pass," strongly suggested those found just below the point where Gunnison's men left it. The chasm is so narrow, and I had to stand so close to the cliff I was photographing, that the distortion in my panorama makes it impossible to satisfactorily compare it with the drawing. This is just the sort of difficult view that an artist can fix up, but in the end I doubt that the drawing and the photograph represent the same subject. I now believe this sketch depicts cliffs that were encountered by the expedition more than a week later and some 70 miles farther along their way, and to be of a scene that a companion

PLATE 172. Composite drawing and photograph:

drawing identifies as "Sunday Septr 11th Un-com-pah-gre Mts" (Plate 274). The two sketches are juxtaposed for comparison in Plate 173, but a discussion of them will be better placed later on.

After Gunnison and his men left the deepening canyon of Pass Creek, they climbed over a divide to the headwaters of today's Prosser and Razor creeks. These merge and then flow northward to become for Beckwith "another branch of Coochetopa creek" because they join the "Coo-che-to-pa Creek" as shown on the expedition's map. Today Coochetopa Creek has been renamed Tomichi Creek, perhaps because it originates not at Cochetopa Pass, but from somewhere to the north. Farther west, Pass Creek also joins

PLATE 173. Juxtaposed sketches of cliffs

Tomichi (Beckwith's "Coochetopa") Creek, at the mouth of today's Cochetopa Canyon, the one that was too rugged for Gunnison and his men to follow.

*(Skip over this paragraph if you wish; it is here only for the sake of geographical completeness. The names of the watercourses in this region have all shifted: In 1853 Pass Creek came down from then Cochetopa Pass; today the same creek is named West Pass Creek and its place of origin is called North Cochetopa Pass; when it is joined by today's Cochetopa Creek, originating farther south near San Luis Peak, the merged streams now take the name of Cochetopa Creek. They flow north through Cochetopa Canyon to join today's Tomichi Creek, the one that Beckwith names "Coochetopa creek." Tomichi Creek originates on the Continental Divide well north of Cochetopa Pass, and from there flows south and then turns west until it reaches the town of Gunnison, Colorado, where it enters what is now the Gunnison River. The Gunnison is the upper portion of what was formerly the Grand River, which farther west joins what is now the Colorado River and flows through the Grand Canyon and on to the Gulf of California. The Grand is occasionally referred to by Beckwith and others as the "Rio Grande," but should not be confused with "El Rio Grande del Norte," which flows out of the eastern slopes of the San Juan Mountains into the San Luis Valley, then south to the Gulf of Mexico).*

The next drawing, "Sept 3rd, Divide between the waters of the Gulf of Mexico & the Pacific Ocean," (Plate 174) was made from the sagebrush-covered ridge that so discouraged the animals. After leaving Cochetopa Canyon the expedition's men encountered their first expansive view of the valleys from which the Grand River originates. The date here is not in Kern's hand. I found it impossible to match distant mountain outlines to the drawing, so I limited myself to three

PLATE 174. September 3: Divide between the waters of the Gulf of Mexico and the Pacific Ocean. 27.1 x 10.5 cm

PLATE 177. 4:45 p.m., September 3, Cochetopa Creek; Top drawing on a sheet of three, 19.6 x 15.0 cm

PLATE 175. Photograph of divide

PLATE 176. Composite drawing and photograph

features that were not so very far away: the hill that enters the composition from the left, with its small bump as it descends; the canyon in the left foreground, out of which the expedition had just climbed; and the hill that rises to the edge of the picture on the right. It is not clear to me if the drawing is complete or if distant mountain ranges have been omitted; nor is it clear how much might have been invisible to me when I photographed the scene because of the clouds that extend to the horizon, or those that made features invisible by the dark shadows they cast on the ground. The actual divide is not in the picture but off to the right and out of view to the northeast. It is rather a view of an expanse from which all waters flow westward on their way to the Pacific Ocean.

Plate 177, "4 45 Sept 3 Coo-che-to-pa Cr.," can be viewed from high up along 14-PP RD about a mile north of the position for the last sketch (Plate 174), and looks northeast toward the Continental Divide. There are two more sketches below this one on the same sheet of paper, one of a very similar scene, but dated two days later, to September 5. The view of this one

PLATE 178. The entire sheet

PLATE 179. Photograph, Cochetopa Creek

PLATE 180. Composite drawing and photograph

is down into and across the valley of today's Tomichi Creek, which flows in front of Tomichi Dome, the large rounded prominence in the middle of the picture. To the right of Tomichi Dome, about 35 miles distant and on the far side of the Continental Divide, is the pointed silhouette of Tabeguache Peak; all the way to the right but closer is another high, rounded hill, today called Lions Head.

"Divide between the Gulf of Mexico and the Pacific Ocean - From 535 Sept. 3" (Plate 181) is a two part panorama on one sheet. When suitably arranged (Plate 182), its central feature is V Rock, named for the inverted "V" appearance of its cliffs, and roughly southeast from where Kern was standing when he made this drawing. On the right is Razor Creek Dome, with a distinctive turret-shaped outcropping on its northern slope. To the left is Prosser Rock, displaying in outline its sheer cliffs on one side and a gentler slope on the other. This is another scene that I found with the help of Pat Richmond, as we drove from Saguache to Gunnison; it is readily seen from 14-PP RD,

PLATE 181. Divide between the Gulf of Mexico and the Pacific Ocean, 5:35 p.m., September 3, 20.2 x 15.2 cm.

PLATE 182. Two-part panorama on one sheet, trimmed and juxtaposed.

PLATE 183. Photograph, panorama on divide

PLATE 184. Composite drawing and photograph

PLATE 185. Camp Rock (Eagle Tail), near camp September 3: Top sketch of two on a single sheet. 20.1 x 15.1 cm

and we were both astonished and gratified to discover that in so economical a sketch Kern had included all the essential details.

A few hours and several miles on, the expedition was approaching its campsite for the evening. The subject of Kern's last drawing of the day, (Plate 185 top, "Camp rock (Eagle Tail) near Camp Sept. 3d") is Prosser and "V" Rocks, two formations featured prominently in the preceding panorama (Plate 182). It shares a sheet of paper with a drawing from August 10, and comes to us with its title tilted at an appreciable angle to the margins of the sheet; otherwise there

PLATE 186. Photograph, Camp Rock

PLATE 187. Leveled sketch

PLATE 188. Composite drawing and photograph

are no clues to horizontal except the sketch itself. The vantage point is from near the junction of Prosser Creek with Razor Creek. Prosser Rock is far more symmetrical in Kern's sketch than its outline in my photograph because he compressed the left side of his representation. After comparing the drawing with the scene, it seemed to me best to rotate the sketch clockwise, under the assumption that Kern's handwriting at the bottom roughly corresponds to horizontal (Plate 187).

Even when rotated by such a sizable amount, the drawing does not do justice to the asymmetric outline of the original. On the left it displays a wooded slope that can readily be hiked up nearly to its top; the crumbling vertical cliffs of the opposite side are a different matter. Kern's name for this distinctive and astonishingly beautiful formation is "Camp rock," and it marks a site with sheltering trees and lush fields of grass along the banks of a nearby creek that would provide abundant fodder for the animals and soft places for the men to sleep. "Eagle Tail" is not an alternative designation for "Camp Rock" but rather the name of the region in which the expedition now found itself; the 1851 Parke-Kern map shows the "Peaks of Eagle Tail" here along the Continental Divide, with "Eagle tail Cr." flowing from them to eventually reach the Grand River; the map accompanying Frémont's 1848 Geographical Memoir upon Upper California calls today's Gunnison River the "Eagle R," and his all-encompassing map, based on his explorations up to 1853-54 but not published until 1886, places the "Eagletail R." here with Cochetopa Creek flowing into it (Shlaer, 65; Frémont, *Memoirs*); finally, *Lippincott's Pronouncing Gazetteer* (Thomas and Baldwin, 1856) contains this entry, perhaps derived from the Parke-Kern map:

> PEAKS-OF-EA´GLETAIL, in the E. part of Utah Territory. near the source of Eagletail River, are in about lat. 38° 40' N., lon. 106° 50' W. (Thomas and Baldwin, 1856, 1447).

By the beginning of the twentieth century this appellation seems to have dropped out of use.

Gunnison and his men left the area of "Camp rock" on the morning of September 5, a day for which the narrative in the *Report* is a bit disordered.

> *September 5.*—Following for three miles the narrow valley of the little creek on which we had encamped... On our right we passed a very large, elevated, and remarkably round butte, standing quite detached from the mountain beyond it. Eight miles brought us to the Coochetopa [today Tomichi] creek, a fine, rapid

> little stream of twenty feet in width, which we were repeatedly obliged to cross and recross as the valley narrowed into gorges, and the stream impinged against its banks, while to avoid this at other points we passed over the artemisia bluffs...
>
> Captain Gunnison ascended a hill one mile W. N. W. from our morning camp, from which he had a fine view of the snow-clad range mountains from which the Puncha and Coochetopa creeks descend. This mountain extends round by the north to northwest (magnetic,) where Grand river passes between it and the Elk Mountains. From this point also he had a view of a snowy peak of the mountains at the head of the Arkansas river, distant in a course N. N. W. perhaps one hundred miles... Reaching the mouth of Pass creek [emerging from today's Cochetopa Canyon], we encamped in a meadow of half a mile in diameter... (G-B, 49).

During the expedition Captain Gunnison made many short excursions like the one Beckwith describes here. It does not seem to have been his usual practice to bring Kern along with him, but this time may have been an exception, for Plate 189 "Sah-watch Mts" illustrates a part of Captain Gunnison's

PLATE 189. Saguache Mountains [September 5] 20.0 x 16.2 cm

"fine view." The sheet appears at first to contain a three-part panorama such as we have seen before. I have juxtaposed the top and middle segments for the purpose of matching the photograph, but the bottom part I have omitted, although it shows terrain that appears to be characteristic of the area, and to be a reasonable continuation of the middle sketch. However, it is not. Tantalizing though it be, it does not correspond even remotely to anything that can be seen from

PLATE 190. Top and middle parts of the drawing juxtaposed as a panorama

PLATE 191. Panoramic photograph of Saguache Mountains

PLATE 192. Composite drawing and photograph

this point of view, nor, indeed, to anything I could find in the surrounding region.

The photograph was made from a hill about a mile east of Razor Creek, along which the expedition was traveling north. This is a rare example of Kern's having exerted himself by climbing or riding away from the group to obtain a view. Gunnison, by contrast, often did so, and this illustration corresponds well to a portion of the "fine view" that Beckwith says Gunnison enjoyed that day. Unfortunately there is no suitable hill to stand on "one mile W. N. W. from our morning camp," which the expedition had just left; the hill that served the purpose is about three miles north of the camp. The best candidate for the "very large, elevated, and remarkably round butte, standing quite detached from the mountain beyond it" is Tomichi Dome, looming against the sky near the middle but too far away for the expedition to have "passed" it; a much smaller, more isolated, and even rounder formation is present off to the right, standing by itself on the floor of the valley, but it is not large or high enough to conform to the description in the narrative. Surprisingly, there is no mention of a high, round butte in Beckwith's diary for the day, suggesting he may have added its description to the text for publication after viewing Kern's sketch of it while he was back in Washington, or after reading Gunnison's journals. The drawing shows a great deal of lateral compression, making the round formation on the right much taller and perhaps even a bit rounder than it actually is. Nor is the drawing complete, for many of the mountains outlined against the sky that appear to the left in the photograph have not been included in Kern's view. Gunnison described them as visible to the north-northwest in the morning, but Kern may not have seen them clearly enough to have represented them in his sketch; according to the table of meteorological observations, most of the latter part of the day was characterized by "dark clouds" (G-B, 101).

PLATE 193. 10 a.m. September 5, Saguache Mountains. Second and third drawings on a sheet 19.6 x 15.0 cm, which on its top contains "4 45 Sept 3 Co-che-to-pa Cr" (Plate 178).

The expedition was at first going north along Razor Creek on which they had camped from the evening of September 3 to the morning of September 5. The normal starting time was

PLATE 194. Photograph

PLATE 195. Composite drawing and photograph

PLATE 196. Photograph

PLATE 197. Composite drawing and photograph

7:00 a.m., so in three hours they had covered about four miles to where, at 10:00 a.m., Kern made this sketch "10 Sept. 5 Sah-watch Mts." (Plate 193). The vantage point is near where 62 RD turns sharply northwest and climbs out of the valley of Razor Creek, and from a nearby hillside there is a view to the east across its flood plain. Here I met Jim Mendonca, who identified the peaks that could be seen in Kern's sketches of the area. At the time I was very uncertain about the route of the expedition, so he offered to get some horses from his ranch and help search for possible vantage points in the more inaccessible areas. This turned out not to be necessary, but I shall always regret not having had the adventure of it.

Plate 193 "10 Sept 5. Sah-watch Mts" shares a piece of paper with a drawing dated two days earlier (Plate 178). At the far left is the familiar shape of Tomichi Dome. The high distant peak in the middle of the photograph, but more leftward in the drawing, is Mount Ouray, while the other one on the horizon but to the right of center is Mount Antero. The distinctive castellated

PLATE 198. West end of Cochetopa Pass [September 5] Bottom drawing on a sheet with three sketches on it

PLATE 199. Composite of two drawings

PLATE 200. Photograph

PLATE 201. Composite drawing and photograph

formation at the bottom left of the sketch appears to be in the foreground of the view, but it is not. Although visible from many other places in the valley, it cannot be seen at all from where I made my panoramic photograph. By climbing farther up the hill I was standing on and down its slope to the north, I obtained a clear view of this prominent, but isolated, formation. Kern's sketch of this rocky mound seems to be tilted to the left but I have chosen in this case not to adjust it; my photograph is properly leveled, however (Plates 196 and 197).

"West end of Coo-che-to-pa Pass" (Plate 198) is the third of three on a single sheet (Plate 137) that looks as if it is part of an intentional sequence to make a narrative of crossing Cochetopa Pass. After searching the valley without reference to my earlier work, I ultimately arrived at nearly the same viewpoint as that of a preceding illustration (Plate 193) , although seen together the correspondences do not seem very compelling (Plate 199).

PLATE 202. Cochetopa Creek (near its junction with Grand River) [September 5]. Top drawing of three on one sheet

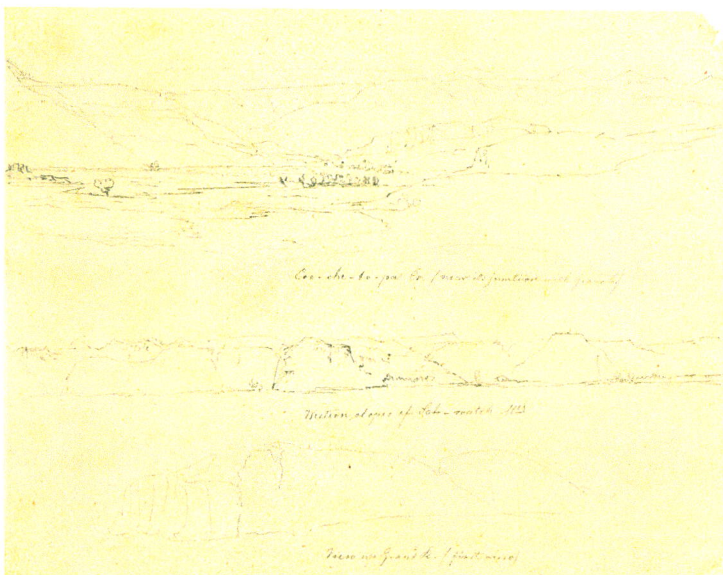

PLATE 203. The complete drawing 19.1 x 14.8 cm

In my illustration for the view "West end of Coo-che-to-pa Pass" I have placed two types of photographs adjacent to each other (Plate 200); the top on infrared and the bottom made with panchromatic film, again to illustrate the dramatically different results to be had from the different photographic materials.

It is hard to imagine that these drawings shown together in Plate 199 are of the same scene, but I have found no alternative. The bottom sketch takes in a much narrower angle of view; the high peak on the left is again Mount Ouray and the one in the center of the photograph is Mount Antero, which may or may not have been left out of the drawing, depending on how a viewer chooses to read the details. Omissions or distortions like this make searching for a scene and for its correct alignment very difficult.

Also from September 5 is "Coo-che-to-pa Cr. (near its junction with Grand R.)" (Plate 202), which is the top drawing on a sheet of three (Plate 203). It looks downstream along the course of Razor Creek from some two miles north of where two previous views (Nos. 193 and 198) were drawn. The sketch is irregularly compressed and distorted, so much so that I could rely on only two details to determine an approximate vantage point: the hill on the far left with trees silhouetted against the sky, and the low cliffs in the center that slope

PLATE 204. Photograph

PLATE 205. Composite drawing and photograph

PLATE 206. Western slopes of Saguache Mountains. Middle drawing on sheet of three

upward to the right. It is not clear how far to the right the drawing extends; Tomichi Dome is visible from here but is not represented in the drawing, so I have cut off the photograph before its slope begins to show. The nominal subject, "Coo-che-to-pa Creek...," (today's Tomichi Creek) is not clearly depicted, but it flows in front of the cliffs at the center of the sketch, downstream being toward the left. Following the names used in the *Report*, the junction of this "Cochetopa" Creek with the Grand River is still some twenty miles distant, near the town of Gunnison, Colorado. The title would be more nearly correct if it had been applied to the bottom of the three sketches (Plates 203, 211), which may be the source of this error.

Plate 206 is another view of the "Sah-watch Mountains" that I cannot locate. It is the middle drawing on a sheet (Plate 203) that contains the previous scene (Plate 202) and a later one (Plate 211). It could be anywhere along the path of the expedition from the San Luis Valley to the town of Gunnison.

"West end of Coo-che-to-pa Pass" (Plate 207) has been trimmed at the right, perhaps cutting off part of an arrow

PLATE 207. West end of Cochetopa Pass [September 6], 19.7 x 14.7 cm

PLATE 208. Unnamed sketch [west end of Cochetopa Pass, September 6?] 14.8 x 10.1 cm

that points left. There is also a small inscription in Kern's hand that I cannot quite read, one that seems to be "C of n" with another arrow pointing left. This distinctive formation, with its advertising sign for a Super 8 Motel (in the photo but not the drawing), is on the north side of US 50 and just east of the town of Gunnison. Then there is a related sketch, with a subject that I did not locate until after this book had been formatted (Plate 208). It is untitled and crudely drawn, yet does have some shadings seemingly in Kern's hand. Both drawings have inscribed arrows with notations that are hard to decipher, and it was on this basis that I first associated them as a pair.

The second drawing has been trimmed at the left edge, cutting off an arrow pointing right along with part of a word in Kern's hand, "ected," perhaps a fragment of "connected." This is an odd coupling, two drawings that are sketched in such different styles: one with a sure, steady hand, and the other shaky and erratic, but with additions by Kern. I imagine that the assistant topographer, James A. Snyder, was trying his hand at topographic art under Kern's tutelage and drew the inferior sketch. Plate 209, "Photograph, west end of Cochetopa Pass" shows the entire rock formation with the outskirts of the town of Gunnison to the left; Plate 210 "Composite of drawings and photograph juxtaposes the three

PLATE 209. Photograph, west end of Cochetopa Pass

PLATE 210. Composite of drawings and photograph

illustrations. A similar pairing occurs later in a view of the Uncompahgre Mountains (Plate 289).

The expedition then traveled westward down Tomichi Creek and on the evening of September 5 camped near its junction with (West) Pass Creek, the watercourse they had followed down from Cochetopa Pass until September 3, when they had to deviate to the north to avoid its rugged lower canyon. The next day they reached the Grand River where Tomichi Creek flows into it.

> September 6.—Seven miles from camp the valley of the Cochetopa...opened into that of Grand river, on the opposite side of which are high ledges of red sandstone—the base of the Elk mountains. This valley, for eight miles after we entered it, is from one-half to one mile and a quarter wide, covered abundantly with grass, the stream being lined with willow and cotton-wood... The Elk mountains tower high above us to the west, the hills immediately along the valley being high and more or less of a table character, or what the mountain men, of Spanish descent,

term mesas—elevated level spaces of land, terminated on one or more sides by precipices and lower levels. Grand river is at present a fine, clear stream of cold water, one hundred feet wide and three feet deep, flowing rapidly over a paving-stone bed... Following the eastern slope of the Elk mountains to their termination, Grand river passes to the south and west of them, where it joins the Nah-un-kah-rea, or Blue river of the Indians and mountain men, which rises in the Middle Park, and is erroneously called Grand river on some of the most correct maps (G-B, 49-50).

PLATE 211. View up Grand River (first view) [September 6] Bottom drawing on a sheet of 3

One of "the most correct maps" that mislabeled Beckwith's "Nah-un kah-rea, or Blue River" as the "Grand River" was the Parke-Kern map of 1851, the one that Richard Kern had helped to compile and draw. In the oblique and inoffensive manner he often adopted on such occasions, Beckwith was now correcting one of its errors. His source for the names of the river would have been Antoine Leroux, who ironically had also been one of the key geographical resources for the Parke-Kern map.

The minimal sketch titled "View up Grand R. (first view)" (Plate 211) is the bottom drawing on a sheet (Plate 203) that

PLATE 212. Photograph, view of Grand (Gunnison River)

PLATE 213. Composite drawing and photograph

contains three. Finding it seemed to be one of the impossibilities, but the title provides a clue: Kern's first view of the Grand (Gunnison) River would have been at its confluence with Tomichi Creek near today's town of Gunnison, Colorado. It seems to be part of an orderly sequence of three drawings on one sheet, although I was unable to locate the middle scene, "Western slopes of Sah-watch Mts." If it were arranged on the sheet in sequence, the middle drawing would be found between the mouth of Razor Creek near Doyleville, Colorado, and the mouth of Tomichi Creek at the town of Gunnison.

I made my photograph (Plate 212) from the campus of Western State College in Gunnison; the view is to the west across the Grand River, not up it. Perhaps "View of Grand R." was the intended title, for at the base of the cliffs is a line of deciduous trees that grow along the river's banks. The peculiarly shaped top of the mesa on the left of the drawing and its associated vertically striated cliffs (Beckwith's "high ledges of red sandstone") are the defining features of this representation. Several contours in the scene sloping down to the right could be associated with those in the drawing, but I believe that the sharp cliffs above the power lines that run down into the valley on the right account for the "notch" between two hills, while none of the more distant shapes on the horizon have been included at all. The expedition forded the Grand River somewhere near these cliffs, and the camp of that evening was on the far bank and downstream, off to the left.

Kern must have made "On Grand River" (Plate 214) before following his comrades across the Gunnison River to camp. The subject is the same sheer cliff as in the previous drawing (Plate 211), but from the south rather than the east. The vantage point is on the north side of Tomichi Creek near its mouth. In the center are the distant peaks of Whetstone Mountain, and to the right is a nearby mesa appropriately called Flat Top. The Grand (now Gunnison) River flows towards the viewer in front of the central cliffs, and then turns to the left among the trees. The out-of-scale tree on the left of the drawing is a device Kern often used, both to close

PLATE 214. On Grand River [September 6] 15.5 x 9.0 cm

PLATE 216. Composite drawing and photograph

PLATE 215. Photograph on Grand River

a scene compositionally and to define the nature of foliage in a scene more clearly than if it were depicted in the "correct" size and place.

The expedition stayed on the right bank as the river turned west and proceeded a short distance down its broad plain to "Camp 57, Grand river (G-B, 101)."

> September 6.—... We encamped in the valley on the west bank of the river, having marched but 14.75 miles... This fine little valley is terminated a short distance below our camp, by the close proximity of the hills on either side, and a deep cañon presents its giant mouth to receive the river (G-B, 49-50).

They were near today's Neversink Campground in the Curecanti National Recreation Area, and the next morning

PLATE 217. The entire sheet. 21.1 x 13.6 cm

PLATE 218. From Camp, September 7 on Grand River Top sketch of two on a sheet

PLATE 219. Photograph near camp on the Grand River

(September 7) Kern made two views on one sheet of paper (Plate 217), both from the north side of US 50 and about one-half mile from camp. In this case the reason for the juxtaposition is fairly obvious: The first looks backward over the previous day's journey, and the second forward toward the morning's approaching labors.

The central mesa in the first picture, "From Camp Sept. 7th on Grand R" (Plate 218) is Tenderfoot Mountain, just southeast of the town of Gunnison. To the left in the distance and hugely emphasized in the drawing are the peaks of Fossil Mountain; hidden on the right among the trees is the Gunnison River. The nearby trees at the far right appear high enough to be silhouetted against the sky and obscure the hills beyond them, as though my viewpoint should be lower. It is possible that the cottonwoods along the riverbank then were spread more widely on the broad flood plain, or taller, or that the riverbed was closer to my viewpoint, but again, and most likely here, Kern has artistically "transplanted" vegetation and emphasized it, to define and illustrate the botanical characteristics of a particular location, as well as to balance the composition against the mountains on the left.

PLATE 220. Composite drawing and photograph

That same morning, by climbing over the small hill that was behind him and descending its southwest-facing slope, Kern made a second view "On Grand R. from Camp Sept. 7th" (Plate 221). It looked downriver over today's Beaver Creek Picnic Ground, to where the expedition was headed that day.

> September 7.—We recrossed the river at our camp, and proceeded down its southern bank 1.80 mile to the head of the cañon, where a small creek enters which we crossed, and immediately began the ascent of the hills to pass around the deep ravines which enter the cañon in deep chasms. The hills were very rocky, but we found little difficulty in ascending and passing them with our wagons, except from the everlasting sage, which was large and rank, and the only vegetation on them, although we approached quite close to the base of the tables or mesas, which are elevated from 300 to 400 feet above our path, and are separated by deep ravines from a few hundred feet to a quarter mile in width. The perpendicular rocks at the head of the cañon are some eighty feet in height, the cañon itself increasing to twice that altitude where a creek enters it from the northwest half a mile below its head [Beaver Creek]. The course of the river in the cañon, for the first mile, is south-southwest (magnetic) and south. It then turns abruptly west, and continues on broken courses towards the southwestern point of the Elk mountains. The rocks are granitic, containing large masses of crystallized quartz, glistening brightly in the sun...(G-B, 50).

The central feature in the scene is Big Mesa, which is on the south side of the Gunnison River, and from here seen beyond the cliffs that stand along its banks forming some of Beckwith's "deep ravines which enter the cañon in deep chasms." On the left in the photograph can be seen an embankment that was built up to support US 50 as it crosses the canyon of Beaver Creek, and where a dense stand of

PLATE 221. On the Grand River from Camp, Sept 7. Bottom sketch of two on a sheet

PLATE 222. Photograph on the Grand River

PLATE 223. Composite drawing and photograph. This drawing is on the bottom of the same sheet as the previous illustration (Plate 218).

deciduous trees obscures its bed. The hills and cliffs of today sustain small stands of evergreen trees, in addition to the carpet of sage that Beckwith noted here in 1853.

This is also the site referenced by the caption on the incorrectly labeled lithograph, "HEAD OF THE FIRST CAÑON OF GRAND RIVER below the Mouth of Coo-che-te-pa Creek, Septbr 7" (Plate 153). The formations here are vaguely similar to those on which the lithograph is based (Plate 151), but the radical change of title explicitly contradicts that of the original sketch (Plate 150). Perhaps the questionable accuracy of Kern's notes on the drawings had become apparent to those responsible for the publication of the illustrations and led them to substitute their own judgment as to the appearances here, where even at its bare beginning the Canyon of the Grand River displays its formidable nature.

Blue Mesa Dam, which is some twenty miles downstream, backs up water almost to the position of Camp 57. I imagined that from this spot downriver to the dam a large proportion of the Grand River drawings would be of sites now inundated by Blue Mesa Reservoir, or if not entirely so, then their proper viewpoints along the expedition's route would be. The presence of the lake did indeed complicate my search, and at one point I contemplated renting a boat to see what might be learned by traveling over the actual bed where the river once flowed, but as it turned out the now submerged riverbanks were so rugged and difficult of passage that Gunnison was forced to cross the river repeatedly to avoid the worst of it, and often led his men high over the adjacent tableland, where many sketches were made from places that are still accessible.

> (September 7.—continued) After making 3.25 miles over the hills, passing the heads of ravines, we came upon a precipitous descent, the first cañon having terminated, and an open grassy valley succeeding for two miles. We had ascended, in this short distance, 735 feet above the head of the cañon, or 715 feet above our morning camp. We had, therefore, to make, in a few hundred yards, a descent nearly equal to this ascent, on a natural grade of about one foot in five, full of igneous rocks of all sizes, from fragments and projecting masses, to mighty ledges. The loose surface stones removed, we attached ropes to the first wagon, which to prevent accidents was held by a number of men. It arrived safely at the bottom of the hill, 547 feet below, and half a mile distant; and we dispensed with ropes, and descended with the remainder of the wagons, separated by a few yards, and soon reached and again crossed the river. This valley was succeeded by another cañon, and we ascended the opposite bank of the river for a similar purpose for which we had labored in the early part of the day. For five miles the ascent was easy, but here we were obliged to cross a deep ravine, and for this purpose were forced close to the base of the mountain to find a practicable descent, which, at best, was very precipitous, as was also the ascent, although not exceeding a hundred yards in length. A mile further on, we again descended to the river, where a narrow strip of grass afforded a night's pasture for our jaded animals, which had been eleven hours in making fourteen miles... On each side of the river to-day, and as we can see, for some days ahead, the banks rise rapidly towards the precipitous sides of the mesas, which extend back from fifteen to thirty miles to the mountains. These elevated tables are in classes, each class preserving the same level, though on opposite sides of the river, and consisting of the same formations—all of them terminated at the top by a capping of greater or less

PLATE 224. September 8, Valley of Grand River [September 7] 22.2 x 14.8 cm

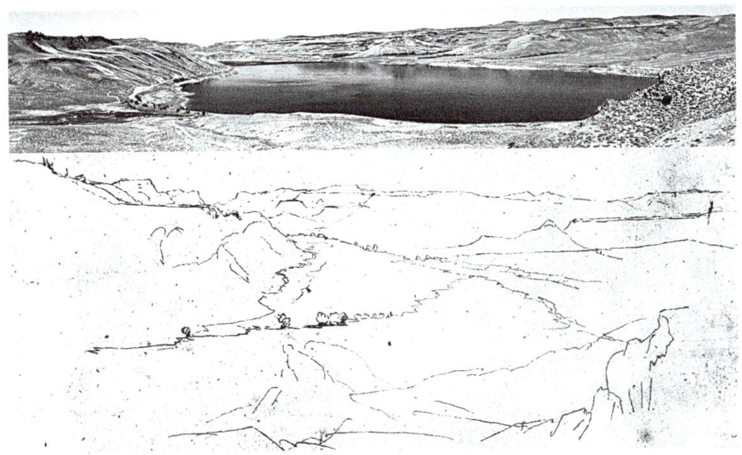

PLATE 226. Composite drawing and photograph

PLATE 225. Photograph, valley of Grand River

> thickness of igneous rocks, overlaid by a few feet of soil, on which, occasionally, small groves of trees may be seen. They were formed, doubtless, by the upheaval of large plains at the same time; and the immense cracks and crevices of those convulsions have been enlarged, in time, by the elements, and now form the cañones, gorges, ravines, gullies, and passes, which in every direction surround us. While the current of the river is rapid, and the descent very considerable, these tables seem to preserve the same absolute level, and consequently become more elevated above the river as it descends. They are judged to be, to-day, 1,200 feet above it, and not less than 1,500 twenty miles west of us. Sage alone flourished along our path (G-B, 50-51).

While searching on the south side of the river I came across a primitive road that appeared to follow the path of the expedition over Big Mesa, including the same steep decline on its western flank. From above I was both surprised and pleased to come upon the view depicted in Plate 224 "Sept 8 Valley of Grand river," one that I did not expect to see from here because of the September 8 date on the sketch; the expedition passed this way on September 7. The title originally read "Side of Grand River," but Kern overwrote "Side" with "Valley." The date, which is off by a day, is in his assistant's hand.

I was plainly on Gunnison's road, and was particularly gratified to find the rocky outcropping in the right foreground (Plate 226). Kern enlarged it to give it more presence, and perhaps to help close the composition as well. The point of view for this scene is from Big Mesa near the commencement of Beckwith's "precipitous descent," where the dirt road I was on makes a steep drop that follows the bed of a ravine lined with large boulders. A broader and more nearly level continuation of that road is in the photograph, pointing to the left towards what is at present the mouth of South Willow Creek. In the drawing this rivulet flows to the right across Beckwith's now submerged "open grassy valley succeeding for two miles" to meet the Grand River, the course of which leads diagonally into the distance from right to left and disappears among the mesas. Somewhere on the right is where the expedition crossed the Grand River again to its north bank, before proceeding farther west through the terrain in the center of the picture. The comparison of drawing and photograph gives a good idea of what was lost to the inundation here by Blue Mesa Reservoir.

The next three drawings are all of a piece. The approaches to the banks of the Gunnison River from the south were

PLATE 227. On Twin Creek, Grand River Country [September 7] 17.7 x 7.8 cm

PLATE 228. Photograph on Twin Creek

impossibly steep and partly on private land, so it was with no little pleasure that I eventually discovered that the three were made from sites close to US 50 on the north side of the river. All the vantage points were accessible, all were within a short distance of each other, and, much to my surprise, none were on Gunnison's route, but rather from several miles east of where the expedition crossed back to the north side of the river.

"On Twin Creek - Grand River Country" (Plate 227) is titled in block letters of a form that has been encountered before, and in this case the title conveys more than just content. Unnoticed by the album's compiler, the drawing was attached to its page face down, so the sketch appears as

LPLATE 229. Composite drawing and photograph:

a mirror image of its subject. The paper substrate is so translucent that this reversal is otherwise inconspicuous, but the mirror writing gave it away; I have accordingly re-reversed the sketch with Photoshop® to show it in its correct orientation. The meaning of "Twin Creek" is uncertain, as there is no creek nearby feeding into the river.

This view of the wonderfully rugged canyon of the Gunnison looks up the river from a site on its bank next to US 50 and about one-half mile east of its intersection with Colorado 149. The river here is beginning to suffer from the presence of the Blue Mesa Dam; although the water is relatively shallow, the deciduous trees once on its banks have been drowned and are gone, while Kern omitted the rocky slope on the right side of the river.

"Grand River Sept 7th 1853" (Plate 230) is a view also looking eastward up the river, and the nature of the terrain is so similar to that shown by the prior illustration that the two views are easily confused. It was, however, made about one-half mile farther downstream from the last one, at the north end of a bridge where Colorado Highway 149 leaves US 50, and it does not contain any of the same subject matter. The deciduous trees along the river have, of course, vanished (Plates 231 and 232).

The viewpoint for Plate 233 "Sept. 7th on Grand River," is from near the same place as the last illustration (Plate 230),

PLATE 230. Grand River, September 7, 1853. 19.0 x 12.5 cm

but looking to the south from high on a hill adjacent to US 50. Again Kern depicted the river lined with cottonwoods, and a rocky prominence that loomed over them is worked out in such magnificent detail that I imagine the sketch was intended to be the basis of a lithograph. The cliffs and ravines that define the hillside are obscured in the photograph (Plate 234) by evergreen trees and by their shadows; they appear now in greater numbers than Kern drew or than Beckwith suggested were present in 1853 (Plate 235). What was then a torrent of rapidly moving water is now a placid lake used by boaters and fishermen.

An unusual thing about this set of three sketches (Plates 227, 230, 233) is that the expedition never visited any of the

PLATE 231. Photograph, Grand River

PLATE 232. Composite drawing and photograph

spots from which they were made, although Gunnison must have. After the men again forded the river to get back to its north side, Kern went east several miles (on foot, or perhaps by horse or mule,) to document the impassable portion of the canyon that the expedition had just spent half the day avoiding. Probably this excursion was at Gunnison's request, since Kern rarely subjected himself to such difficulties for the sake of drawings. Obstacles of this sort along the Grand River constituted a far greater impediment to a railroad than did the passes in the Sangre de Cristo Mountains and over the Continental Divide.

> (September 7.—continued) Captain Gunnison rode into the cañones several times during the day. He says of the first, "that it would require blasting one-third of the distance for the construction of a road, and solid masonry, with many arches for culverts on the whole line—a stupendous work for an engineer. The second is less formidable, the rocks being more friable, and the curves of larger radius, while the cliffs are but 100 feet in height." The river, at high water, he judged to cover the bottoms in places to the depth

PLATE 233. September 7, on Grand River, 19.8 x 15.0 cm;

PLATE 234. Photograph

PLATE 235. Composite drawing and photograph

of six and eight feet; and from a neighboring hill, he esteemed the country "the roughest, most hilly, and most 'cut up,' he had ever seen. Hills with flat tops, hills with rounded tops, and hills with knife edges and points, and deep chasms, are on every side" (G-B, 51).

At the end of the day the expedition's men made their "Camp 58, Grand river" (G-B, 101), near the mouth of today's East Elk Creek, where "a narrow strip of grass afforded a night's pasture for our jaded animals." I imagine that after his

PLATE 236. Side valley of Grand River [September 8] 16.6 x 9.5 cm

PLATE 237. Photograph, side valley of Grand River

PLATE 238. Composite drawing and photograph

exertions of the day, Kern did not illustrate the camp's location until the following morning, September 8. The expedition then tried to move west but was soon forced to cross the river repeatedly to circumvent obstacles and covered only a disappointingly short distance. The map accompanying the *Report* is hard to decipher at this spot because the hachures (line patterns used in maps of the time to indicate topographic detail) are locally so dense as to obscure the dashed line of the expedition's path, which is not clearly laid out here in any case. The map does not indicate the expedition's multiple crossings of the river, probably because they were made in such close proximity to each other.

The campsite, which is depicted in "Side Valley of Grand River" (Plate 236), was easily discovered because its features are so distinctive and because it is adjacent to US 50. Although Kern renders a few trees on the slopes to the right, most of the vertical forms turn out to be freestanding rock formations of a sort the expedition would encounter more frequently farther downriver. I photographed this scene for the first time in 2001, and had trouble trying to decide which

PLATE 239. "from 10.20 Sept 8 Affluent of Grand R." 15.4 x 11.3 cm

of the high cliffs on the right corresponded to particulars in the drawing; I also could not correctly align the small prominence, silhouetted on the nearby slope to the left, with the more distant hills. I passed by here again in the drought year of 2002 when the lake was very low, making it possible to get farther away and lower by walking out onto the exposed lake bottom; the resulting alignment in this second photographic attempt, as shown here, looks almost perfect.

Returning for a second time also resolved the problem of precisely what is represented on the right side of the picture: In the drawing the cliffs just to the right of center lack the rounded "cap" visible in the photograph; it turns out that Kern simply did not draw it in. Perhaps this seems a minor point, but on site it was hard to distinguish the central formation in the sketch from the repeating ranks of similarly shaped slopes and flat-topped cliffs that continue farther to the right.

"From 10.20 September 8th, Affluent of Grand R." (Plate 239): if the date and time are correct, they would place this sketch within a very small region downstream from Camp 58. Its appearance is characteristic of the area, but the view has eluded me. Perhaps it is now partly under water, or the sketch is incorrectly dated.

### THE FIRST SIGN OF UTAH INDIANS, BRINGING JUST THE SLIGHTEST PRESENTIMENT OF COMING DISASTER

Schiel describes a disquieting experience he had somewhere in this vicinity while out riding, accompanied only by Creutzfeldt.

> we were surprised by one of those adventures that could have been a menace but had a comic ending. We had been riding down along the river for several hours...when Creutzfeldt suddenly cried "Indians" and stopped his mule, looking sharply toward the open space where we were to meet the wagon train.

> If Creutzfeldt had observed correctly we were in a spot and our situation critical; we could not think of turning back for it would have been twenty miles to get back to the other side of the river and reach our people again by following the wagon tracks. Besides they would have left but faint traces on the rocky ground which we could easily miss in the darkness. Consequently all we could do was to go forward and this we did cautiously by making use of the ravines and using bushes for cover. But when we got to the spot that we had taken for an Indian village, we found nothing but a row of rocks in the shape of wigwams. The "village dwellers" were a few stags that fled at our approach. Soon our wagon train came along from the other side of the mountain and encamped after having crossed the Grand river. When I told Leroux about our experience he said I had better omit any such further excursions—if I wanted to keep my scalp (Schiel, 81-82).

Could the pyramidal rocks on the slope in Plate 236 be the formations that Creutzfeldt mistook for a village of wigwams? Gunnison describes such a scene from a spur on the north side of the river, and Beckwith makes note of a Utah smoke signal that gave Leroux's warning some added emphasis.

> September 8.—...We were obliged to cross the river twice at this camp to pass around a bluff from a spur of the Elk Mountains, and to avoid ravines on the south, which enter the river at a gorge a short distance below. Leroux had gone in advance, leaving a man who had been over the road with him the previous day to point it out to us, but he wandered off in search of mountain sheep, and our pilots, after crossing a spur, descended to the river again, where we lost much time in searching for a ford, the river being narrow and too deep for our wagons; and we were eventually obliged to return to the hills, and follow them for a short distance, when we again crossed to the southern bank of the river and proceeded immediately from it towards the base of the high tables on that side. We ascended rapidly, having, however, but one sharp ravine to cross, the opposite bank of which we ascended only by dint of hard labor, and descending into another ravine, where we found a small spring of cool water, encamped, with abundant grass on the hills for our animals, having traveled but

four miles, our camp being 346 feet above that of the morning, although 200 feet below the crest of the ravine. A large smoke ascending from our last camp, from the grass taking fire after we left it, a larger counter-smoke was seen during the day directly on our route ahead, made doubtless by the Utah Indians, in the heart of whose country we have been traveling for several weeks, and whom we expect daily to meet, as we are approaching their summer hunting-grounds...

As the train left the river, Captain Gunnison ascended a spur on the north side, whence "...the reason was apparent why the guides pronounced the further progress of the wagons along the river impracticable." "The stream is imbedded in narrow and sinuous cañones, the dark top outline of which resembles a huge snake in motion, as the wavy atmosphere conveys light to the eye. And the little spurs appear merged into one great connecting ridge, from the mountains at the head of the Rio del Norte to the great Elk mountains on the north... The side creeks from the mountains have cut deep valleys, with perpendicular sides, in the softer rocks; and there are left standing many hills of sandstone... To

PLATE 240. Grand River Canyon, September 8, 1853. 19.9 x 11.0 cm

look down over the tangent plane to the cañon below, it seems easy to construct a railroad; but immense amounts of cutting, filling, and masonry would be required. There is no timber to speak of nearer than the mountains, and that difficult of access for such a work. Cotton-wood in clumps on the rivers, and dwarf cedar and pine scattered on the cliffs and hills, will furnish fuel for wagoners" (G-B, 51-52).

The first ravine the expedition encountered after that day's third crossing of the Grand River was today's Cebolla Creek, and the next one, in which they finally camped, is now Fourmile Gulch. It enters Blue Mesa Reservoir from the south

PLATE 241. Northern slope on Grand River, September 8. 19.5 x 13.1 cm

PLATE 242. Lithograph by John Mix Stanley titled "View of Ordinary Lateral Ravines on Grand River From Camp Septebr. 8

near a bridge for US 50 over the lake, and contains the spring that watered the nearby grass in an otherwise arid landscape. Two drawings dated September 8 (Plates 240 and 241) were made from high above the east side of the gulch and belong together.

As in "Side valley of Grand River" [Sept. 8] (Plate 236), the subject of the first one (Plate 240) is visible from US 50 and exceptionally easy to find; on the south side of Blue Mesa Reservoir and just west of a bridge that crosses it is a scenic pull-off, with a highway department sign to indicate that the view of Dillon Pinnacles was worthy of being photographed. Kern's viewpoint is a bit of a hike east from the bridge along a

PLATE 243. Composite of two drawings and lithograph

PLATE 244. Photograph, northern slope on the Grand River

service road that parallels a power line, then makes a detour south to cross Fourmile Gulch above its spring. If one continues east and climbs above the road, the scene comes into alignment.

There is also a further drawing of the same date "Northern slope on Grand R. Sept. 8th" (Plate 241): Kern erased the"f" in "of Grand R" and changed it to "on Grand R", an oddly fastidious bit of attention to detail for him, in view of the plethora of erroneous captions for which he was otherwise responsible. When I found the Dillon Pinnacles and climbed to Kern's vantage point for the first drawing I did not at the time recognize that Dillon Mesa, which is just to its right, is the subject of this additional drawing from September 8th. When I later examined some snapshots I took in the area I noticed my error, and so returned to the site to photograph both, to see if they were a panoramic pair. They are. Some of the pencil markings that touch the left edge of the right-hand drawing appear to have been trimmed off, but the sketches can be fitted together nicely, and nothing of significance has been omitted at their junction. They originated from points of view so close together as to be for practical purposes identical. The drawing on the left was also used as the basis for a lithographic illustration in the *Report*, *"View of Ordinary Lateral Ravines on Grand River from Camp Septbr. 8.* (Plates 242 and 243), where Stanley remained true to the outlines of the drawing, but gave the cliffs a much flatter and more featureless texture.

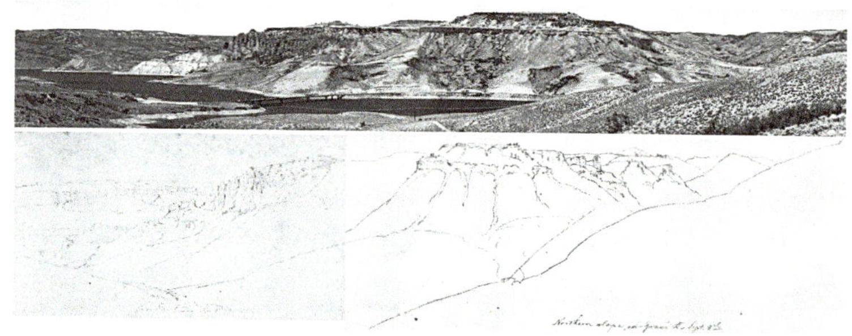

PLATE 245. Composite drawings and photograph

When the drawings are compared to the photograph (Plate 245), the only incongruous detail is the foreground slope on the right, that in Kern's drawing seems to rise higher than the distant mountains. Moving the point of view to the right does not help here because the actual hill is nowhere high enough to reach the horizon. Moving ahead (downhill) will indeed make the foreground on the right appear to rise above the background, but then it obscures some of the detail on the lower slope of the mesa, and the move results in some other obvious misalignments. The strongest argument for not going forward and lower is that against the sky near the middle of the right-hand picture, Kern has carefully drawn the summit of today's South Baldy Mountain, which is in the distant West Elk Range. It is just visible in my photograph, but going even a few feet lower makes it disappear entirely. I think it likely that Kern exaggerated the rise of the foreground hill simply to close the composition on the right. Among other details, Fourmile Gulch can be seen entering the lake at the bottom just in front of the bridge, and the mouths of "two fine streams" that Beckwith would note in his diary for the next day are visible at the far left, beyond some light-colored hills that extend down to the lake.

The following day the men of the expedition came face to face with the most difficult crossing of the entire trip, that of Lake Fork of the Grand River:

September 9.—For the second time our guide returned to camp last night ill at ease, and it was evident that his two morning's examination of the route ahead had not only proved less successful than he desired, but had quite surprised his memory. But we were too close upon his trail to admit of longer delay in informing us that we had a serious obstacle before us in the passage of the Rio de la Laguna, or Lake fork, coming into Grand river from the south, through almost one continuous cañon from the mountains to the river, and that he failed to find an easy crossing. This morning, therefore, large working parties of soldiers and employés started forward, under their respective commanders, to prepare the crossing of the creek; and at 2 o'clock p.m. we received orders to move on with the train. Ascending from the ravine on which we had encamped, we were forced high up on the mesas, to avoid numerous deep ravines, which we succeeded in turning successfully, when a short, steep ascent around the rocky wall of the table to our left, brought us, four miles from our morning camp, to the top of the difficult passage—a rapid descent 4,055 feet in length, and 935 in perpendicular height above the stream, covered with stones

PLATE 246. Side canyon of Grand River [September 9] 20.3 x 14.3 cm.

PLATE 247. September 13, Canyon of Grand River [September 9], 21.1 x 14.3 cm

of all sizes, from pebbles to tons in weight, with small ledges of rocks cropping out at various points. Some of the stones had been removed in the proposed road; but the wagons, with locked wheels, thumped, jarred, and grated over the greater portion, especially those too large and deeply imbedded in the soil to be removed, until their noise quite equaled that of the foaming torrent creek below. At one point, as they passed obliquely over a ridge, it was necessary to attach ropes to the wagons, and employ a number of men to prevent their overturning. Two hours were thus employed in descending with our eighteen wagons, and in twice crossing the creek, in the bed of which we had to descend for a quarter of a mile, before we could gain a permanent footing on the west side. The creek is sixty feet wide by from one to two deep, with an impetuous current falling with a loud noise over a bed of rocks and large stones. Just above its mouth two fine streams, half a mile apart, enter Grand river from the Elk mountains. Day's march five miles, through a heavy growth of sage (G-B, 52).

Four drawings on this day are views over the canyon of Lake Fork from high up on its east side (Plates 246, 247, 248, and 253) and must have been done before the expedition descended into its depths and crossed it. Finding the place

PLATE 248. Grand River Canyon, September 9. Top drawing on a sheet with two sketches on it

PLATE 249. The entire sheet with two drawings 19.5 x 15.3 cm

or places from where these drawings were made was another adventure in misidentification. I did not imagine at first that three of drawings went together, since one is dated September 9, one September 13, and one not dated at all, and I overlooked the fact that they all bear similar titles relating to the canyons of the Grand River. Since the expedition would be traveling farther along the river or near its tributaries until the 13th of September, I put Plate 247 aside and went looking for the other two. I eventually found myself high on Sapinero Mesa above the canyon of Lake Fork, and several miles southwest of the camp on Fourmile Gulch. I located a single vantage point that served for both "Side cañon of Grand R—" (Plate 246) and "Grand Riv. Cañon Sept. 9th" (Plate 248). Once back home I belatedly realized that if these two sketches were placed on either side of the evidently misdated "Sept 13th Canon of Grand River—" (Plate 247), the set was a continuous panorama. I had to return to the site that overlooked Lake Fork and photograph it properly.

Kern included a group of several distant mountains on the horizon of the center sketch. The high summit just to the right of its center is Uncompahgre Peak; seemingly joined to it on its right is Silver Mountain. On the far right, with a pinnacle that slopes down to the right, is the outline of Sheep Mountain. Zigzagging away from the observer in the center of the picture is the chasm of Willow Creek, a tributary to Lake Fork. Its walls suggest in miniature just how extreme the

PLATE 250. Three sketches joined into a panoramic drawing

PLATE 251. Panoramic photograph of the Grand Canyon

problem was that confronted Gunnison, but the sheer cliffs that line the thousand-foot-deep canyon of Lake Fork can no longer be appreciated from here because they are under water. The probable location of the expedition's crossing is inaccessible for the same reason.

The canyon of Lake Fork of the Gunnison crosses this scene from left to right, but is too low to be visible; from this position its cliffs would be obscured by the foreground, even if they were not now submerged. The left-hand sketch is correct in its label, "Side cañon of Grand R—," even though the slopes in the foreground obscure the canyon itself. "Sept 13th Canon of Grand River—" in the center is misdated by four days, and aside from the canyon of Willow Creek it barely includes the far slope of Lake Fork's chasm, and nothing of the Grand at all—two errors that together deflected me into a variety of dead-end searches. The right-hand panel, "Grand Riv. Cañon Sept. 9th," is correctly dated but the slopes in it are really of Lake Fork as well; the Grand River is just out of view on the far right.

Plate 253, "Lake Fork Sept 10th," was also made from east of Lake Fork and overlooking it, but September 10 is a day too late. The expedition made camp deep in the canyon on the 9th, and on the following morning crossed Lake Fork and climbed out on its west side. The drawing is the bottom one on a sheet that also contains another from almost the same place (Plate 249). To make this view on the morning of September 10, Kern would have had to backtrack out of the canyon, and then descend again to the crossing. The viewpoint is from high on Sapinero Mesa, somewhat north of but very near the spot from which the panorama encompassed by the three previous drawings (Plate 250) was made. It looks directly west down the canyon of the Grand River and could well have been a fourth panel continuous on the right of the last set of three. I considered and rejected that idea in the field because of certain difficulties of alignment that I felt required a slightly different point of view for this drawing, and because there seems to be a gap between what the two sketches

PLATE 252. "Grand River" drawings and photograph, juxtaposed

represent. I may be wrong here, and it would not do the presentation an injustice to assemble all four of them as a complete panorama, but I prefer to regard this one as separate.

The angular chasm that contains the Grand River is clearly marked out as it leads diagonally away from the lower right corner toward the center of the picture. Here is the beginning of today's Black Canyon of the Gunnison, and the expedition avoided its 2,000-foot sheer cliffs by staying to the left of it, going up and away from the river.

The lithograph "View Showing the Formation of the Canyon of Grand River near the Mouth of Lake Fork with indications of the formidable Side Canyons" (Plate 256) is the only one in the Gunnison-Beckwith *Report* that did not originate with Richard Kern. By its title it is a closer view of the same part of the canyon of the Grand River that the previous

PLATE 253. Lake Fork, September 10 [September 9] Bottom drawing on a sheet of two

PLATE 254. Photograph, Lake Fork

PLATE 255. Composite drawing and photograph

sketch (Plate 253) shows at a distance. In some versions it may be without attribution, but others carry in the lower left "Sketch by Egliffstein," "Sketch by F. W. Egliffstein," or "J. W. Stanley from Sketch by F. W. Egloffstein." Egloffstein was not in this area with Gunnison's party, but rather passed by here a few months later in his capacity as topographer for Frémont's fifth expedition. He may have made a sketch and retained it, or else he reconstructed the view from memory afterwards, but his original drawing is not in the Newberry album.

It is possible to make some tentative inferences about what is actually represented in the lithograph. Egloffstein was with Solomon Carvalho, Frémont's photographer, who here made a daguerreotype of the Dillon Pinnacles, which is the same formation that Kern drew from the south side of the river the summer before (Plate 240). From the very precise engraving of the scene in Frémont's Memoirs, Carvalho's viewpoint can be located on the north side of the river (Shlaer, 115-117), and the rest of Frémont's company, including Egloffstein, would have been in the vicinity. About a mile from where Carvalho was making his daguerreotype, West

PLATE 256. *right,* Lithograph by John Mix Stanley from a sketch by F. W. von Egloffstein, "View Showing the Formation of the Cañon of Grand River near the Mouth of Lake fork with indications of the formidable Side Cañons."

PLATE 257. Photograph looking downriver from the face of Blue Mesa Dam

Elk Creek enters the Gunnison River from the north. There Egloffstein may have seen it as it appears in the lithograph, flowing toward the lower left. A USGS topographic map of the area includes the contours of the land before Blue Mesa Reservoir inundated it. Here the creek ran immediately next to a very steep cliff on its right bank, while on its left was a narrow floodplain, both of which correspond to what is depicted by Egloffstein. Upon closer inspection, the lithograph shows a small stream entering through the cliffs from the left, and the topographic map includes just such a detail flowing into West Elk Creek from the northwest. All this is to suggest that the Egloffstein lithograph is a view he obtained by looking north up West Elk Creek from a vantage point on its left bank, a place that was once high above the scene but is now perhaps close to or under water. Today the only direct evidence of what the canyons in the immediate area must have looked like is downriver from Blue Mesa Dam, which is about four miles below the mouth of West Elk Creek. A photograph made from partway down the face of the dam shows the beginnings of the Black Canyon of the Gunnison (Plate 257), clearly evoking, as does the lithograph, a sense of sublime, frighteningly steep, terrain.

> *September 10.*—After considerable labor in removing surface-stones and digging down a few yards of the opposite hill, too sideling for our wagons, we doubled our teams, and with ten mules, but not without severe labor—detaining us, however, but six hours—pulled up the load of six to the crest of the western bank of Lake fork, ascending 480 feet in forty-one hundredths of a mile. By the line followed by our wagons, it is 1.50 mile from crest to crest of the banks of this creek, but in a right line it is only 2,639 feet, or about half a mile, while the perpendicular descent from the east, as already given, is 935 feet. The most practicable means by which this immense ravine can be passed by a road, will be by ascending one of its banks by a heavy grade into the mountains, crossing it by a bridge, and descending the opposite bank—a stupendous labor, for it will be necessary to cut through miles of rocks and to cross large side-ravines. But it becomes narrower below the crossing, and proportionally steeper; and Captain Gunnison, after examining it, thought it, perhaps, not impossible, but very difficult to bridge it (G-B, 52-53).

PLATE 258. From 2:35 p.m. September 10 (Salt Creek Canyon towards Grand River) 27.1 x 12.4 cm

"From 2.35 Sept 10th (Salt Creek Canyon towards Grand R.)" (Plate 258) was drawn at 2:35 p.m. just after the expedition crossed Lake Fork. The vantage point is near Cove Road on the northeast slope of Pine Creek Mesa looking north across the Gunnison River and up the valley of Salt Creek (today Soap Creek). My position is a compromise because of houses that now block the correct view, so the foreground slope on the right appears to be too far to the right (Plates 259 and 260). One-quarter of the way in from the right and in a notch between some closer formations the sketch outlines the two distant pinnacles of West Elk Peak (only one of which is visible in the photograph), while high near the right edge is

PLATE 259. Photograph

PLATE 260. Composite drawing and photograph

the rounded silhouette of South Baldy Mountain, which was also visible in a drawing of September 8 from above the east side of Lake Fork (Plate 245). The spit of land that descends from the right in the foreground of the drawing separates the Gunnison River flowing in from the right from the mouth of Lake Fork that comes in diagonally from the lower right. Its slope is now half-submerged so that it reaches only to the center of the photograph before disappearing beneath the waters. The high cliffs along the river valleys prevented Kern from seeing any of the three streams that once flowed through the confines of those deep, narrow canyons. A modern highway bridge over the mouth of Lake Fork (not visible in this view) is in about the same place as the one Gunnison thought would be nearly impossible to construct, and the water below it is more than 300 feet deep.

There are five sketches (Plates 261-265) that, by their titles, are from along the Grand River, but which I cannot locate. I include them here because by date and place the first one belongs at this point, and I have no good argument for inserting the others anywhere else along the Grand.

The terrain in Plate 261, "Grand River Canyon (leaving the river) Sept. 10th," looks much like that in the previous sketch (Plate 258), and if the date and title are correct it must have been drawn from somewhere nearby. It seems to be from a high vantage point, looking over a deep canyon, or possibly two, but the distant mountains do not match anything to be seen from the west side of Lake Fork.

Plate 262, "Canyon on Grand R," is a well worked-out drawing, one made from just above the level of the plateau through which the canyon of the Gunnison River has been cut by its waters. The trees there look like spruce or fir, high altitude vegetation found along the river's upper reaches.

Once again there is a familiar sense of place in "Grand R. Canyon," (Plate 263), which was made from a high point of

PLATE 261. Grand River Canyon (leaving the river), September 10
19.7 x 15.4 cm

PLATE 262. Canyon on Grand River. 19.8 x 8.9 cm

PLATE 263. Grand River canyons. 16.2 x 12.4 cm

view, but I cannot find the distinctive faraway mountains that might help to locate the foreground.

"Grand River" (Plate 264) is a striking view of a mesa that has written on it "broken brown," yellow," "red," and "white," along with some undecipherable notations. The viewpoint is low and overlooks the river; a tree defines the near bank in the foreground. Kern's elaborately worked out drawing has all the earmarks of having been intended for a lithographic illustration.

Another "Grand River" (Plate 265) is very similar to Plate 264, and is attached to the same page in the album. I believe the two are of the same formation but from slightly different points of view, the second one being seen from slightly farther

PLATE 264. Grand River. 22.4 x 12.3 cm

PLATE 265. Grand River. 22.1 x 9.7 cm

PLATE 266. "Grand River" drawings, juxtaposed

to the right. In the center of the drawing the notation "red" appears on its cliffs over some diagonal hatching, a position that corresponds to where the word "red" is found in the previous drawing. Plate 266 juxtaposes the two "Grand Rivers" sketches .

The expedition's men now left the Grand River, but at the mouth of the Uncompahgre they were to meet it again. From there they would follow its mostly inaccessible bed from above, traveling on high tableland, then descend to its confluence with the Blue (now Colorado) River, just east of the city of Grand Junction. Leaving it yet again to avoid the impassable gorges of Horsethief and Ruby canyons to the west, they finally touched upon the Grand (Colorado) once more at Westwater Canyon, Utah. In none of those places could I locate this distinctive mesa, the two views of which are juxtaposed in Plate 266. Were it along the river upstream from the Black Canyon of the Gunnison, it might now be under water.

# 5

# In the Company of Indians

*Encounter Utah Indians, Who convey Warnings About Violence in the Great Basin; Into the Uncompahgre Valley, Back to the Grand River, and Down to the Blue*

SEPTEMBER 10.—(CONTINUED) Leaving Lake fork we continued along under high bluffs, over very rocky hills with deep intervening gullies, which forced us southward into a valley gorge, which we reached by a steep ascent, and encamped, after a march of 4.69 miles, under a vertical wall of igneous rocks 100 feet in height, at a beautiful spring of cold water in a fine grassy meadow, through which a creek descends to the river, distant two miles. This little valley is part of a depression some four miles in diameter, like a basin in the high table-land among the mesas, which on all sides enclose it to the eye, although Grand river passes through it, and small streams enter it through deep, wide gorges in all directions... (G-B, 52-53).

This lovely drawing "Grand River Canyons" (Plate 267) bears only a general title, but from it Stanley made a lithograph with a much more specific legend, "Rock Hills Between Green and White Rivers Octr. 3d Wahscatch Mountains in the distance." It is about 250 miles from where the drawing turns out to have been made to the scorched desert region in Utah that corresponds to the lithograph's caption. It would take the expedition two weeks to travel from one of these locales to the other.

PLATE 267. Grand River Canyons [September 10], 22.5 x 13.1 cm

As usual, Stanley did an excellent job transforming Kern's sketch into a lithograph, while adding a rocky foreground to balance the composition. The sketch was trimmed so that some lines of Kern's pencil were lost at both sides; Stanley's reproduction shows perhaps a bit more of the view to the left but a bit less on the right, so it is hard to determine whether it was cut down before or after Stanley used it. Of greater importance, Stanley altered and added to the vegetation, to make the scene more desert-like. He turned what in the left foreground appear to be rushes—or similar plants indicating the presence of water—into a flowering, arid-land yucca. He added a smaller yucca plant in the middle of the

PLATE 268. Lithograph by John Mix Stanley, "Rock Hills Between Green and White Rivers Octr. 3d Wahscatch Mountains in the distance"

PLATE 269. Composite drawing and lithograph

foreground, and to further emphasize the dryness of the scene introduced a prickly pear cactus at the lower left corner.

To distinguish between the two captions required locating the scene, and it turned out that the view was not of "Rock Hills" in the deserts of Utah as the lithograph claims, but rather from the site of "Camp 61, Mountain Creek" (G-B, p.101); the drawing closely matches my photograph looking north from there (Plate 271). The expedition had crossed Lake Fork successfully on September 10, and now was forced south, away from the Grand River and its impassibly deep canyon, today the Black Canyon of the Gunnison. The campsite is just as Beckwith described it, "under a vertical wall of igneous rocks 100 feet in height, at a beautiful spring of cold water in a fine grassy meadow, through which

PLATE 270. Photograph, Grand River Canyon

a creek descends to the river, distant two miles." That would be today's Pine Creek, flowing northward beneath the cliffs of Pine Creek Mesa looming on the right, while a few miles away the Gunnison River travels invisibly through the gorge of its Black Canyon. Spruce and fir trees dot nearby slopes, and there is not a yucca plant or large cactus in sight. It is unclear why the lithograph was altered to suggest a desert and its title modified accordingly. Perhaps it was to illustrate a part of the expedition's travels for which no other drawing seemed suitably evocative, following the reasoning that I imagine was behind the drawing and lithograph of a nonexistent mountain in "Peaks of the Sierra Blanca" (Plate 110). In the *Report* this lithograph is placed opposite page 63, where the White River of Utah and its adjacent deserts are discussed.

PLATE 271. Composite drawing and photograph

Another surprise emerged from the John Mix Stanley *Papers* when I looked them over to find samples of his handwriting. Attached to a page in his diary from 1854 is a sheet of paper with a rectangular border (Plate 272), and on it a copy of this September 10 sketch by Kern (Plate 267), but in mirror image. It is just there; it does not relate to anything Stanley recorded in his journal.

The original is not available, so I do not know its exact size. I cleaned up a microfilm of it with Photoshop® and made it into a negative, with white lines on a black background. I

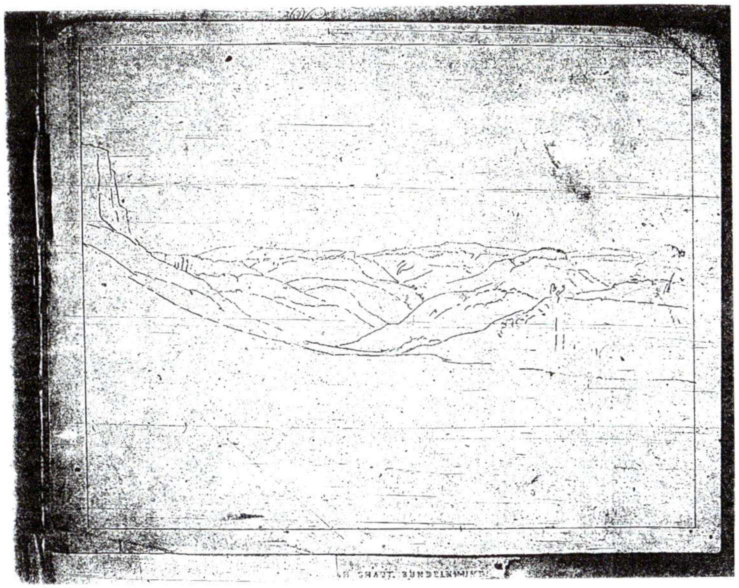

PLATE 272. Sketch found in Stanley's diary

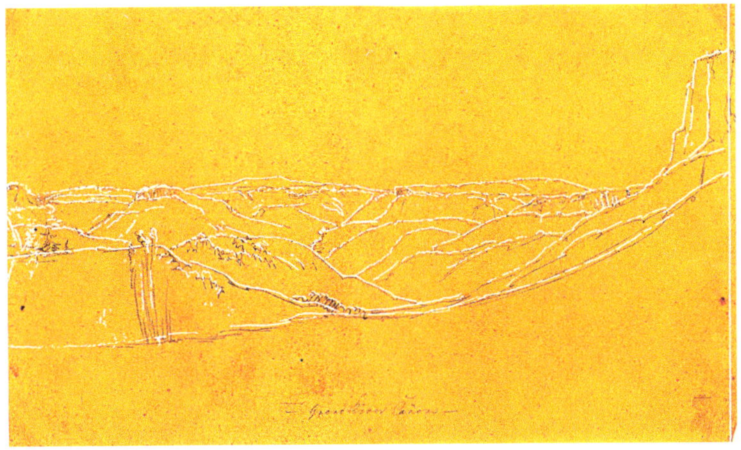

PLATE 273. Superimposition of the two drawings

then adjusted its size, returned it to the same orientation as the scene, and superimposed a semi-transparent version of Kern's sketch onto it (Plate 273).

The match is so precise that it is hard to decide if Stanley's drawing is a freehand copy or a tracing, but either way it was done more carefully in some places than in others. He left out material on the right, and included some on the left that probably was present in Kern's original sketch before it was trimmed and mounted. The rushes on the left have retained their character, and not yet been turned into a yucca plant.

But why is it a mirror image, and why did Stanley retain it in his diary? A reversed drawing would have no purpose if, as I have supposed, transfer lithography was the method used for the illustrations in the Gunnison-Beckwith *Report*. Perhaps in preparation for making the lithographic transfer Stanley inadvertantly copied from the back of Kern's sketch. After detecting his error and making a new drawing, he was, for whatever reason, free to retain this one. Another possibility is that after producing this drawing Stanley was asked to redo it, and to alter parts of the scene so they would correspond to the arid desert conditions implied by what was to be its new title.

The right edge of "Sunday Septbr 11th, Un-com-pah-gre Mts" (Plate 274) has been trimmed so as to cut several of

PLATE 274. Sunday, September 11, Uncompahgre Mountains. 22.7 x 9.7 cm

PLATE 275. Photograph

the pencil lines. This piece is mounted on the same page as another drawing "West of Summit in Coo-che-to-pa Pass" (Plate 173), and they appear to be representations of the same subject. These cliffs are on the face of Blue Mesa, part of the Uncompahgre Mountains, into which the expedition would soon be headed. The actual path Gunnison took was over the mesa off to the left. Plate 276 juxtaposes both drawings with the photograph I made of the subject.

To distinguish the underlying formation that I believe is represented in this view it is necessary to "see" through the trees that in my photograph obscure the contours of the cliffs. The date on Plate 274 is Sunday, September 11, and the site is some two miles north from "Camp 61," where the expedition took its Sabbath rest. The implication is that Kern left camp to make his drawings and then returned, although such excursions were not typical of his practice. I imagine that he did so in the company of Leroux, who would have been looking for the best way forward for the next day's travel. To my eye, that best way approximates the route of US 50 today, a course notably without obstacles and one that passes in front of the mesa's cliffs. But the next day the expedition did not follow that seemingly easy route; rather, it went south and west up onto Blue Mesa, then across a number of the ravines and streams to be found on its top, after which it rejoined what is now US 50 near the route that I suspect Leroux had urged on Gunnison in the first place. Perhaps the two men were again grinding together in personal conflict, and now, as was often the case, Gunnison determined to follow his own counsel.

> *September* 12.—Crossing the creek [Pine Creek], we followed the ravine valley of our camp southward to the top of the mesa, and turning westward, passed for two miles along its summit, and descended with

PLATE 276. Composite of the photograph and both drawings

difficulty to a creek two hundred feet below, only to ascend again, by an equally abrupt path, to the same level, and again immediately descended, by a similar path, to another creek, difficult to cross only because of the dense thicket of willow bushes which line its banks, and again ascended to nearly the same level as before, and then wound more gradually down a long descent to a larger creek, coming through a deep gorge to the south, from snow-peaks, plainly in sight, of the Sierra de la Plata (G-B, 53).

Creutzfeldt echoes this account:

> Early in the morning we travel in S.W. direction a rivulet upwards and reach soon the mountain top, that offers here a splendid view, beautiful wood, good grass and open tracts being arranged in picturesque variety. Our journey, though fatiguing by going up and down the mountain leads through an interesting region, where nature wears its summer garment still in all luxuriancy with woods, as yesterday, running rivulets, and small lakes... (Creutzfeldt, September 12).

Traveling south from the Pine Creek camp kept the cliffs of Blue Mesa to the right of the expedition for several miles before it reached a way up that was suitable for wagons. Ascending there and traveling westward, Gunnison's expedition emerged from the woods to find itself on a hillside above today's US 50 and overlooking the gorge of Blue Creek, where Kern made the drawing "Valley of the Cibolla Cr" (Plate 277). The words "All Pines" appear written across some of the nearer

PLATE 277. Valley of the Cebolla Creek [September 12] 19.7 x 12.6 cm

PLATE 278. Lithograph by John Mix Stanley, "Summit of the nearest ridges south of Grand River traversed in passing around lateral canones 12 o'clock, Septbr. 12"

hills, and Kern has used lines of irregular rounded forms to suggest their presence.

This drawing resulted in a lithographic illustration, and as usual Stanley rendered the scene with excellent fidelity to the original. The title on the lithograph is much more elaborate than that on the drawing: "SUMMIT OF THE NEAREST RIDGES SOUTH OF GRAND RIVER traversed in passing around lateral Canones 12 O'clock, Septbr. 12" (Plate 278).

A tree bare of foliage that appears in heavy strokes at the right edge of the sketch is seemingly drawn on top of the outline of distant hills, but not over some nearer details, where allowance has been made for its trunk. It may be part of a much denser stand of trees that was just out of the field of my camera to the right, or perhaps it was simply an afterthought to balance and close the composition against the steep slope on the left. Stanley faithfully retained it and elaborated it into a tree of a species that I cannot identify. The scraggly, pointed evergreen in the bottom center of the sketch, along with an adjacent grove, have been fittingly made into fir or spruce, while the distant trees cannot be identified.

The search for this scene consumed a great deal of time; the view is not of the immense drainage that is Gunnison's "Valley of the Cebolla Creek" (now the Cimarron River), where I spent weeks searching in vain. This is one occasion where my inclination to trust the caption on a drawing and give it precedence over that on a corresponding lithograph led me far astray. The scene is actually one overlooking the valley of today's Blue Creek as it flows to the Gunnison River through a deep gorge that is partially visible on the right side of the photograph. The description on the lithograph is exactly correct; the expedition encountered this view at about noon on September 12, then climbed over the divide and descended into the next drainage, which was that of Cebolla Creek (today the Cimarron River). Because of limitations imposed by fenced private land, the alignment obtained from my viewpoint is less than satisfactory, nor did nearby trees allow my photograph to extend far enough to the right; nonetheless the picture communicates the most important aspects of the scene. Among the remote snowy mountains visible on the horizon to the left of center, the highest is Sheep Mountain, while the last one discernible farther to the left is the more distant Uncompahgre Peak. These are the ones that Beckwith later describes as "... snow-peaks, plainly in sight, of the Sierra de la Plata."

PLATE 279. Composite lithograph and drawing

PLATE 280. Photograph, Uncompahgre Mountains

PLATE 281. Composite drawing and photograph

In the unusually detailed log for the day (G-B, 102) are two entries—"On small creek 10.20 a.m." and "On second small creek 1.30 p.m." that bracket noon, the time indicated on the lithograph. The "second small creek" flows in front of the wooded hill on the left in the photograph, where the sage-covered slope in the foreground that extends all the way across in my foreground hides it. Also hidden by that slope, and surprisingly close to the vantage point of the photograph, is US 50 as it here begins its twisting course down the side of Blue Creek Gorge to cross Beckwith's "second small creek." A third watercourse the expedition finally encountered as it "wound more gradually down a long descent to a larger creek, coming through a deep gorge to the south, from snow-peaks, plainly in sight, of the Sierra de la Plata..." is Blue Creek itself, which would have been crossed at the very bottom of the chasm on the right in the photograph. How the lithograph came to be completely and correctly captioned despite the erroneous label on the drawing remains a mystery.

### UTAH INDIANS IN CAMP—WHAT DO THEY KNOW ABOUT WHAT LIES AHEAD? HINTS OF THE WALKER WAR BETWEEN MORMONS AND UTAHS

Later that day Beckwith recorded the expedition's first direct encounter with Utah Indians:

> September 12.—(continued)... We left this creek [Blue Creek] by a more gentle ascent than we had climbed for a week before, through luxuriant fields of grass, in which, indeed, we had traveled during most of the morning, in rear of the mesa adjacent to Grand river, and passing one or two small ponds of water on the way, descended for five miles to the first branch of Cebolla or Onion creek, the last two miles through a level artemisia field, in which we encamped, on a small grassy space near the creek, having traveled 13.18 miles. While Captain Morris and myself were out in search of a suitable camp, a few Tah-bah-was-chi Utahs exhibited themselves on their war steeds, near enough to call out to us. We advanced to meet them, and a crowd of men, women, and children soon gathered at our camp (G-B, 53).

From here on, contact with Indians was a recurring event, and it elicited a comment by Beckwith only when it was out of the ordinary. This afternoon's visit of the Utahs is described in the *Report* as if it were a relatively minor affair, despite the anxieties that such an event, long expected though it may have been, was bound to arouse in the members of the expedition. Now that the impending had materialized, Creutzfeldt displayed a rising note of annoyance at their presence, and recorded what must have been a dismaying story from them that the Beale-Heap expedition, which had passed this way in July, had been totally wiped out by the Navajos.

> Towards the evening we meet a considerable tributary Creek of the Grand river, where we encamp and soon are surprised by Yutah Indians, who, men wives and children, approach at full speed; There may be 40-50 of them; they conduct themselves amicably and are on a hunting excursion to the Quitchitopas. Our journey is about 14 m. in changeable weather, sunshine, rain and thunderstorms (Creutzfeldt, September 12).
>
> We remain a pretty long time in the camp in the morning, the captain making presents to the Indians and some trifling bargains besides. We move then only for some miles, where the animals are able to refresh themselves in good pasture, they having been tied in scanty grass last night on account of the Indians. These are molesting us all the day long, trying to bargain for guns and gun powder, but are disappointed. According to their report Lieut. Beal and 6 men were killed by the navahah Indians; they tell also of difficulties with the Mormons (Creutzfeldt, September 13).

It would have been difficult to immediately sort out which of the Indians' stories were fabrications, and which might be the truth. Creutzfeldt's note that the Utahs spoke of having "difficulties with the Mormons" is the first mention by a member of the expedition of the uneasy relations between the Latter Day Saints and the Utahs. During this first encounter the possibility of theft and perhaps violence must have impressed itself deeply on the minds of the men, and intensified their watchfulness. Kern was never an admirer of Indians and must have found the presence of the Utahs particularly galling, since it was they who had been responsible for the deaths of his brother Benjamin and his friend Old Bill Williams, when the two men attempted to recover some of the equipment that had been cached in the San Luis Valley after the dissolution of Frémont's fourth expedition. I imagine that captains Gunnison and Morris must also have been led to consider carefully their future expectations of safety for the expedition, and to take appropriate measures during travel farther west. From both Creutzfeldt's and Schiel's version of events it is clear that the Utahs spoke unmistakably about troubles to the west with Mormons. The unavoidable conclusion is that the officers, and presumably the men as well, had received an explicit description of the disturbed state of relations between the settlers in the Great Basin and Walker's band of Utahs, and of a rising climate of violence into which the expedition was heading. Still, uncertainty about the intentions of the Indians in camp must have been a more immediate source of anxiety than the ominous but distant intimation that the Utah Indians were at war with the Mormons. In this anxious moment Schiel describes a speech by Leroux to the Indians that appears to have helped maintain calm.

> ...on the banks of Onion creek we found ourselves surrounded by a crowd of Tabeguache Utes who seemed to have sprung from the earth. There were several hundred men, women, and children... Their language at first was haughty, almost menacing, for they soon let it appear that if we did not give the presents, they would take them... According to Leroux, who spoke their language perfectly, they let it be known that there were 2,000 Ute warriors in the neighboring hills, that they had just been engaged in a big battle with the Comanches and had chased them over the mountains, that the Utes had not yet been vanquished by any other Indian tribe, that they were at war with the Mormons, had killed a lot of them, and much other edifying talk along the same

> lines. Then Leroux made them a speech, something like this: "We have good weapons, much powder and lead. If you want to fight, come on, we will kill many of your warriors. The White Father has many brave warriors, he will punish your transgression. He has sent us to travel through your country and to see what his red children are doing." (Schiel, 83-84).

Beckwith's account of this event in his personal journal is slightly more complex than is his narrative in the *Report*; it echoes Creutzfeldt's reference to the possible destruction of the Beale expedition and then dismisses it as unlikely.

> Septr. 12... While we were out looking for a camp the Utahs were bold enough to exhibit themselves on their war steeds on the hills near and to call out to us—we advanced to meet them and a crowd soon appeared at our camp, men, women, & children. They report that the Navajos killed Mr. Beale and party who are known to have passed here in June or early in July for Cal;—Seven Americans and four New-Mexicans they report have been killed—the exact number of his party—but we do not give credit to it and least of all to its having been done by the Navajos in the middle of the Utah Country! Distance marched 14 miles (Beckwith, *Journal*).

Because the claim that the Navajos had massacred the Beale-Heap expedition seemed dubious on its face and was later found to be indeed false, Beckwith omitted any reference to it in the *Report*. The Utahs probably invented the tale and must have known it was fictitious, but may have related it to subtly intimidate the members of the expedition in the hope of enhancing their prospect for favorable trades through an unspoken but clearly implied threat of violence. They were able to lend their story an aura of authenticity by detailing the exact number and ethnicity of the men traveling with Beale, for they had encountered his expedition a few months previous. The two groups had remained in intermittent but friendly contact for several weeks, during which time the Utahs had ample opportunity to observe the ethnicity of Beale's companions (Heap, 66-70).

Camp 62 was directly on a branch of Cebolla Creek (today the Little Cimarron River) next to US 50, so it was a simple matter to find it. This is where the Utahs first visited the expedition, and Kern must have drawn "From Camp 62, Septr. 12, 1853" (Plate 282) while his companions at the camp were dealing with their guests. In the left foreground are trees that

PLATE 282. From Camp 62, Sept. 12, 1853. 19.5 x 10.5 cm

PLATE 284. Composite drawing and photograph

PLATE 283. Photograph near Gunnison's Camp 62

line the Little Cimarron River, and directly above them on the horizon is Poverty Mesa. In the center are slopes of Black Mesa that lead down to the Black Canyon of the Gunnison from the north side of the Gunnison River. The deciduous trees in the middle of the sketch might at first glance indicate the presence of the riverbed, and although there was some leeway in locating my camera here, if I got close enough and low enough to put such trees into the center of the photograph the result would be to misalign and partially obscure the background features. That this stand of trees has been drawn on top of part of the slope that goes up and to the right suggests their presence in the sketch is again an afterthought to illustrate the sort of flora present at the campsite.

In the text of the *Report* for September 13, Beckwith describes leaving the next camp (63, on Cibolla creek) and climbing west to the high ridge of today's Cerro Summit. From there he was able to view much of the path the expedition had followed from the Continental Divide, preview a portion of what was yet to come, and describe some of the visible features of the surrounding territory.

> *September* 13.—Captain Gunnison, this morning, made presents to the Indians... They were very importunate for powder and lead, everything else appearing of little value to them. We were anxious to purchase horses, but they would sell them only for arms and ammunition.
>
> We crossed the creek a short distance above our camp [number 62], where a practicable ravine afforded us a descent, the bank being forty feet high and very steep, and passing down it ascended the other bank by a similar ravine, opposite our camp, to the rolling sage plain which we crossed to the main branch of Cebolla creek [today the Cimarron River], which we forded, and encamped, after a ride of only 3.75 miles, on a grass field near by, at the base of a connecting mountain range, which here crosses the valley of Grand river from the Elk mountains towards the Sierra de la Plata—it being necessary to find a path for our wagons before attempting the passage. Captain Morris and myself, therefore, with Leroux as guide, and a party of men, rode forward by one of the two routes followed by Indians and hunters in passing this range, and reached the summit in two hours; the scenery becoming more beautiful as we ascended, especially through the gorge of Onion creek to the south, where vertical columns of rocks stood out high and clear against the sky, being part of the Sierra de la Plata—a range of mountains to the west of the Sahwatch and Sierra San Juan—whose sharp summits are broken into a thousand points and angular forms, and its sides streaked with banks of snow. Our route far behind us lay clear and distinct at our feet to the mountains about the Coochetopa Pass; and the course of Grand river, with the Elk mountains to the north extending round to the northwest with a level summit for many miles, terminating with a vertical descent of a few hundred feet, and then apparently subsiding into a plain. At our feet to the west lay the

Uncompahgra river, rising in the Sierra de la Plata, and flowing northwest through a valley of considerable width, beyond which a range of high land was overlooked by more distant mountains, among which the Salt and Abajo peaks were pointed out to us. The former is directly upon the noted Spanish trail leading from California to Abiquiu, New Mexico, and is a favorite resort for the Utah and Navajo Indians for trade; while the latter is near the junction of Grand and Green rivers, considerably below the fords for this trail, or, as Leroux says, below any ford on Grand river known to the New Mexicans, and hence its name. But we had little time to enjoy this majestic scenery, and hastened to examine the descent to the west, which we found very difficult, and at various places, as on the ascent, thickly covered with scrubby oak bushes and aspens. The soil is light, but covered with luxuriant grass. We thought it possible to pass this route with wagons; but the other route, followed by the Indians from our camp to the Uncompahgra, lay directly below us while ascending the mountain, and appeared much preferable to the one we had examined; and a small party, sent out to examine it a short distance, reported it passable (G-B, 53-54).

PLATE 285. Uncompahgre Mountains, September 13, south of Grand River, 19.8 x 11.0 cm

There are two similar drawings from this day or the next that share the same subject and close or identical viewpoints. The path that Beckwith's scouting mission of September 13 followed was an Indian trail leading over Cerro Summit and into the Uncompahgre Valley. There is today an irregular way west out of the valley, partly along dirt roads, that I assume are the modern expression of that ancient trail; first it ascends southwest on Cimarron Road to an intersection with P77 RD, then goes north and northwest on the latter to reach US 50 at Cerro Summit. This I imagine is the one Beckwith and Captain Morris took on the scouting trip of September

PLATE 286. Photograph, Uncompahgre Mountains

PLATE 287. Composite drawing and photograph

13. Where the second trail that Beckwith describes might be located is hard to say, but US 50 is visible from high up on P77 RD as it takes a more direct route to the summit, so it is likely the other Indian trail that "lay directly below us while ascending the mountain" is roughly paralleled by today's paved highway. According to the maps of the *Report* the expedition climbed from the Cimarron Valley along the hillsides in an almost direct route to the summit, but from that route nothing of the scene in the drawing can be observed. Beckwith's "gorge of Onion creek to the south, where vertical columns of rocks stood out high and clear against the sky—a range of mountains ...—whose sharp summits are broken into a thousand points and angular forms, and its sides streaked with banks of snow" can only be viewed in full from midway up P77 RD or somewhere near to it. Kern must therefore have accompanied captains Beckwith and Morris on their reconnaissance of September 13, on which "Un-com-pah-gre Mts Sept 13th South of Grand River" (Plate 285) and the following sketch "From 910 Sep 14 Un-com-pah-gre Mts" (Plate 288) would have been produced.

This view depicted on Plate 285 looks almost directly south up the valley of the Cimarron River, and the formations on the right are major constituents of the Cimarron Ridge. At the far left horizon are two peaks that rise over a nearer hill; the first is Sheep Mountain and on its right Silver Mountain. The high, broad summit that stands alone against the sky is

Uncompahgre Peak, which was also visible in an earlier drawing (Plate 277). Almost exactly centered in my photograph is the squared-off crest of Wetterhorn Peak; the next high mountain silhouetted against the sky is Precipice Peak, while just to its right and partially obscured by it is the still discernible shape of Coxcomb Peak. Little details in the drawing such as the protuberance on Coxcomb that barely appears above Precipice Peak offer assurance that my choice of vantage point was substantially correct. The photograph was taken on September 1, 2001, and the presence of early snow on the irregular shapes and north-facing slopes of these mountains corresponds to Beckwith's mid-September 1853 description; Schiel also noted the exaggeratedly rugged landforms here.

> On the steep slopes of the mountains which form those wild romantic valleys of the Elk Mountains and the southern Sierra de la Plata, one frequently finds formations hanging there like towers of old castles... (Schiel, 80).

The second drawing of this view is dated September 14, which is probably a day too late. On the 14th the expedition climbed out of the Cimarron Valley and over Cerro Summit into the valley of the Uncompahgre River by a direct route

PLATE 288. From 9:10 [?] September 14 [13], Uncompahgre Mountains. 13.7 x 4.9 cm

from which this scene would not have been visible. The vantage point and therefore the view is apparently the same as for the previous one, but contains some puzzling elements. Beckwith describes the ascent to Cerro Summit as having been completed so rapidly that it is unlikely that either of these sketches could have been done on the way.

> *September* 14.—It was 3.80 miles by this route to the top of the steep ascent of the ridge, and three hours were occupied in its ascent... (G-B, 54).

The evidence of the expedition's narrative and map indicates that on September 14 Gunnison took a direct path to the summit, moving almost straight west. This is the only way for wagons to get from the camp along the Cimarron River

PLATE 289. The two drawings juxtaposed

PLATE 290. Photograph looking toward summit

PLATE 291. Composite of drawing "From 910 Sept 14 and photograph

up to Cerro Summit in only four miles of travel and in less than three hours of time, but is over a route that would never yield a completely clear view up the Cimarron Valley or of the mountains represented in the sketches. They reached the summit at 10:00 a.m., a time that makes it barely possible for a view up the valley to have been drawn at 9:10 even if a suitable viewpoint could be located. Since there are none to be found along this route, I think it almost certain that Plate 288 was drawn on September 13 as well. If so, the time of 9:10 a.m. is implausible because the expedition did not reach its camp of the 13th on the main branch of Cebolla Creek until noon, and Beckwith in his *Journal* indicates that the party sent forward to scout the route left camp at 2:30 PM.

Therefore both the date and the time on the second drawing must be incorrect, and the sketch was made the day before, at about the same time and from about the same position as the previous one (Plate 285). Plate 289 shows the two drawings juxtaposed. The Cimarron Ridge and the more distant San Juan Mountains, the subjects for this pair of sketches, are made up of the wildest, steepest, most fantastically picturesque formations imaginable; they are hard to mistake, and nowhere else along the path of the expedition is anything like this composition to be seen. The best I could do was to make a picture from as far up P77 RD as possible before the view is lost behind nearby hills, and very close to where I made the previous photograph (Plate 286). The most significant among the discrepancies between this drawing and the photograph (Plate 291) is that Uncompahgre Peak, a major landmark, is missing.

In view of its artistic and representational shortcomings, the second drawing is possibly by James Snyder (as I have supposed to be the case in other similar instances) and was an attempt to render a work of topographic art under Richard Kern's tutelage. The sketch, and its purpose, remains an enigma, and it is doubtful that all my efforts to find a matching view for it produced anything significantly better than the photograph used for the previous sketch. I believe both drawings not only are views of the same subject, but were made from practically the same position.

#### ONCE AGAIN, CLEAR WARNINGS FROM THE UTAH INDIANS ABOUT THE VIOLENT STATE OF AFFAIRS TO THE WEST

The sequence of drawings in the album now begins to show some large gaps. The expedition followed the site of present day Montrose in the dry bed of Cedar Creek down from Cerro Summit to the Uncompahgre Valley, then descended NNW along the Uncompahgre River to the locale of present-day Delta. On September 17 the men again came to the Grand River, which they had left almost a week before.

> *September* 16.—We traveled 18.25 miles down the Uncompahgra to-day… encamping this evening a short distance above its junction with Grand river… We met several parties of Indians that day, all of whom followed us to camp; and others continued to arrive until a late hour at night, filling the air as they approached with yells and calls, which were answered by their friends in or near camp—consisting of inquiries and directions as to how and where they were to pass—until we were heartily tired of them.

> The most of them were sent out of camp, but they built their fires only a few yards from ours, and their noise was little abated by the change, and our safety but little increased. They had, much to his regret, recognized our guide; but he neither showed fear nor want of confidence in them, although he had once shot one of their chiefs, who was attempting to rob him of his horse; and he shared his fire, pipe, and blankets with the chiefs who remained all night with him (G-B, 55).

Here again the camp was filled with Utah Indians, and their noisy, active presence cause some discomfort among the members of the expedition, as well as difficulty sleeping. No violence ensued, even though the Utahs recognized Leroux as the man who had slain one of their number, and against whom they undoubtedly held a grudge. Scheil described the same event:

> By evening about two hundred warriors were gathered around our camp when suddenly there resounded from several sides a warwhoop. This, however, had only been done out of cockiness or to test our courage for they had recognized our leader and the latter had once killed one of their chiefs when he wanted to steal his horse. Leroux did not show the slightest trace of fear, although he expressed his regrets that we should be molested by the redskins on his account and he shared his part of the camp with the chiefs who spent the whole night with him (Schiel, 86-87).

From exchanges with this formidable but ultimately peaceful crush of guests in the camp came again the suggestion of possible difficulties to the west.

> *September* 17.—Si-ree-chi-wap, the principal chief of the band, who is now so old that he exercises but little authority directly—intrusting it to his son, who accompanies him—arrived during the night, and, followed by his sub-chiefs and warriors, this morning repaired to Captain Gunnison's tent to talk and smoke. The Captain informed them that "the President had sent him to look for a good road by which his people, who live towards the rising sun, can visit those who live upon the great water where it sets; that the President was their friend, and had authorized him to make them a few presents in his name."

> The son of Si-ree-chi-wap replied; "This is your land, and you can go over it at any time. There are bad Indians over the mountains, who kill white men, but the Utahs are good, and glad to see the Americans" (G-B, 55-56).

In his diary entry for September 17 Beckwith discusses the presence and appearance of the Utah chiefs in camp that morning, but relates nothing about conversations that may have taken place in Gunnison's tent (Beckwith, *Journal*). I imagine that in the *Report* he is quoting or paraphrasing Gunnison's own journal, and that the words of Si-ree-chi-wap's son, with their explicit warning, were not something Beckwith directly witnessed or heard at the time. Indeed, Beckwith may have been entirely unaware that Gunnison had received this counsel of caution until too late, when, after the massacre, his late commander's papers were recovered by the Mormons, and he took custody of them. Fragmentary evidence like this suggests that Captain Gunnison did not always confide in his second-in-command, even on more mundane matters; he may in particular have kept his observations and opinions on the practicability of their route, as well as the information he received about Indian affairs, private. Perhaps in his ambition to succeed he did not want open discussions of these issues among fellow officers or with Leroux, discussions that might force him to exercise sensible precautions and perhaps slow the progress of his expedition. Gunnison clearly had received a warning but did not take it to heart, nor did he communicate it to Beckwith.

PLATE 292. Elk Mountains [September 16 or 17] 19.5 x 11.0 cm

> *September* 17. (Continued)...We crossed the point of land lying between the Uncompahgra and Grand rivers, reaching the latter at Roubideau's old trading fort, now entirely fallen to ruins... A mile below the fort we crossed the river at an excellent ford; the bottom being a mile in width, and covered with abundant grass.

PLATE 293. Panoramic photograph of Elk Mountains

> The cañon which we have been so many days passing around, terminates several miles above the junction of the Uncompahgra with Grand river, where the latter receives a large affluent from the Elk mountains known as Smith's fork. The high ridge, varying from 500 to 1,500 feet in height above our path, back of which we passed from Lake Fork in avoiding this cañon, and which is itself cut with deep cañones by the Cebolla and other streams, terminates, towards the valley of the Uncompahgra, in buttes and clay hills, of which there are two ridges... From our camp below the mouth of the Coochetopa creek [at today's town of Gunnison], to the junction of Smith's fork with Grand river, there is nothing deserving the name of valley. Now and then there is a small open bottom, from a few yards to a mile or two in length, but at the season of high water the river sweeps over these spaces, and the stream is never followed even by an Indian trail (G-B, 56).

Kern's view of the "Elk Mountains" (Plate 292) is visible to the east from the town of Delta, Colorado, and constitutes the western limit of that mountain range. The Uncompahgre River, which the expedition was following down to its confluence with the Gunnison, flows through the town, on the future site of which Gunnison's men made their "Camp 66, Uncompahgra river" of September 16 (G-B, 102). Because Delta has been heavily planted with trees, the

PLATE 294. Composite drawing and photograph

mountains cannot be seen from near the river. By ascending a high bluff on the west side of town and looking between the houses there I located an unobstructed, if distant, view of the scene.

The air in this region seems to be continually hazy, and its lack of transparency affected my photographs to such an extent that to make it possible to distinguish details in the distance I had to inordinately increase the contrast. Since this project led me through Delta on many occasions I would each time scrutinize the view, always finding the "seeing" to be discouragingly poor, occasionally photographing it again, but never improving the result.

In this view (Plates 292, 293 and 294) the Gunnison River flows unseen in its deep canyon, before the distant mountains but behind the long ridge in front of them that slopes down from the right; it then turns towards the viewer and meets the Uncompahgre River out of sight to the left. The drawing is incomplete, for the background mountains on both sides have been omitted. On the left is Mount Lamborn; then comes the broad irregular crest of Coal Mountain, and the high conical form that stands in front of it is Landsend Peak.

Now that the expedition was exiting the Rocky Mountains for the deserts of Utah, there appears to have been a moment's reflection on the suitability of the terrain along the Gunnison River for a railroad. The observations in the following paragraph from the *Report* do not appear in Beckwith's private *Journal,* and the prose style is in places so reminiscent of Gunnison's that I imagine it to be in part an extract or paraphrase from the latter's papers. In it the concept of the Central Route to the Pacific is neatly buried beneath an overwhelming mountain of disapprobation.

> *September* 17. (Continued) The difference of elevation between the head of this cañon section [just west of the town of Gunnison] and our camp, a few miles below its termination, on the Uncompahgra, separated from Grand river by a level bottom only, is 2,077 feet; and as the distance between these points by the river does not exceed seventy miles—of which, perhaps, sixty preserves its cañon character—the average descent will vary but slightly from thirty feet to the mile. But the continuance, for so great a distance, of vertical rocky walls along the river, ranging from 80 to 1,000 feet and more in height, upon which the road must be carried, and which can be cut only by blasting, and, from the deep side-chasms to be passed (as described by Captain Gunnison on the 7th instant) only by the heaviest masonry, it is evident that a railroad, although possible, can only be constructed in the vicinity of this section of Grand river, at an enormous expense—for the accurate estimate of which, situated as the work is at so great a distance from civilization, where not only laborers, but their subsistence, must be transported by land carriage nearly 1,000 miles, and where scarcely a stick of timber has been seen for the last 100 miles on the route, nor will be for the succeeding 150 miles, suitable for a string-piece for a small temporary bridge, or even a railroad tie, it is not too much to say, no data exists, nor will until such a labor shall be undertaken. And it would be a waste of labor to add even a rude estimate of the cost of so impracticable an undertaking (G-B, 56).

Despite Gunnison's opinion that the route they were following could never support the construction of a transcontinental railroad, Beckwith remained tirelessly concerned with details of engineering and topography as the expedition descended along the Grand River toward its junction with the Blue (today the Colorado) River, for which the Indian name was "Nah-un-kah-rea." Perhaps Beckwith was never told of his commander's dismissive judgment of the route they were evaluating, and then was surprised to read of it in his late commander's papers—just as he must have been taken aback to see the warnings of possible violence ahead that Gunnison received both here and elsewhere, but ignored. From the mouth of the Uncompahgre River and down the Gunnison to near the Utah border, Beckwith's geographic narrative continues, as does his concern for the practicability of a railroad, but there is a gap in the visual record from September 17 until September 22.

Creutzfeldt occasionally displayed a grudging admiration for Gunnison's energy but was more often than not contemptuous of the captain, whom he often calls in German "Röhrle." The word has no translation, but perhaps is an idiomatic term of disparagement meaning something like "high-pitched pipe." Creutzfeldt now begins to seriously question Gunnison's judgment in substituting his own plan of action for that suggested by Leroux. Even if we discount Creutzfeldt's negative attitude and perhaps curmudgeonly nature, it more and more appears that Gunnison was impatient to hurry the expedition forward, even when Leroux counseled a more circumspect approach. This conflict between Gunnison's seeming impetuousness and Leroux's considered restraint is a recurring theme in Creutzfeldt's journal. Nor did Creutzfeldt enjoy the close contact with the Indians whom Gunnison had permitted to remain in camp.

A very pretty journey is made to day, the Campagre down, over desolated, waste plateaux to the Grand river, which, though wide has here a shallow bed; we cross it, leave behind us good grass and wood, travel on in dreadful deserts till late in the night, and encamp without pasture, water, wood, supper and c. in beautiful stone fragments with impertinent cactus peeping out in order to disturb also the sleep of the tired. All this is a natural consequence of our Rohrle's energetic arrangements; Leroux had advised him to encamp near the river, because the nearest water is 30 m. distant... In the morning we had been detained till 10 o'cl., by nearly 100 Indians, who had surrounded our camp last night, who had to get their presents from our coward who soils his pants at their sight, allows the copper dogs all liberties, which they use with impudence, looking all over, molesting by begging and finding the most convenient opportunity to propagate their lice.

Though it is Sunday to day and after the opinion of our resurrectionists a criminal offense to travel, still we are obliged to obey in preference the command of the grumbling stomach and hungry and thirsty dito

> mules to set out and look for better luck. We travel along the Sahara-soil for 8 1/2 miles, find, what we badly needed, water, grass and wood... In the East of us is the range of the Elk mountains, cutoff abruptly and showing nothing but barren yellowish sides, consisting of sand stone, slate, gypsum and sandy soil. In the West are similar mountains but smaller (Creutzfeldt, September 17-18).

The expedition stayed on the northeast side of the Grand River and followed it by traveling on the adjacent high tablelands, from which there was rarely any access to the river or other sources of water; Kah-nah Creek (today Kannah) was a notable exception. On September 19 the men crossed the Blue (Colorado) River near its junction with the Grand.

> *September* 18.—At break of day we moved forward... and encamped on a small stream from the west end of the Elk mountains, which are on our right, our course being northwest. This little stream the Indians who visit us call Kah-nah...
>
> *September* 19... The light friable soil of the last two days continued to the Nah-un-kah-rea river, which we reached in a march of 12.32 miles. The eastern bank of this stream, for miles above and below where we struck it, is perpendicular, and from forty to eighty feet in height... A small gully afforded us the means of cutting a very steep path for our wagons to the river, which we crossed a few hundred yards below, at a point where it was but a little over two feet deep and a hundred yards wide... The river enters this valley through a cañon or immense gorge, which separates the Elk mountains on the east from the Roan or Book mountains to the west, and, bending from its southern course, unites with the Grand river just below us. Roan mountain, which derives its name from the color of its sides of red, gray, white and blue clay, in horizontal strata, destitute of vegetation and washed into many deep gorges and fanciful forms, sweep round to the west, following a course some miles from the river (G-B, 57).

The Roan Mountains have three other names that are used interchangeably: Book Cliffs, Book Mountains or Roan Mountain. Beckwith often uses this singular even though the formation has no clear peak and is spread over a huge area. According to Beckwith, the south face begins at the junction of the Gunnison and Uncompahgre rivers (near today's town of Delta, Colorado), and extends to just beyond the Green River (near the town of Green River, Utah), where it turns to the north; it was continually visible on the expedition's right for two weeks. Here Schiel makes note of something Beckwith does not mention: It was the Indians who pointed out a place where the wagons could ford the redoubtable Colorado River.

> A march of twelve miles over sterile ground brought us the next day to the bank of the Naunkara or Blue [Colorado] River. At this point it emerges from a huge canyon which separates the Elk Mountains from the Roan Mountains on the west, and flows into the Grand River valley. The Blue River here is probably 300 feet wide and its bed is deep for the most part. The current is swift and we had a great deal of trouble getting our wagons across. After some Indians had showed us a place where the water was not over two feet deep, we worked on the banks with hoes and spades and after about three hours we brought the wagons over to the right bank with great difficulty. The sight of the Roan Mountains, which we had on our right for more than a week while following the Grand River, is very picturesque. Eroded green sandstone and red clay slate cover the jagged steep slopes of the mountains, giving them an unusual vivid coloring whose charm, however, is diminished by the almost total absence of all vegetation (Schiel, 88).

On September 20 Gunnison took the opportunity to write to his wife, so that the letter could be carried back to Taos and posted by Leroux, who would be leaving the expedition in a few days. In it he expresses a certain envious regard for Lieutenant Beckwith, whose obvious competence led the men of the expedition to prefer his leadership when difficulties arose, and to credit him for their success when they had overcome them. The kvetches about Gunnison that appear frequently in Creutzfeldt's Memorandum-book may not be entirely without cause.

> Some parts of our route for the last month have been very laborious and I have worked very hard, and flatter myself that my energy and determination have got us forward not a little—so that the men say, when we are in difficult straits, I am told, "Just send for, or wait for, Mr. Beckwith, who will get us through—with him nothing is impossible!" Egotistical enough no doubt you will think but as I do not

> expect much credit for my exertions why, to you, I may be a little vain (Gunnison, *Letters*).

This just hints at a rising disaffection with Beckwith. During the following month tension between the two over Gunnison's decisions may have increased to the point where Gunnison withheld crucial information from his second in command about more threats of violence in the territory. Then came Gunnison's fatal decision to divide the party in order to hasten completion of the last of his surveys for the season. By so doing he ran straight into a band of Pahvant Indians who were hell-bent on revenge for the killing of their fellow tribesmen by emigrant whites.

FROM THE COO CHE TO PA PASS TO THE WAHSATCH MOUNTAINS

# 6

# Into the Deserts of Utah

**ARGUMENTS WITH LEROUX AT THE EDGE OF THE UTAH DESERTS; ON THE SPANISH TRAIL TO THE GREEN RIVER FORD; REACH THE EASTERN BASE OF THE WASATCH MOUNTAINS**

*From Blue River crossing to Green, White, and San Rafael rivers and the eastern foot of the Wahsatch Pass.—September 20 to October 13, 1853 (G-B, 58).*

AFTER CROSSING THE COLORADO RIVER the expedition made its Camp 71 at Little Salt Creek on September 21-22 (Plate 295), near what is today Mack, Colorado. Ahead were the inhospitable deserts of Utah. This is the second "Salt Creek" the Expedition encountered; the first one is now Soap Creek, on the north side of the Grand River across from Lake Fork. This one retains its name, with East and West Salt Creeks joining to form Salt Creek, which flows south into the Gunnison River.

> *September* 21.—... Seven miles below camp the [Blue, or today, the Colorado] river again enters a cañon, near which we filled our canteens for the night, and continued on for 7.30 miles over the same grease-

PLATE 295. Salt Creek Canyon, Sept. 21, 1853. 12.0 x 4.8 cm

PLATE 296. Photograph of Salt Creek Canyon

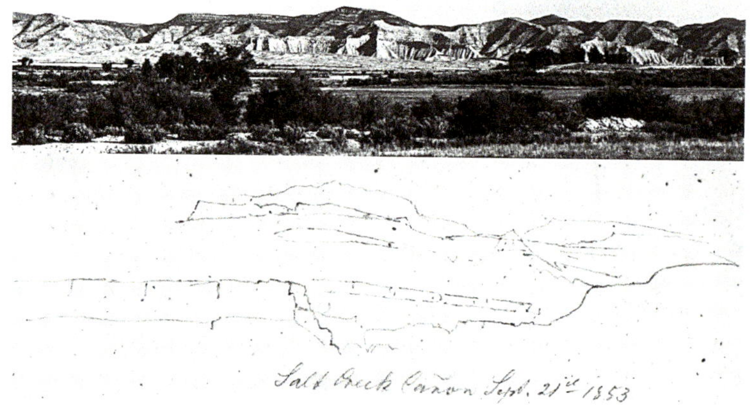


PLATE 297. Composite drawing and photograph

wood plain to Salt creek, which we found a mere rivulet of miserably brackish water, the sands of the bed being covered with incrustations of salt… Near this creek the plain is washed into little valleys, leaving small knolls and ridges standing, which give it a rolling appearance… Many trails lead up this creek, and the Indians inform us that they are used in visiting their neighboring band, the Uintas (G-B, 58).

In this view today's East Salt Creek is just out of the picture to the right, and Beckwith's "small knolls and ridges" are visible in the distance. They are part of the almost continuous cliffs of the Roan Mountains, before which the expedition would travel for more than a week to the Green River crossing. In his sketch Kern has exaggerated the vertical separation of the lower cliffs from the more distant hills. Here Beckwith made a note in his *Journal* of Indian activities that he did not include in the published *Report*:

> Sept 21st… Indian signal smokes streamed high above the mountains on which they were built to our left all day as we passed down the valley—doubtless to give notice to their friends on our route of our approach (Beckwith, *Journal*).

PLATE 298. Desert between Grand and Green rivers [September 28?]22.0 x 14.5 cm

From the camp on Salt Creek until it crossed the Green River, the expedition was never very far from the path of US Highway 6 and its more recent replacement, Interstate 70. It took nine days to reach the Green River; for the first seven of those we have no dated sketches. There is one drawing with a title that places it along here "Desert between Grand & Green R." (Plate 298), and though it should be readily discoverable in such open terrain, I cannot locate it. The sketch does have a quality appropriate to the face of the Roan Mountains, of which there is a continuous, unobstructed view from the expedition's path. I place it here as a challenge to eyes other than mine.

The expedition was now entering the deserts of Utah, where water and grass were often scanty or nonexistent, and access to the Grand River possible only at a few widely separated places.

> *September* 22.—... We left Salt creek without a guide—Leroux having gone forward some four days since to examine the route, and show those who accompany him the best road to the Spanish trail, and not yet returned... We found no point at which we could approach the river until too late an hour in the afternoon to reach it with our train, for it was impossible to travel at night with wagons without a road. We encamped, therefore, without grass, near the dry bed of what proved to be a small intermitting creek of bitter water... So many of our animals gave out, that several of the wagons did not reach camp during the night.
>
> We were here about four miles from the river, which, by following the ravine cut through the cañon wall by the creek, was easily reached on horseback, (and only obstructed for wagons by a dry channel cut deep in the clay,) at a narrow bottom of fine grass two or three miles in length, with shady groves of cotton-wood on the banks of the stream. The red sandstone cañon walls are nearly vertical, and two hundred feet high; beyond which smaller ledges rise above each other, terrace-like, for some miles towards Salt mountain, which bears south from our camp, some twenty miles beyond the river. The cañon [today Westwater Canyon] narrows to the width of the river below the groves of cotton-wood (G-B, 58-59).

Creutzfeldt expressed his unrestrained displeasure at the events of the day and attributed the difficulties to Gunnison's failure to follow Leroux's advice.

> We go on to day senselessly in a desolate waste land without an idea, where to get water or grass, in all directions of the compass, and finally stop in this Arabia late in the dark night, on a Creek with some little water trickling in, but for its salty and bitter taste unpalatable. Men and beasts are suffering dreadfully. One wagon is left behind, the mules fatigued to death being unable to go on. All this because of our great genius whom La Roux instructed not to proceed with our journey before he explored the route for some days... We have of course nothing to eat but bacon and bread; this Devil lives only for himself, uses

ham, molasses, pickles, fresh butter, sardines and so on for himself and has the audacity to call it private property whereas we have to eat bread and bacon to keep body & soul together. La Roux having searched for us half the day and having used up his munition in signaling us to follow him, arrives in the evening very angry about Röhrle's kind of management, and frankly pronouncing his opinion (Creutzfeldt, September 22).

> Forced to refresh our mules tired to death and ourselves, we are compelled to remain here, in a distance of 5-6 m. from the river in deep barren sand, seasoned with a little Sage, rattlesnakes, and scorpions; we drive the animals to the water and let them graze in the bottom lands where they find plenty of grass. La Roux and the captain are arguing all day long; La Roux's critique not too flattering; besides called him a picayune man but in the afternoon the captain gets his instructions, how to come out of this hell; since La Roux intends leaving us tomorrow. How we will fare only Belzebub & Company know, when this dog of a Captain takes over who is too cowardly to make advance explorations of our route... Some of the soldiers had gone to the river and had caught great many fishes, but all of one sort, called Pikerell by Sancho Pansa [a derisive reference to Beckwith] (Creutzfeldt, September 23).

Beckwith's entry in the *Report* for September 22 is longer than usual, and he does not separate material by date until the 26th, perhaps because the expedition was stationary for the intervening period. The following excerpt is from no earlier than September 24, the day Leroux began his journey back to New Mexico.

> *September* 22. (Continued). Leroux, with three companions, left us at this camp to return to New Mexico, having completed his engagement as guide. He expects to travel much at night, and trusts to his tact and knowledge of the country for passing safely through the Indian bands along his route (G-B, 59-60).

Schiel was discomfited by the prospect of crossing the desert without a guide.

> We had more than one occasion...to deplore the absence of our leader, for already at the Grand river

Leroux had left us to fill other engagements and we were on our own. The trip back to New Mexico Leroux had to undertake at night, as they had to hide during the daytime. For if they had fallen into the hands of the Utes, they would have been scalped. It took a man fifty year's experience to be able to deceive the sharp eye of his enemies and successfully terminate such an adventure.

> Before Leroux left us he had given us an exact description of the locale in which we were to reach the Spanish Trail and by following this could cross the Grand [here he means the Green] river (Schiel, 92).

From September 22 until the morning of September 26, the expedition remained at Camp 72, Bitter Water Creek (G-B, 103), at what is today Westwater Wash, and from where the exhausted animals had access to plentiful grass and water along the Colorado River. From here and for several days farther on in their travels the expedition's men had a clear view of the Salt Mountains on their left and of the Book Cliffs or Roan Mountain on their right. Perhaps the undated Plate 298, "Desert between Grand and Green R. is from this time, but I cannot identify the scene. Gunnison led them over a direct route to the Green River, a course that was much shorter than the one Leroux counseled him to take, and that was possible only because of torrential rains that by happenstance provided water. Beckwith indirectly expresses some wonderment that they got through, for usually their route was so dry that all the animals would likely have died. When the desert did get that fortunate dousing by a rainstorm, the soil turned into a heavy mud.

> *September 27.*—It continued to rain most of the night, and increased in violence until 10 o'clock in the morning, when it ceased, and we moved slowly forward over a very slippery and miry soil—all the beds of creeks, recently dry, pouring down torrents of water, and water filling every little depression on the surface of the ground; yet the earth was not moistened more than two inches deep... Our route here lies but two or three miles from the base of the Roan mountain, and is much more direct from Salt creek than by following the river to the Spanish trail, and thence crossing to the ford on Green river, and is less interrupted by deep gullies; but in wet weather it would be impossible to follow us with heavy loads, and in the dry season no water is known to exist on this path, between Grand and Green rivers.

Captain Gunnison indicates the choice of localities for a railroad track as lying still nearer the base of the mountain, where, however, "much cutting and filling would be required, and many large culverts necessary." The thunder-showers of the morning covered Salt mountains with snow, the effects of which we feel as the wind sweeps round from that quarter, for we can get no wood, and only sage enough to cook our coffee.

*September* 28.— We delayed our march until 8 o'clock, to derive as much benefit from the sun and morning drainage as possible, and it was difficult, even at that hour, to make any progress—mules miring and wagons stalling...

The mountain on Grand river is very broken, and during the day presented many beautiful rocks standing high above the adjacent ledges and ridges. From one position a majestic shaft stood out clear against the sky; and chimney rocks were almost hourly presented as we rode along, with piles occasionally resembling ruins of immense churches and dwellings, and one or two on eminences, resembling the ruins of mighty cities of adobe buildings (G-B, 60-61).

Creutzfeldt interrupted his grumbling to write appreciatively on the scenic qualities of the distant views to the south, but found nothing appealing about the immediate wasteland through which the expedition was traveling.

> The ground is as before a miserable desert and the mountains in sight bare and barren, but in Southern direction shaped in interesting forms. First appear in mighty height the prominent mountain ridges in beautiful formation, their summits covered with snow and looking quite winter-like. At their feet smaller chains giving the appearance of Obelisks, Pyramids, Ruins of castles in all variations but with no trace of vegetation; they consist mostly of slate and sandstone. We live in the hope to see the Green R. soon, but after 16 m. traveling not a trace of it is to be seen; all is a continuation of the desert in which we might probably have lost all our animals, if not the rain had provided us with water which though dirty, was drinkable, for nothing can be found between the so called Springs and the Green River. Our Röhrle calls it the commencing of the rainy season (Creutzfeldt, September 28).

PLATE 299. September 28: Desert between Grand and Green rivers. 21.1 x 8.2 cm

PLATE 300. Photograph of desert between Grand and Green Rivers

PLATE 301. Composite drawing and photograph

"Sept 28 Desert between Grand & Green R" (Plate 299) bears a title identical to that on the previous drawing, but here Snyder usefully appended the date. In any event there can be no doubt of the subject; finally we have a view of what Beckwith and Creutzfeldt have been describing, of the jagged cliffs that line the Canyon of the Grand River and of the immediately recognizable features of the Salt Mountains beyond it to the south. The best alignment for this I could find is from a hill overlooking Nash Wash, just north of Interstate 70 at Exit 202. This is near or at the site of "Camp 74, on hill" of September 27-28 (G-B, 103).

"Sept. 28 Desert bet. Grand & Green Ris. (Plate 302) is the third drawing from the region, along with Nos. 298 and 299,

PLATE 302. September 28: Desert between Grand and Green rivers. 21.7 x 8.4 cm

bearing the identical title. I thought that such a distinctive formation as the one in this sketch, silhouetted prominently against the sky, would be readily visible from the path the expedition took. This was not the case. Time after time I returned to the area and scoured the desert, but found only the roughest approximations to the scene, all of which I was ultimately forced to reject as being matches in my imagination only.

How could I fail to locate a subject so unusual, one so high, isolated, and in seemingly open desert terrain, and one that was somewhere within the distance covered by only one day of the expedition's travel? Years passed before my efforts met with success, and then it was only by happenstance. I was south of I-70 looking for the subject of the next drawing, "Book Mountains, September 29" (Plate 305), and climbed a hill along Yellowcat Road to scan the desert with binoculars.

PLATE 303. Panoramic photograph of desert between Grand and Green Rivers

PLATE 304. Composite drawing and photograph

This splendid turreted formation swam into view, nestled in an amphitheater of surrounding hills of similar or greater height, so that from the distance it is hardly visible, and not at all from most directions. Beckwith's "From one position a majestic shaft stood out clear against the sky" can be read as his response to seeing this dramatic tower of sandstone suddenly come into view.

The butte that is the drawing's dominant feature is placed far to the left, in front of which is a dry wash that becomes gradually deeper toward the right. On its turret is the notation "dark," and on the lower slope "gray." The letter "f" seems to occur in two places, but if it is indeed a letter I cannot decipher its meaning. In the center of the scene the Salt Mountains (today La Sal Mountains), which marked the route of the main branch of the Spanish Trail and were the subject of the previous drawing (Plate 299), are left out. The day was reported to be clear, so this omission was not the result of great distances or of poor visibility, and the Salts loom recognizably on the horizon in the middle of my photograph (Plate 303). Remarkably, on the right side of the sketch is the partial outline of the much more distant Henry Mountains, which are also present in the photograph. This mountain range was visible to the Gunnison expedition during many days of travel but remained entirely unremarked upon. Frémont must also have seen them when he came through Utah in January of 1854, and again they were in his view for weeks, but there is no mention of them in the surviving documents of the journey, even though they appear under a different name on Frémont's summary map of his five expeditions (Frémont, 1886; Shlaer, 2000). It was John Wesley Powell who, during his 1869 exploration of the Colorado River, finally described this range and gave it its first formal name, "Unknown Mountains," thereby becoming its official discoverer. It is the last major mountain range in the United States to be so "discovered" and named; in 1872 Powell changed its designation to "Henry Mountains."

"Book Mts Sept. 27th (Plate 305) is both mistitled and misdated. Starting with the date, September 27, I was led into an unavailing search over the expedition's path for the day that led me instead to the difficult-to-find scene in the previous drawing (Plate 302). This view here is not of the Book Mountains, and it was only when I realized that the shapes outlined on the right possess the characteristic silhouette of the distant Henry Mountains that I was able to locate the view, by traveling along the route of the expedition for September 29 until the foreground appeared in alignment. This occurred near the junction of Valley City Road with US 191; the spot is on the slope of a nearby hill that overlooks the Spanish Trail.

> *September* 29.—For a mile, in the morning, we continued our course of yesterday, W. S. W., and then changed to S. W.for seven miles, when we came upon the noted Spanish trail which passes the foot of Salt mountain. We then turned W. N.W., following this trail, and encamped after a march of 14.07 miles, in which we descended 12 feet 3 inches per mile, at a

PLATE 305. Book Mountains, September 29. 14.8 x 3.4 cm

PLATE 306. Photograph

PLATE 307. Composite drawing and photograph

rain-water pool, a neighboring ravine furnishing a limited supply of grass; but, for once sage was even more scarce than grass, the country being entirely destitute of wood, and presenting only a picture of aridity and barrenness.

From an elevated bluff near camp, Captain Gunnison describes the view as desolate and disheartening in the extreme. "Except three or four small cotton-wood trees in the ravine near us, there is not a tree to be seen by the unassisted eye on any part of the horizon. The plain lying between us and the Wahsatch range, a hundred miles to the west, is a series of rocky, parallel chasms, and fantastic sandstone ridges. On the north, Roan mountain, ten miles from us, presents bare masses of sandstone, and on the higher ridges, twenty miles back, a few scattering cedars may be distinguished with the glass; Salt mountain, to the east is covered half down its sides with snow; and to the south, mass after mass of coarse conglomerate is broken in fragments, or piled in turret-shaped heaps, colored by ferruginous cement from a deep black to a brilliant red, whilst in some rocks there are argillaceous layers, varying to gray or glistening with white. The surface around us

> is whitened with fields of alkali, precisely resembling fields of snow" (G-B, 61).

Gunnison could not have seen the Wasatch Mountains from here, although he knew where they were. Rather, he was gazing at the face of the formidable San Raphael Reef and perhaps into its desert beyond, a harsh landscape that perfectly accords with his description as "a series of rocky, parallel chasms, and fantastic sandstone ridges."

> September 29. Continuing our journey in the S. direction over triste hills and valleys, we reach at noon the so called Spanish trail, which coming from the foot of the Salt mountains takes its course towards N.W. We follow the path hoping to reach or to see the Green River; but disappointed in both we have nothing before us but broken hills and waste valleys and encamp with little dry grass and pool-water; small crippled Griswood merely sufficient to make some coffee. Of flowers and plants no trace. Weather clear and fine, even hot (Creutzfeldt, September 29).

The poor quality of the photograph (Plate 306) is a result of the unclear atmosphere that now seems to be a permanent condition over a large portion of the deserts of Utah. The haze mostly consists of particulate matter, so infrared film was of limited use in penetrating its obscuring murk, and I had to compensate by increasing the contrast of my photographs to the point where they take on a truly ugly appearance. This miasma arises from vehicle-raised and wind-blown dust, as well as from the smokestacks of power plants built here to exploit the huge nearby deposits of coal, some of which Captain Gunnison originally discovered.

"From 4.10 Sepb 29, Book Mts" is the top drawing on a sheet of two (Plate 309).Perhaps it is a stretch, but the two drawings on this sheet are related because they both depict a valley as seen by the men of the expedition before they entered it; in this case that of the Green River, and in the lower one that of the Sevier River, which would first come into their view on October 17. The scene in Plate 308 includes on its right a detailed representation of a high mesa, from here twenty miles away, with a pyramidal spike on its heights. This landmark is visible for great distances in the desert, and would have guided sojourners heading west on the Spanish Trail from New Mexico to a practical ford on the Green River. It is part of what is now the Beckwith Plateau, which is north of the town of Green River, Utah. In modern terminology it marks the westernmost extent of the Book or

PLATE 308. From 4:10 p.m., September 29, Book Mountains. Upper drawing of two on a sheet, 20.1 x 15.0 cm

PLATE 309. Sheet with two drawings. 20.1 x 15.0 cm

Roan Cliffs, at the point where their ramparts turn north. Beckwith sometimes regards the Book Cliffs (or interchangeably Book Mountain or Roan Mountain or the Roan Mountains) as reaching their terminus at the Green River, but also notes that the mountains to the west of the river partake of the same characteristics and so are really a continuation of them. The far-off shapes outlined in the center and to the left are part of the San Rafael Reef, some 30 miles distant. It is a massive, impassable uplift that forced travelers on the Spanish Trail far to the north, a detour Gunnison's expedition would have to make as well. The position from which I took my photograph is near the Ruby Ranch Road where a power line crosses it, and the view again looks through miles of hazy air.

> *September* 30.—Our course for six miles this morning was the same as that of last evening, following the direction of the hills and dry beds of creeks. We then passed through the range of hills on our right, and again resumed our course along the base of Roan mountain; these hills present precisely the appearance of immense beds and fields of ashes, being more saline and friable even than those of previous days, and even more destitute of vegetation, the un-

PLATE 310. Panoramic photograph of Book Mountains

PLATE 311. Composite drawing and photograph

dulating descent being relieved near the Akanaquint or Green river by scattered tufts of grass. Groves of cotton-wood lined the stream, and a narrow bottom afforded grass for our animals for the night, after a march of 14 miles. The distance from Grand river to this ford, by a very direct course, is 70 miles, and from Bitter creek, 67 miles by our route, which, except during rains, is entirely without water. By following Grand river, however, some miles below Bitter creek, until the Spanish trail is reached, and following it, crossing a more broken and gullied country, a spring is said to be passed; but its locality is not known to me. This entire section is, however, not only crossed with great labor and difficulty, but is utterly valueless for occupation and settlement by civilized man...

Many Akanaquint or Green river Utahs were on the opposite bank as we encamped, and soon crossed it to beg tobacco, and, if possible, to trade; dressed deer-skins being the only article they offer for this purpose (G-B, 61).

Creutzfeldt must have been delighted to finally reach the plentiful water of the Green River, even though the expedition was unable to immediately cross it.

Having dragged along for 14 m. in this abject land following the Sp. Trail, we reach at last the Green

> River so much longed for; we try to ford it, but find it too deep and sandy (Creutzfeldt, September 30).

> Before Leroux left us he had given us an exact description of the locale in which we were to reach the Spanish Trail and by following this could cross the Green river. Finding a ford...was made easier for us by the help of some Akanaquint or Green river Utes who swam the river with their horses when we reached its banks in order to call upon us (Schiel, 92).

"Grand [Green} River Country" (Plate 312) is obviously mislabled, but I did not notice it for years because its subject is so obvious; clearly the high mesa north of the town of Green River, that rises sharply from the western bank of the Green River, and that overlooks the ford that the Gunnison Expedition would use to cross it. It is the same one so carefully represented on the right in the previous sketch (Plate 308), on top of which lies the Beckwith Plateau. The point of view is low on the east bank of the river, from where only a hint of the pyramidal turret is visible. When the expedition continued its journey it went around the left side of this mesa and turned north to follow the Spanish Trail. The tree on the left, probably a cottonwood, helps define the riparian environment where the sketch was made as it closes the composition; such trees still occur on the banks of the river today. Here Beckwith first mentions a "Little Mountain," and the "Little Mountains" appear on the expedition's map, extending north from the Green River crossing and then bending around to the west, where they become part of the Wasatch Range. There is a sketch in the album titled "Little Mountains," so from here on I kept a constant lookout for Kern's view of them. It turned out to be a scene that was encountered by the men almost two weeks later, when they camped at the eastern base of the Wasatch Mountains near the entrance to Wasatch Pass (Plate 335).

## THE MOST EXPLICIT POSSIBLE WARNING OF NOT-SO-DISTANT VIOLENCE; CLEAR REPORTS OF WAR IN UTAH AND NO INDIAN WILLING TO ACT AS GUIDE

> *October* 1.—We crossed the river by an excellent ford, which we had observed the Indians crossing, from a few yards below our camp (on the Spanish trail) to an island opposite, and from its upper end to the shore. The river is 300 yards wide, with a pebbly bottom, as we forded it, but with quicksands on either side of our path...
>
> Indians thronged our camp for several hours. They are the merriest of their race I have ever seen, except the Yumas—constantly laughing and talk-

PLATE 312. Grand [Green] River country [September 30] 21.3 x 11.9 cm

PLATE 313. Photograph, Green River country

ing, and appearing grateful for the trifling presents they receive. A wrinkled, hard-faced old savage, with whom I shared my luncheon of bread and bacon, quite laughed aloud with joy at his good fortune. They confirmed the reports we had before heard, of a war between the Mormons and Wah-ka-ra's band of Utahs, and his absence in New Mexico to dispose of a herd of cattle which he had stolen from them.

The Roan mountain, along which we have travelled for more than a week, extends quite to Green river, and forms one side of the cañon through which it descends a few miles to the north of our present camp. Three miles to the north, if our recent guide is not mistaken [it is more nearly twelve], White river [today Price River] cuts the opposite side of this cañon, passing, itself in a cañon, through the southern point of Little mountain, which lies chiefly between White and Green rivers, and forms the western side of the cañon of the latter stream. But in reality Little mountain, which is united to the Wahsatch range on the west, is merely a continuation of the Roan, whose character and appearance at a distance I have described at Blue river. Here, however, we are but a mile or two from its base, and its stratified rocks, nearly horizontal, are distinctly visible, extending on each side of the river on the same level. The moun-

PLATE 314. Composite drawing and photograph

tain itself, as we see it here, is but a few hundred feet high, generally level on its summit; yet there are a few peaks and ridges rising above this common level, but their character is the same as the lower mountain, which has the appearance on the side towards us of recently-broken earth, as though the valley had just been sunken or the mountain thrust up, leaving its sides almost vertical—indeed quite so with the higher strata, the talus having only accumulated at the base. This mountain wall, however, is very irregular; deep ravines and gorges extend back into it, giving it, with its regular strata presented to us, where no sign of vegetation exists, the appearance of an unfinished fortification, on a scale which is pleasing to the imagination, and contrasts the works of men strongly with those of nature. These walls may be in height from 300 to 500 feet; and its strata, in color, are red, blue, gray, and white. Desolate as is the country over which we have just passed, and around us, the view is still one of the most beautiful and pleasing I remember to have seen. As we approached the river yesterday, the ridges on either of its banks to the west appeared broken into a thousand forms—columns, shafts, temples, buildings, and ruined cities could be seen, or imagined, from the high points along our route. Fifty miles apparently below us on the river, the high snow-peaks of the Sierra Abajo are visible.

Efforts were made to obtain a guide from among the Indians, but no one could be induced by a display of the trinkets, cloths, paints, and blankets they so much covet, to accompany us even to the Wahsatch Pass (G-B, 62).

PLATE 315. Green River, October 1 22.4 x 13.9 cm

PLATE 316. "View of the Roan or Book Mountains At the Spanisch Trail Ford of Green River Oct 1st"

Now Gunnison had received an explicit warning of the ongoing war between Wah-ka-ra's (Walker's) band of Utahs and the Mormons, the menace of which prevented any of the local Indians from acting as guide, no matter how great an inducement they were offered. On October 1 the expedition forded the Green River, and Kern made a sketch looking back over it to the Book Cliffs along which they had traveled for more than a week "Green river Oct 1" (Plate 315). He drew it on paper that in the nineteenth century was commercially available for watercolorists; it had a toned area with the shapes of clouds already in place, all within a border that Kern did not entirely respect. This paper is found only a few times in the album, and it is not clear why Kern drew on it at all, but the sketch with its well-worked-out trees is the basis for one of the *Report's* lithographs "View of the Roan or Book Mountains At the Spanisch Trail Ford of Green River Oct. 1st".

This version is without an attribution, but another that I have seen is marked simply "Sketch by R. H. Kern." The usual reference to Stanley was again absent, and "Spanish" in the title was spelled correctly. The lithograph is a reasonable version of the details in Kern's sketch, but it lacks the grace

PLATE 317. Juxtaposed drawing and lithograph

and sure hand of the other prints. Perhaps an attribution to Stanley was omitted because this one is not his work. It is the last illustration in the Gunnison-Beckwith *Report*, and may have been added as an afterthought.

My view looks to the northeast up and across the river, and was taken from the bridge on E. Main Street in the town of Green River. The accepted Spanish Trail ford is upstream a few miles from here, but there is evidence that travelers crossed elsewhere; that, and the lability of river beds in general, makes the exact location of the expedition's ford uncertain.

PLATE 318. Photograph, Green River

PLATE 319. Composite drawing and photograph

In Beckwith's and Schiel's accounts the river ford was discovered by simply observing where the Indians crossed it, but Creutzfeldt implies a more active participation on their part.

> Yesterday evening some Indians came across the river and did show us a ford, where we after some mendings of the road and the raising of our things in the wagon, easily traversed the river and encamped on the right bank, where our animals might become refreshed by the existing good grass. The river is pretty well overgrown with Cotton-wood, willows and Sumach, has extraordinary dirty water and a nearly S. course (Creutzfeldt, October 1).

"Oct 2d Rock Hills" (Plate 320) shows some of the rugged landforms that are part of what Beckwith calls the "Little Mountains." My vantage point is next to N. Long Street, about 1.5 miles north of Main Street in Green River, near both the Green River ford and "Camp 78, west bank of Green river." (G-B, 103-104). The striking flat-topped, castle-like formation to the right of center is now called Gunnison Butte, which rises from the plateau and looks down on the Green River from its west bank. The hills to its right in the picture are all on the east side of the river. The row of cottonwoods that crosses the entire view of the photograph is following an irrigation ditch and not the river itself, which is too low to be seen from here. Kern must have made his sketch in the morning as the expedition was leaving camp to follow the Spanish Trail as it led around the southern face of the Beckwith Plateau, and then turned northward.

> October 2.—Our course this morning, for two hours, was a little south of west, gradually leaving the river. It then gently changed to northwest—our march being 16.76 miles, following the Spanish trail... (G-B, 62).

PLATE 320. October 2, Rock Hills 17.5 x 11.7 cm

PLATE 321. Photograph, Rock Hills

PLATE 322. Composite drawing and photograph

Creutzfeldt didn't miss an opportunity to aim his private jibes at the increasingly impatient Gunnison, who had forgone his custom of resting men and beasts on the Sabbath in order to hurry the expedition forward:

> Though Sunday, the captain seems to turn a free-thinker and continues our journey. We follow the Span. Trail leading through broken mountains, sandy plains, beds of rivulets and square sandstones until in the evening we find good fresh water running or trickling from out of the sandstones (Creutzfeldt, October 2).

The next day the Spanish Trail curved to the west, and because Gunnison thought the terrain in that direction appeared to be too broken for wagons, the expedition continued off the trail in a northerly direction.

> October 3.—Travelling sometimes in the bed of the creek, (dry above the [Akanaquint] spring,) and at others over the rocky, friable soil of the hills,

> we made but slow progress this morning—about six miles in as many hours—on the Spanish trail. Its course then bore off more strongly to the west, over very rocky, broken hills—and we left it, taking a northwest and a north-northwest course by compass, leaving these rocky hills to the left, and skirting along others to the right, as rocky but perhaps less broken and cut up transversely by cañones (G-B, 63).

Creutzfeldt had a more emphatically negative view of what seemed to him to be pointless, indiscriminate meandering over a barren country.

> We travel in all directions of the compass over a broken, desolate, God-forsaken country...but still as triste a region as ever on the Gila. Nothing but sand mixed with gypsum and sandstone in a great confusion, intersected by dry Creeks. We leave after a few miles the Sp. Trail behind us and follow a Creek toward N.W.S. and E. The captain calls it the nearer road to Salt Lake city and therefore avoids the Span. Trail, because it leads to little Salt Lake and has good camp places. One is inclined to believe that the Donkey has lost all his sense to lead us randomly through this unknown desert which will probably lead us to misery, but this could be expected under leadership of him and Sancho Pansa... According to the odometer we made 16 m., but in a straight line probably not amounting to more than half of it (Creutzfeldt, October 3).

On page 63 of the *Report* there is a discussion of Utah's White River, and opposite that page is bound the incorrectly titled lithograph "Rock Hills Between Green and White Rivers Octr. 3d Wahscatch Mountains in the distance" (Plate 268); the view is actually of the "Grand River Cañons" that Kern drew in Colorado on September 10 (Plate 267). With its rugged cliffs, rocky ground, and altered foreground foliage, the lithograph does at least suggest the harsh deserts of Utah rather well.

The next day, October 4, was much like the previous one, and Beckwith had little specific to say about it.

> *October* 4.—We followed the dry bed of the creek in which we had encamped for five miles, turning northwest as we approached White river [now the Price River], which we crossed nine miles from camp... We encamped a mile above the crossing, on the thin bunch-grass of the hills (G-B, 63).

Creutzfeldt, on the other hand, was becoming more and more contemptuous of the leadership of the expedition and discouraged by the bleakness of the landscape.

> First we are changing again our direction to all points of the compass, following the creek for some miles yet; then we take a nearly N.W. direction and meet a path leading to the White River. The country, of course is unchanged poor as before... all around the river deadly silence is reigning; no fish nor bird to be seen (Creutzfeldt, October 4).

On the afternoon of October 4 Kern made a drawing of this forbidding terrain not far from the camp "On White river Ocbr 4th near to the Spanish trail." (Plate 323). This bluff is adjacent to US 191, north of Green River, Utah. Bonnie Hardwick discovered it for me when, on one of her trips between New Mexico and California, she took this circuitous route just to help me in my searches. Posted land along the river prevented me from getting to the perfect vantage point, but the essential quality of the scene is well presented in my photograph. The high, pointed summit is Mount Elliot. The bottom through which the Price River pursues its winding course is in the foreground, along with a few small trees. A mile or so away and near the actual encampment there were large cottonwoods, and Kern has "transplanted" them downstream to indicate the position of the riverbed and the wooded nature of the campsite, as well as to close the right side of the composition. The expedition arrived in camp at 3:00 p.m., and "Sunset" is noted on the drawing, so Kern must have sketched it later in the day. The drawing is incomplete in a way that casts some light on Kern's working methods: The mesa that obstructs a view of the face of Mount Elliot is missing, but room for it has been left in the drawing. This demonstrates again that Kern occasionally sketched the background details before adding those closer up; in this case the sketch was not finished and that foreground never filled in.

> *October 5.*—... White [Price] river winds very much among high hills, frequently impinging against their bases, and at various points passing through narrow cañones, rendering it quite impracticable to follow near it. Turning more westerly, we descended a dry creek for two miles and came upon Clever creek, a small branch of White river from the northwest, winding between high hills and bluffs, and encamped after a march of 8.72 miles—being timid about leaving the grass, which was here more than usually abundant (G-B, 63).

PLATE 323. From Camp 81 at Sunset, On White River October 4. Near to the Spanish Trail. 21.5 x 9.1 cm

PLATE 324. Photograph on White River

Where Beckwith mentions the all-important presence of grass here, Creutzfeldt took note of the trees that Kern would draw.

> Following an Indian path we are traveling near the river through broken land and in all directions but mostly N.W.... Our camp is on a small Creek either a branch of the White river, or the river itself... Pretty large trees of Canadian Poplars, growing here, begin to look autumnal already... (Creutzfeldt, October 5).

Like the sketch from October 1 (Plate 315), "On Clever Creek Oct 5" (Plate 326) is on watercolor paper readied with

PLATE 325. Composite drawing and photograph

the outline of cloud formations; Kern has once more drawn beyond its prepared area. Clever Creek is an exposed place with little water, but below the surface there must be enough to keep alive its small, widely separated stand of perhaps a dozen cottonwoods. The distinctive form of their trunks is a result of the harshness of the environment. Among these dwarfed, twisted, wind-blasted trees I chose the one most closely matched to that in the sketch, although in their gnarled appearance any of them would have served. So evocative is my photograph of Kern's subject that I have been asked repeatedly if the two could be identical; the answer is no, because cottonwoods are a relatively short-lived species, but the importance of this seeming identity is that the shape of both trees reflect the environment they held in common, and their characteristic appearance conveys a sense of the climate and conditions of the location.

From here the expedition went north along the Price River, turned west, then south in front of the Wasatch Mountains and rejoined the Spanish Trail near the San Rafael River. Not until the men traveled almost 50 difficult miles in five days and made camp on the "Garambulla river" (today Farron Creek) is there another drawing by Kern in the album.

> *October 6.*— Our northwest course was continued for four miles and a half, when we left the branch [of the

PLATE 326. On Clever Creek, October 5

PLATE 327. Photograph on Clever Creek

White River] on which we had encamped, turning west up a narrow valley, which we followed for some three miles, and then took an Indian trail leading W.S.W., crossing a low ridge to another creek, which the trail descended for a couple of miles, and then ascended a hill towards White river, until we overlooked that stream just at our feet. But the descent was so steep that we were forced to turn from our southwest course directly north; and we were occupied two hours in descending the half mile of bluff to the river bank, crossing the stream and encamping on the opposite hill, having travelled by an unnecessarily serpentine path, 11.11 miles...

The Little mountain, sometimes from the regular appearance and variegated color of its strata, like the Roan, called the Book mountain, lay during to-day's march plainly in view from Green river north and west, to where it apparently joins the first range of the Wahsatch—a low mountain, resembling the former in all respects, which extends around to the west and southwest... (G-B, 63-64).

PLATE 328. Composite drawing and photograph

Once again "Little mountain" is said to be continually visible from the path of the expedition here, and there is confirmation in the expedition's map; thus I spent an inordinate amount of time along this desolate, difficult part of the route looking for the subject of the drawing with that title (Plate 335), but to no avail. I began to understand more clearly the displeasure that Creutzfeldt expressed at the activities of the day.

> Unhesitatingly marching on, first over somewhat better hills, more rounded and richer in grass, we make in a straight line certainly only a few miles; following a path, soon lost in inaccessible cavities, we have to open another path over steep mountains to the white river, cross it, climb up a mountain on its right bank and pitch our tents there among stone fragments of every description. What may be our intention, is entirely unknown, since we are making circles, curves, angles and all kinds of figures, the theorems of a Pythagoras could be enriched with... (Creutzfeldt, October 6).

In the published *Report* Beckwith is fairly circumspect when discussing the events of the following day.

> *October 7.*—...Passing from the bluff on which we encamped last night, over rolling barren hills, we entered a small valley coming from the southwest, in which we again came upon the trail we were forced by the hills to leave yesterday and followed it during the day in a very direct course...without reaching the summit of the hills drained by White river (G-B, 64).

But to his private diary he confides doubts that the indirect route over which Gunnison was leading the expedition around the San Rafael Desert was the best choice. He also ruminates on their failure to obtain an Indian guide from the throngs of them that were at the Green River crossing, and makes it clear that he was alert to the increasing hazards to the expedition as it approached the conflict between the Utahs and the Mormons.

> *October 7...* a series of plains, running parallel with the Wahsatch mountains on our right and the Rocky Hills which the want of water and a knowledge of what route exactly to pursue to assure the best wood and a supply of grass and water we have moved so great a circuit to avoid on our left...
>
> I have not myself seen any apparent insurmountable obstacle to passing much with in the limit of the circuit we have taken from Green River; but, as the country is very broken and generally arid, only actual

exploration can determine this; which, at present, however, I cannot think more difficult than the route we have followed; and it would certainly be much shorter.

> Exertions were ineffectively made with the Indians on Green River to procure a guide for this part of our route —they being afraid to go near Mormony — and we have since met no Indians (Beckwith, *Journal*).

The next day Gunnison encountered an Indian who unambiguously declared that there was a state of war between his tribe and the Mormons.

> *October* 8.—Two miles from camp we passed the divide between the waters of the White and San Rafael rivers; and in eleven miles reached and crossed the latter stream... Captain Gunnison, who was in advance as we approached camp, observed an Indian ascending the opposite side of the valley, and, discharging his pistol, made signs for him to approach, which he did after some hesitation, galloping at a rapid rate with his rifle held ready for action, fearing we were Mormons, with whom he informed us his people were at war, boasting of their feats of prowess (G-B, 64).

Warning after warning of the conflict in Utah had been delivered to Gunnison, and this time from an Indian who was in all likelihood a participant. In his private *Journal* Beckwith elaborated on that day's contacts with Utah Indians.

> *October 8*... An Indian visited us as we were encamping and after a short absence returned with his squaw Moyna and child of two years of age & one companion & two or three horses and a few dressed skins to trade. We purchased a fine horse for a few beads, brass bells, yards of cloth & knives —but they were not satisfied because they could get no ammunition which they need in their hostilities with the Mormons; a material difference from the account given us by their friends on Blue river (Beckwith, *Journal*).

The terrain was becoming slightly less arid; on the west side of the San Rafael Desert the streams coming out of the Wasatch Mountains were larger and more consistent than those encountered earlier. Away from the streams, however, it remained a desert.

We go along in S.W. direction in a level valley towards the mountain and reach at noon a pretty considerable creek with much water, the banks of which are well overgrown with good grass... We cross it without difficulty and pass over a height to another creek, tributary to the first and on our course only 1 mile distant. The name of the former is given as Rafael R. and of the latter, which we encamp on: Garanbuga [Garambulla] R. Here cotton wood, Sumach and Eleangus are growing; the water is good and the river must in the rainy season be quite considerable. Nature becomes a little more lively. Hawks, Ducks, Sky and Field-Larks, Sparrows, Fishes and a couple of Indians are to be seen. We shall remain here tomorrow in order to give the animals opportunity for sufficient grazing (Creutzfeldt, October 8).

Here nothing exists, besides what I mentioned yesterday. Nature, harmonizing with the country is dead, and sometimes disturbingly quiet so that ghosts and apparitions could amuse us (Creutzfeldt, October 9).

However mildly it may be phrased, the *Report*'s narrative for October 10 contains what must be read as a reproach of Captain Gunnison's choice of route. Its substance is taken from Beckwith's diary entry of October 7, and confirms again Creutzfeldt's grumbling observation that the path the expedition took was unnecessarily circuitous and offered no advantage over a more direct course.

*October* 10.—Two miles from camp, in a nearly southern course, we came again upon the Spanish trail, which we left a week ago to avoid the rocky hills which lay in front of us, passing to the north by a route which, from a want of knowledge of what route exactly to pursue to secure the best road and a supply of grass and water, may have been extended too far. We struck lower down on White river than it would be necessary to do if the march from Akanaquint spring to the river could be made in one day, or if water could be found at some intermediate point. The distance from the spring to the river, at a point near the northwest end of the Rock hills, can probably not exceed twenty-five miles. The Spanish trail itself, however, if it can be followed with wagons, is much shorter than the route here indicated; and I see no reason to apprehend any insurmountable obstacle from the appearance of the country, much of which was in view as we passed around it. But the distance from the Akanaquint spring to the San Rafael by this trail may reach thirty miles; and although there was water on it at a point ten miles from the spring when we passed it, I did not see it, and am not informed as to its permanence. But, as the country is very broken and generally arid, only actual exploration can determine its practicability, which, however, I cannot think more difficult than the route we have followed, and it would certainly not be one-half the distance... The third branch of the San Rafael, called Garambulla by the Indians...we reached six miles from the morning camp and crossed at our present one (G-B, 64-65).

PLATE 329. On the Garambulla Creek, October 10. 10.7 x 7.9 cm

Creutzfeldt briefly described Garambulla Creek, and Kern sketched some of the trees that grew along it "On the Garambulla Creek Oct 10" (Plate 329). On the creek some willows and popular trees (Creutzfeldt, October 10). After five days without a drawing we finally have this one. As was the case for the preceding sketch, "Clever Creek" (Plate 326), the vegetation defines the character of the place. Sheltered and well watered, it is today a farming community with fields irrigated by what is now Ferron Creek. Here I met Sam Singleton, who was kind enough to give me the names and phone numbers of several ranchers he knew whose properties lay along my route, and where I ultimately located three of Kern's scenes.

I had my choice of several similar stands of cottonwoods from which to make a photograph for comparison here, and the strong, straight trunks that grow on the creek are in stark contrast to the windblown, crooked specimens at Clever Creek. Visible beyond the trees are the foothills of the Wasatch Mountains to the southwest near Youngs Point. They

PLATE 330. Photograph on the Garambulla Creek

are only about six miles away, but the murkiness of the air has reduced them to a hazy, indistinct presence.

> *October* 11.—the Spanish trail, though but seldom used of late years, is still very distinct where the soil washed but slightly ... Specimens of coal were brought in from the hills near camp, Captain Gunnison and Dr. Schiel differing in opinion as to its quality (G-B, 65).

The buttes to the right of center in Kern's sketch "Near Wah-satch Pass, 130 Oct. 12" (Plate 332) have writing on their cliffs that I decipher tentatively as "yellow hills." In the lower

PLATE 331. Composite drawing and photograph

left-hand corner is some script to which I cannot ascribe a meaning. At the lower right is a face in profile wearing a hat, also to no purpose that I can discover. At this point the expedition was being accompanied by some Utah Indians, of whom one would later consent to be their guide, and Kern, with his distaste for Indians, may have caricatured one of them. The time of 1:30 is too early because the expedition was crossing a stream 8 1/2 miles away at noon, and the first entry for the camp that evening at Oak Springs is 6:00 p.m. The pencil stroke for "1" looks heavier than the rest of the inscription, as if a change was made by overwriting something; enlarging it and comparing it with the "1" in "12" makes it possible to read the time as perhaps 7:30.

PLATE 332. Near Wah-satch Pass, 1:30 [7:30?] p.m., October 12. 23.6 x 14.8 cm

This is another scene that Bonnie Hardwick located for me; she was on Utah Highway 10 near its intersection with I-70 when she spotted the distinctive top of the isolated "chimney." It is on the Oak Creek Ranch, on the south side of which is an entry gate accessible from the service road along I-70 near Fremont Junction. The gate was locked, but next to it was a sign with a phone number for Brad Johnson, the owner, one that Sam Singleton had also given me back in Ferron. When I called him, Brad gave me the days and times that it would be open, and told me just to go onto the ranch and explore it as I saw fit. I did so, and as I was driving down one of the ranch's main roads a man in a pickup truck came along in the opposite direction. We stopped opposite each other, and his first words were "How may I help you?" He turned out to be Clint Johnson, Brad's son, whom Brad had not told that I might be coming. This is the sort of reception a stranger can count on among ranchers of the West, especially in Utah. He looked over my copy of the drawing and suggested how I might best approach the scene. I also learned that the Spanish Trail went through a ranch on the west side of Wasatch Pass that belonged to Stewart Johnson, Clint's uncle, for whom he gave me contact information in case I needed to search for something over there.

Much to my delight, as I continued on my way I unexpectedly came upon "Little Mountains" (Plate 335), photographed it, and then continuing came upon a clear view of "Near Wah-satch Pass" (Plate 332), the whereabouts of which I already knew. For the latter I started close to the subject and

PLATE 333. Photograph near Wah-satch Pass

PLATE 334. Composite drawing and photograph

moved gradually away from it to try to find Kern's vantage point, but as it turned out the terrain in front of the scene is crossed by a series of deep but dry washes, some of which some are visible in the photograph, and I was occupied for half a day going up, down, and over them before I finally emerged at what seemed to be the right spot. Behind and to my left were some hills that prevented me from backing up any farther without either going too high or having one of them obscure the view on the left.

The viewpoint I was practically forced to adopt makes the tall, narrow "chimney" on the right protrude above the horizon, which it does not do in the sketch. Climbing the hill immediately behind me remedied that, but at the price of misaligning everything else. Thunderstorms were swiftly approaching, and so as not to be caught in the open when they arrived I had to make a rapid decision; consequently I took the photograph from the lower point of view. Then I walked out the easy way, which would have been the easy way in as well if I had only known where I was going. That was to follow the route of the power lines on the left in the photograph, which lead directly back to where I was parked. It was only after I got home and studied this drawing and my photograph at leisure that I realized the sketch is incomplete, and my hastily adopted point of view was the correct one; Kern left a gap in the background mountain through which he must have meant to extend the "chimney" to its full height, but he never did so.

PLATE 335. Little Mountains [October 12 or 13] 12.8 x 7.7 cm

PLATE 336. Photograph, Little Mountains

In the *Report* Beckwith points out several times that "Little Mountain" north of the Green River ford turns west and connects with the Wasatch Range, and that the two share a similar appearance. His observation had drawn me into an extensive search over the deserts for this subject, and, tantalizingly, the character of the mountains in many of the places I visited very much reflected that seen in the sketch. Ultimately the scene depicted in "Little Mountains" appeared before my eyes when I was not looking for it, as described above. It is in the foothills of the Wasatch Range just west of a large irrigated alfalfa field, 130 miles of travel and almost two weeks away by expeditionary reckoning from Beckwith's first mention of "Little Mountain." The title is in the block letters that have occurred on a few other sketches, and I can only speculate that it was given its name on the basis of its general appearance, of the similarity in topography between the Wasatch and the Little Mountains (Plate 335), and from the suggestion by Beckwith that since the two merge they are really part of the same mountain range. The two buttes that are the subject of this drawing are also visible in the previous illustration (Plate 332), as the left center and right center background formations.

### AT LAST! AN INDIAN WILLING TO ACT AS GUIDE!

The appearance of the terrain in the two previous drawings (Plates 332 and 335) that Kern made from "Camp 88, Oak

PLATE 337. Composite drawing and photograph

springs" (G-B, 105) conforms to Beckwith's description of the eastern face of the Wasatch Mountains, in front of which the expedition traveled toward its encampment that night. At Oak Springs one of the Indians the expedition had met a few days previous, Tewip Narrienta, agreed to guide them over the mountains and into the Great Basin.

> October 12.—... A series of sandstone spurs, rising one above another, sets down from this southern range, joining the Rock hills to the east, whilst numerous small lateral valleys branch off to the west towards the gorges, among sandstone peaks and tables overlying clay, which form the eastern range of the Wahsatch mountains. These bluish clay cliffs, from two hundred to three hundred feet high, are capped with red and argillaceous sandstone a hundred feet thick, and thence sweep gently up to the summits of the mountains... We encamped...at Oak spring...
>
> Tewip Narrienta, or Powerful Earth, one of our Utah acquaintances of four days' standing, came up with us to-day, having overcome his fear of the Mormons so far as to determine him to accompany us three or four days as a guide... (G-B, 65).

> Our journey, following the direction of the Span. Trail, leads through valleys and hills, and over two creeks containing water, we cross a valley in the mountains and encamp on the West end... One of the Indians we met at the Garambuga overtakes us today, to go with us as a guide over the mountains. Another we find single on our camp. It seems they are whipped by the Mormons and roam about separated, living on berries, roots, insects viz. like beasts. (Creutzfeldt, October 12).

Nephi City
Fillmore
FROM THE VALLEY OF GREEN RIVER TO THE GREAT SALT LAKE
HON. JEFFERSON DAVIS SECRETARY OF WAR

# 7

# Rushing to the Massacre

**OVER THE WASATCH MOUNTAINS AND INTO THE GREAT BASIN; FOLLOWING THE SEVIER RIVER TO ITS LAKE, WHERE GUNNISON AND KERN MAKE CAMP FOR THE LAST TIME**

*From the eastern base of the Wahsatch mountains, via the Wahsatch Pass and Sevier river, to near the Sevier lake, the most western point of explorations, and back to Cedar springs, after the death of Captain Gunnison.*

*—October 13 to 28, 1853 (G-B, 66)*

THE EXPEDITION LEFT ITS CAMP at Oak Springs and by the end of the day had crested Wahsatch Pass and entered the Great Basin, making camp at Salt Creek, on the western slope of the Wasatch Mountains.

> *October* 13.—Passing a low break in a ridge of hills to the south of our camp, after a ride of a mile we reached the Akanaquint, a small mountain brook... [O]ur Indian guide...told us that a circle in red, high up on a sheltered rock on the face of one of the hills, where some rude human figures are seen, also sketched in red lines, was called Akanaquint. These rude figures, in the place in which they are seen, were a great wonder to him, and he had often attempted to describe them to us during the previous day, telling us that they had been made by an American captain—all chief men of parties are captains with these Indians—who had passed here on his way to California, which the Indians know by the name of Monterey; and in pointing them out to us, he seemed to think he was showing a remarkable sight...
>
> Salt creek [today Salina Creek], our Indian guide says (as well as we can understand him, and the appearance of the mountains confirm his statement,) enters a large cañon two miles below our camp, in a very direct course to the Sevier river. Through this cañon, he says, there is a horse-trail, but that it is impossible for wagons to pass through it without removing the rocks. The stream, to where it enters this gorge, continues its easy descent (G-B, 66-67).

This is the only mention of rock art in the *Report*, and there is only one sketch of an example in the album, apparently of a pictograph (Plate 338). It depicts an Indian with bow, shield, and lance mounted on a stallion, and since the horse is a Spanish introduction to the New World it must date from historic times, but the drawing cannot be directly associated with the narrative account. The bluff on the left

PLATE 338. [Bluff and Pictograph], 11.2 x 3.2 cm
VIEW PLATE 338: www.Kernsketches.com/plate/338

side of the sheet may be the site of the pictograph, but it is not detailed enough for me to hope to find it.

The gorge leading into the Great Basin does indeed become very narrow, and the early automotive highway built here had to have several tunnels cut into the rock walls overlooking the stream. To avoid this impassably constricted defile, the expedition first ascended southwest along Yogo Creek and then crossed over to Niotche Creek.

> *October* 14.—Leaving the little valley of Salt creek... we passed over a small hill to the south, and almost immediately struck a fine little stream [Yogo Creek], which we ascended for half a mile, and then crossing another divide to the southwest, reached the Swam-bah [Niotche Creek], an ice-cold creek, two or three feet wide, falling over a rocky bed. This stream rises to the south in one of the highest ranges in the vicinity, on which are large banks of snow, and flows in a narrow ravine, in a nearly direct line for ten or fifteen miles, as seen from the summit of a high peak ascended during the day. It is densely lined, throughout its entire length, with willow-bushes, interspersed with aspens and a few spruce and pines. The Spanish trail, leading for a short distance up this creek, the guide represented as being much more practicable than any other for wagons; and we therefore followed it for two miles and three-quarters, to where the trail leaves it. The labor on this short space was very considerable, occupying a large party the whole day in cutting willows and digging down the banks to allow us repeatedly to cross and recross the creek, and to pass along the narrow ravine; two wagons having overturned after the road was deemed practicable. Our progress was five miles during the day, encamping at sundown at the mouth of a beautiful ravine of abundant grass, with fine groves of aspen on the hill-sides... (G-B, 67-68).

In the pass we find marshy ground, which after the report of our Indian goes on increasingly downward and is impracticable. Therefore we turn towards S.W. and are obliged to follow a creek upwards, where, though a trail is running we have great difficulties in transporting our wagons. The mountains with its valleys are very pretty and must have a luxuriant growth, the soil being good; fragments of many plants are to be seen and good grass, but wood is scarce though splendid specimens of *Abies alba*

PLATE 339. Sierra de Wahsatch on White Pine Creek, October 14, 1845 [1853], 11.0 x 14.6 cm

> [silver fir] are growing on the creek perhaps 150 high (Creutzfeldt, October 14).

Niotche Creek and the Spanish Trail go through the ranch that belongs to Brad Johnson's brother, Stewart. I went to the ranch headquarters to meet him, and he gave me permission to search on the ranch property. Then Stewart's son, Jared, appeared; I showed him the sketch "Sierra de Wahsatch On white pine Creek Oct 14, 1845" (Plate 339) and his response was: "I think I know where that is. I grew up here." I gave him a copy of the sketch and he went off on his motorcycle to look, while I spent the rest of the day fruitlessly searching along what I thought was the most likely route of the expedition. I later met Jared back at the ranch house, where he told me he was sure he had found it, so we made arrangements for him to take me there the next day. He did so by using an all-terrain vehicle, and because the site was heavily overgrown he thoughtfully brought rope so we could tie back trees if necessary—which it was. This was a most unlikely find, and never in my wildest imagination could I have succeeded in locating it on my own.

The trees in the ravine are perhaps more dense than was the case in 1853; by moving around, observing its cliffs through the overgrowth, and constructing a mental image of

PLATE 340. Photograph on White Pine Creek

PLATE 341. Composite drawing and photograph

them, I seemed to have found the subject of Kern's drawing, but it is impossible to visualize it as a whole in a photograph. The same problem occurred on Mission Creek at the Kansas River (Plate 6). By looking through the obscuring trees in the photograph one can make out parts of the cliff, the mental sum of which does a fair job of approximating those represented in the drawing. The only vantage point that avoided most of the trees and included a view of both the near cliffs and the distant mountain was on top of a very large boulder; there was no choice. Jared tied back the nearest trees and

I scrambled up the giant rock with my camera equipment, where there was room enough for the tripod and just barely for me as well. To provide a sense of scale for the picture he ascended the opposite side of the ravine and stood near the edge of its high, steep precipice. Is it possible that the tree with the double trunk in the sketch is the same one to the left of Jared in my photograph?

A day later, on October 15, the men of the expedition made "Camp 91, Ungottahbikin creek" (G-B, 105). along what is today Gooseberry Creek, where they rested over the Sabbath and departed on the morning of October 17. Here their Utah Indian guide took his leave and turned back towards his home, but Indian names for geographic features continue to appear on Kern's sketches, in the narrative of the *Report*, and in Beckwith's *Journal*; they probably originated with two Mormon guides whom Gunnison hired a few days later.

### TEWIP NARRIENTA PRUDENTLY TURNS BACK—NOT A GOOD OMEN, BUT WHO WAS PAYING ATTENTION?

> *October 17.*—Our Utah guide, Tewip Narrienta, left us this morning to return to his squaw and papoose, for whom he expressed much fear lest in his absence they might suffer for want of food; but, as they were subsisting when he left them on the still abundant en-carpe, or buffalo berries, gathered by the squaw, there was no doubt that his anxiety was attributable to our proximity to the Mormon settlements. He repeatedly warned us against these people. His services for the few days that he was with us were valuable; for he was one of the best guides I have ever seen, and was as good a judge of natural wagon roads as any one, and was of course familiar with his own hunting-grounds.
>
> ... "I have reconnoitred," says Captain Gunnison, "much of this mountain and hilly region while the party has been engaged in its passage. From a high ridge which I ascended on the 14th instant... On all sides were mountains, peaks, and ridges, abrupt bluffs with white cliffs capping the summits; and the deep cañon, which has driven us over a mountain much higher than the summit of the pass itself, lay three miles to the north. Through this a railroad track might be made, but, owing to the cutting of rock, at a very great expense."...
>
> A pleasant sight to us...was a few wagon-tracks, after months of toiling without a road, and frequently without trails even, in an unexplored and wild coun-

> try. These wagons had been here, as we subsequently learned, to procure salt... (G-B, 68-69).

Once again there were clear warning signs in the cautious behavior and repeated admonitions from a friendly Utah Indian who had done good service as a guide, and whose departure came the same day that the expedition discovered tracks of Mormon wagons. In the densely wooded Wasatch Mountains an Indian like Tewip Narrienta could find plentiful cover, but on the open plains of the Sevier River Valley he would become easy prey for the settlers, should they choose to kill him.

In the narrative of the *Report* for September 17, Beckwith inserts a long excerpt from Captain Gunnison's notebook. The Wasatch Mountains had been crossed and the expedition was entering the Great Basin; the difficult tasks assigned to Gunnison in his original orders seemed to have been largely accomplished. Now Gunnison took the opportunity to privately exult over his achievements, and their import for the country and for his reputation.

> *October* 17.—(continued)... In entering this valley, Captain Gunnison, with two or three men, rode forward, in advance of his party, "and enjoyed the scene extremely. On reaching this plain a stage is attained," he says, "which I have so long desired to accomplish: the great mountains have been passed and a new wagon road open across the continent—a work which was almost unanimously pronounced impossible, by the men who know the mountains and this route over them.
>
> "The result is, a new mail and military road to Taos, in New Mexico, by way of Fort Massachusetts; which, with a little work on Gunnison's creek and a hill near Taos, will be very direct and easy, with excellent feed and water all the way.
>
> "2d. A road for the southern States to California, and for emigrants who are late in starting from the States.
>
> "3d. A military road to, and command of, the Utah country, passing into the center of the territory of that people at Grand river, from whence radiate trails to all points of the compass.
>
> "4th. It is demonstrated that, for a railroad route, it is far inferior to the Middle Central, by Medicine Bow river, and Laramie plains. It passes some thousands of feet higher, and also lower, and is much longer from St. Louis.

“To the energy, zeal, and ability of Lieutenant Beckwith, and Brevet Captain Morris, in superintending the working parties and conducting the train, the expedition is greatly indebted. That a road for nearly seven hundred miles should have been made over an untrodden track, (except in some places by pack-mules and footmen,) through a wilderness all the way, and across five mountain ranges, (the Sierra Blanca, San Juan, Uncompahgra, Sandstone, and Wahsatch,) and a dry desert of seventy miles between Grand and Green rivers, without deserting one of our nineteen wagons, and leaving but one animal from sickness and one from straying, and this in two and a half months, must be my excuse for speaking highly of all the assistants on this survey” (G-B, 70).

The pride he exhibits here may to some degree have contributed to his demise, because, in thrall to its force, he divided his command in order to complete the survey before winter. Otherwise Gunnison exaggerates only to a small degree the extent of the expedition’s success, and includes high praise for his fellow officers and assistants that was no doubt well deserved.

PLATE 342. From 1:10 p.m., October 17, entering the Sevier River Valley from Wasatch Pass. Bottom sketch of two on a sheet

The expedition continued down the valley and reached Salt Creek a few miles above where it enters the valley of the Sevier River; here Kern made a sketch that included mountains on the far side of the valley “From 1.10 Ocb 17 entering Sevier R. valley - from Wah-satch Pass” (Plate 342). This view can be seen from I-70, and is another that Bonnie Hardwick first located for me by noting the mountain in the center with its distinctive pointed summit; today it is called Beehive Peak.

This is the bottom sketch on a sheet of two (Plate 309) that both depict the landscape ahead as the expedition entered a valley. In the photograph (Plate 343) I-70 is on the right descending toward the Sevier Valley, and FR 037

PLATE 343. Photograph entering the Sevier River Valley

PLATE 344. Composite drawing and photograph

can be seen in front of the stand of trees; it has replaced the Indian trail the expedition followed down from camp along Ungottahbikin (today Gooseberry) Creek. A few miles west of this site the expedition reached the Sevier River and traveled northward down its valley, while Gunnison went in search of the Mormons.

> October 18$^{th}$. Captain Gunnison, who had been out during the day in search of a settlement, returned to camp not having succeeded in his object (Beckwith, *Journal*).

The next day they made Camp 94, Sevier River (G-B, 106) at a site that is now underwater near the eastern shore of Yuba Lake, also known as Sevier Bridge Reservoir. The mountains Kern drew that evening "From 4.10 Ocb. 19 Kah-kah-nak-ah-nit. Wah-Satch Mts (Plate 345) are to the north, and not visible from the campsite; he traveled several miles over intervening hills in what is now Yuba State Park to obtain his view. This scene shows territory into which the expedition was not immediately going to travel; it includes most prominently Mount Nebo on the left, which is the highest peak in the Wasatch Range and a landmark that is visible for great distances. Beckwith mentioned it in his private journal the next day, but it is not alluded to in the *Report* until a week

PLATE 345. From 4:10 October 19, Kah-kah-nak-ah-rah-nit, Wasatch Mountains 15.0 x 4.5 cm

PLATE 346. Photograph, Kah-kah-nak-ah-rah-nit

later. On the right and somewhat nearer is Salt Creek Peak. From its camp the expedition turned west and south to follow the Emigrant Road to California.

The haze in the Sevier Valley seems perpetual and severe, but it was still possible to get a just satisfactory photograph of the scene on one of my visits to the site. I have not, however, been able to track down the origin of

PLATE 347. Composite drawing and photograph

"Kah-kah-nak-ah-rah-nit"; it is not mentioned in the *Report* or in Beckwith's *Journal*. I imagine it to be a transliteration of the Indian name for Mount Nebo.

The following day the expedition moved just a couple of miles west to a campsite that today is also under Yuba Lake, "Camp 95, on north bend of Sevier river, one mile above bridge" (G-B, 106). In his private journal entry for the day, Beckwith described, in addition to Mount Nebo, the ruins of a bridge and some of the surrounding scenery.

> October 20... At this point there are still standing the base of a Mormon bridge which has been swept

away by high water, some of the timbers having been found and preserved on the shore and are doubtless intended for use in rebuilding the bridge... Through the break in the first range of mountains to the east, the Moot-se-neah peak is seen in the midst of the snow, still towering beautifully above all the other peaks near it... [L]eaving apparently an open passage on each side of it, Mt. Nebo stands detached & solitary & precipitous, a fine, large mountain of itself with its summit high above the nearest ranges (Beckwith, *Journal*).

None of this fine literary rendering of the scene was included in the *Report*, displaced perhaps by more ominous information that came with the return of Captain Gunnison, who had gone the previous day through some of the Mormon settlements in search of supplies and a guide.

#### THE DEFENSIVE PRECAUTIONS TAKEN BY THE MORMON SETTLERS ARE OBSERVED AND DESCRIBED BY CAPTAIN GUNNISON

> *October* 20.— ... Captain Gunnison left us at our camp of yesterday morning, and proceeded up the valley of San Pete, or the northeastern extension of the valley of the Sevier river, to the settlement at Manti City, eighteen miles from that camp. He found the settlers, a hundred families, all gathered into a village for mutual protection against the Utah Indians, who have killed several of the citizens, destroyed their mills, and driven off some of their stock; but this has been accomplished by no means with impunity. A strong guard was posted at this settlement at night. Having procured some necessary supplies and guides (two brothers, G. G. and William Potter) to accompany him to the Sevier lake, Captain Gunnison rejoined us at a late hour (G-B, 71).

Creutzfeldt recorded an account of Gunnison's return to the expedition that echoed Beckwith's.

> We wait here for the return of the captain, who arrives in the evening with a wagon, two Mormons and a Spaniard. They bring with them fresh meat and will serve as guides. They tell of bloody conflict with the Indians having murdered six of their men and carried away 200 cattle. The distant settlers had for their safety to move to Salt L. City, from whence they are

returning now. The captain met about 16 m. from our camp of the day before yesterday nearly 100 families of these settlers... (Creutzfeldt, October 20).

While in Manti Gunnison anticipated that from Utah he would be able to send mail, and so wrote what was to be his last letter to his wife. In it, among other things, he acknowledged that he had been somewhat cavalier in his attitudes and actions with respect to the war between the Utahs and the Mormons. The date should probably be October 19 or 20.

> City of Manti, Oct 18 1853
> My Dear Wife
> ...I have to go back to find my camp in the morning & have hired two guides around to Utah from Sevier Lakes—This will take ten or twelve days, & then I shall send for my letters. There is a war between the Mormons & the Indians & parties of less than a dozen do not dare to travel. We did not know what a risk we have lately been running until coming here —for I have been riding carelessly in the mountains hunting roads ahead and other curious capers —but I made friends with a Utah Indian who has been with me for a week until Sunday when he put'back to his squaw and papooses, not daring to come near these people...
>
> ...may the favor of Heaven attend us until the work is accomplished in a like manner as heretofore... (Gunnison Archives, Huntington Library).

"The favor of Heaven" was not to endure. Against all advice, in the face of the unanimously apprehensive demeanor of Indians with regard to the conflict in the Great Basin, and despite his own clearly expressed understanding of the situation, Gunnison determined to divide his party and rush to complete his surveys in time to go to winter quarters before the onset of cold weather.

If the sight of the town of Manti "forting up" was unsettling to Gunnison, it still did not lead him to take appropriate precautions. During this period he also met with Anson Call, the president of the community of Fillmore. Call's position of responsibility obliged him to constantly monitor the activities and moods of nearby Indians, and his warning couldn't have been more explicit. Call reminisced in his autobiography about the meeting with Gunnison:

> These outrageous proceedings [the killing of some peaceful Indians by a party of emigrants traveling through] enraged the Indians, so that they became infuriated and could not be pacified. They were so

> excited that nothing short of blood would appease their wrath...In this time of excitement, Captain Gunnison and his exploring party came along...he came to Fillmore and I had an interview with him...I invited him to rest a while till the Indians became cooled down...I entreated him to exercise great caution and disclosed to him my fears that the Indians would if they could have satisfaction from the first white man or men they met...
>
> Captain Gunnison, however, did not accept my invitation, but went on, with about twelve others and Potter the guide, to explore the lake (Call, 1986).

After hearing this, and even though he had observed firsthand the defensive measures being taken by the settlers, Gunnison politely declined to follow Call's advice. He also appears to have been less than candid with his second in command about the counsel he had received, both from Anson Call and no doubt from other Mormons as well.

> It was known to the party that a band of Indians was near them for we had seen their fires daily since entering the valley; but an unusual feeling of security against them was felt, as Captain Gunnison had learned that a recent quarrel, resulting in several deaths which they had with emigrants, had terminated, and that notwithstanding this difficulty they had remained at peace with the neighboring settlers, which had been confirmed and guarantied for the future in a "talk" held with some of the Indians of this band, by an agent of the governor of the Territory, during our stay near Fillmore. This information, Captain Gunnison told me before leaving, relieved him from any apprehension he might otherwise have felt regarding this band... (G-B, 73-74).

The intelligence Beckwith received from Gunnison was exactly the opposite of the warning that Gunnison had been given by President Call. Why this pretense? Perhaps tensions and disagreements between the two officers, which the tactful Beckwith often implies but never describes explicitly in his writings, lay behind it. The conflict may have originated in Gunnison's lack of rapport with the guide Antoine Leroux, whose expert advice Gunnison repeatedly disregarded. Strains between the two officers seem to have increased over this and over Gunnison's inexplicable choices of more difficult routes across Utah; its rising intensity perhaps now led Gunnison to avoid an unpleasant, time-consuming confrontation by being less than candid with his underling, for if he had been more forthcoming about what he had learned from Anson Call, the cool-headed Beckwith would undoubtedly have expressed the strongest possible disagreement with his superior's reckless decision. The officers of the Mounted Riflemen, Captain Morris and Lieutenant Baker, should also have been part of the discussion but apparently were not.

While these difficulties and uncertainties swirled about his commanders, Kern made a three-part panorama, "From Mormon Bridge, Sevier River Oct. 20th" (Plate 348). The drawings are on two sheets that are attached to a single page of the album, one above the other, and have alignment marks. The horizontal scale is irregular, so it cannot be fitted well to a photograph; as before in such cases I simply aligned the ends and let the rest fall as it may. The view is westward toward part of the Un-kuk-oo-ap Mountains, and in the foreground is the floodplain through which the Sevier River winds its way from left to right. Beckwith described the area on October 17 when the expedition had just entered the Sevier Valley and gained its first unbroken view of the valley, then again on the 21st.

PLATE 348. From Mormon Bridge, Sevier River, October 20. Upper sheet 16.8 x 9.7 cm; lower sheet 16.8 x 6.3 cm

> *October 17.* (Continued)... we entered the broad valley of the Sevier river... on the west a range of the Wahsatch mountains, Un-kuk-oo-ap, extends to

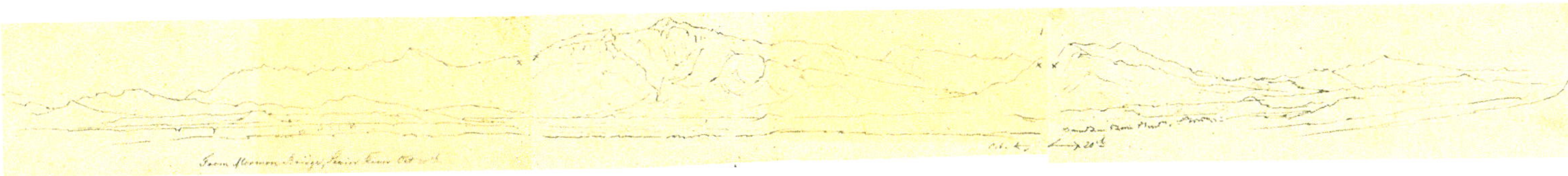

PLATE 349. Continuous panoramic drawing

PLATE 350. Panoramic photograph from Mormon Bridge, Sevier River

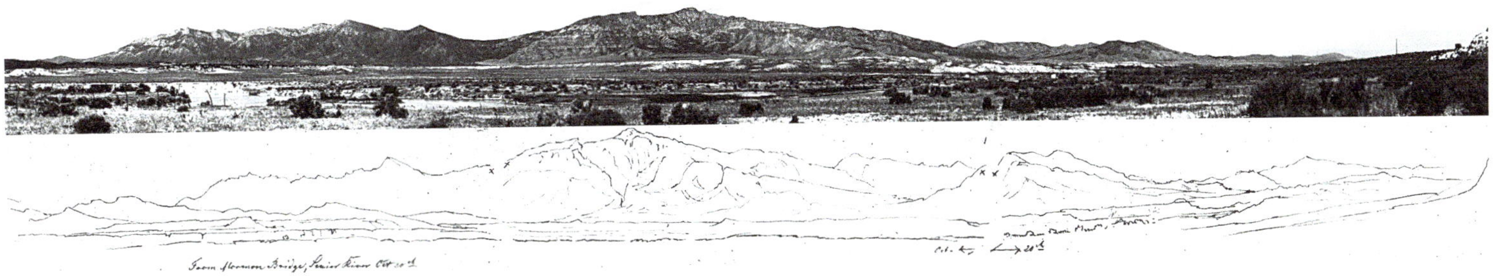

PLATE 351. Composite drawing and photograph

the north, until broken by the passage of the river, beyond which, in a low range, it still extends to the north... (G-B, 69).

October 21.—... The country from our camp to the cañon of the river being broken, and the guides never having passed through it, we crossed the river and followed the California road, passing a low range of hills, within a short distance, into a small valley in the Un-kuk-oo-ap mountains—the Indian name of the range lying in the bend of the Sevier river.

PLATE 352. From 11:00 a.m., October 21, Wasatch Mountains

This valley, from a small pond which stands several miles to the south of the road, is called Lake valley. To the south of this pond there is said to be an easy pass descending by a creek to the Sevier river. This, if practicable, would lessen the distance considerably from the point where we first came upon the river, westward to this point (G-B, 71).

In the muted, respectful-sounding style he adopts for such occasions, Beckwith points out that the expedition once more took the long way around an obstacle by staying close to the Sevier River, instead of sending out a scouting party to determine the best way forward. Of course these failings are more obvious after a century and a half of surveying and settlement, but he is correct; the corridor he describes is a relatively easy one and is now taken by US 50 northwest from Salina to the town of Scipio.

PLATE 353. Continuous panorama

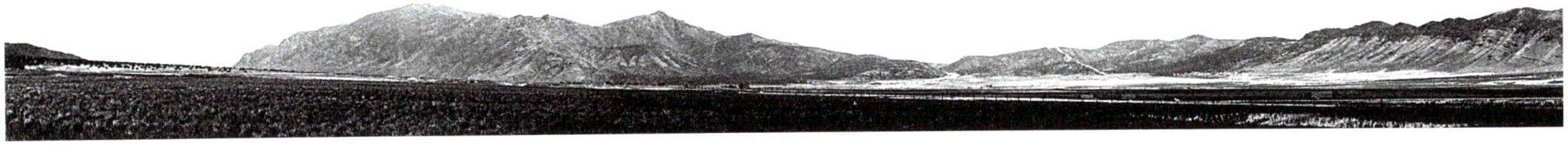

354. Photograph, Wasatch Mountains

The California road passed not far from Camp 95, which was at or under today's Yuba Lake. In the late morning, as the expedition moved south along it, Kern made a highly schematic two-part panorama of some of the Un-kuk-oo-ap Mountains to the south and west "From 11 Oct 21. Wah-satch Mts" (Plate 352). The low level of detail is characteristic of this and of the last two surviving works, made as the expedition wended its way down the Sevier River towards disaster. Because the exploring season was nearly over and because of the exhaustion that afflicted both animals and men, Kern may have husbanded his remaining energy in anticipation of a winter's respite in Salt Lake City from the rigors of travel. The impending task would be to create the maps of the expedition from his field notes, and with that to look forward to he may have become less and less involved in what was, all considered, only a secondary concern.

Today a portion of the California road from Mormon Bridge has become Utah 78; here it intersects I-15, which in

PLATE 355. Composite drawing and photograph

PLATE 356. October 25, 1854 [1853], Great Basin. 20.4 x 14.1 cm

turn can be seen in the center of the photograph (Plate 354) curving and climbing into the same low gap the expedition followed over the Pahvant Range into the valley of Sevier Lake. The high peaks here are identical with those seen on the left in the previous drawing (Plates 348 and 349), but now, from much closer up, they occupy half the panorama.

There is a four-day interval before the next surviving sketch in the album "Oct. 25th 1854 - Great Basin" (Plates 356 and 357), during which time the expedition moved about in the Sevier River Valley; this drawing again shows a diminished attention to the task. "Camp 98, Sevier river" (G-B, 106), occupied from the afternoon of October 24 to the morning of October 25, was in the middle of the present-day town of Holden, Utah. As far as I can determine the sketch was made from the campsite; it was out on a plain and would have afforded a clear view of the mountains to the north and east. Because of trees in town the campsite no longer offers an unobstructed view of the mountains; I had to move my vantage point about a mile to the north, from which US 50 and the outskirts of Holden are visible on the right side in the photograph (Plate 358). The surrounding hills are all part of the Un-kuk-oo-ap; the highest peak on the left is Blue Mountain, in today's Canyon Mountains. The hills on the right are the same part of the Pahvant Range that was prominent in the previous two illustrations, but this time seen from the west, so their contour is roughly reversed. This is the last dated sketch by Richard Kern that we have, though ironically it is misdated to 1854. It must have been made in the morning because later that day Kern left camp with Gunnison for Sevier Lake, not knowing that this was to be his final, fatal journey.

> *October* 25.—Captain Gunnison, with Mr. R. H. Kern, Mr. F. Creutzfeldt, and Mr. Wm. Potter, (guide,) with John Bellows, and a corporal and six men from the escort, left camp at a late hour this

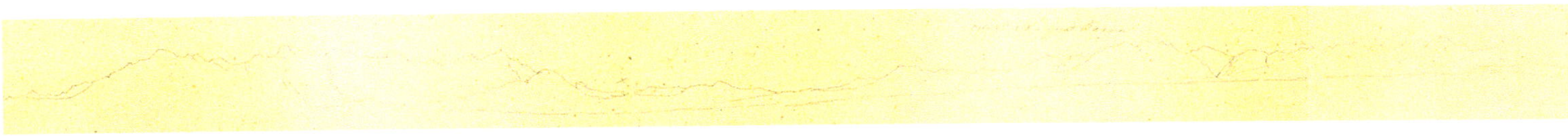

PLATE 357. Continuous panoramic drawing

PLATE 358. Photograph

morning to explore the vicinity of Sevier lake, supposed to be distant some fifteen or eighteen miles (G-B, 72).

Later Beckwith described the unfortunate sequel in his usual restrained manner, no doubt taking into account the sensibilities of Gunnison's widow. In a respectful, indirect style, he nonetheless lays the blame squarely on the shoulders of Captain Gunnison, who had received but ignored multitudinous warnings about the climate of violence then prevalent in Utah. Ironically, it was a revenge killing that destroyed the lives of Gunnison, Kern, and the others, rather than an incident in the war between Walker's band of Utah Indians and the Mormons, concerning which there had been so many portents. Nonetheless, appropriate precautions against that threat and against the level of violence then prevalent in the

PLATE 359. Composite drawing and photograph

PLATE 360. Jo-on-Kah-Pa-ga-mu [October 25?] 14.8 x 5.2 cm

PLATE 361. Photograph, Jo-on-Kah-Pa-ga-mu

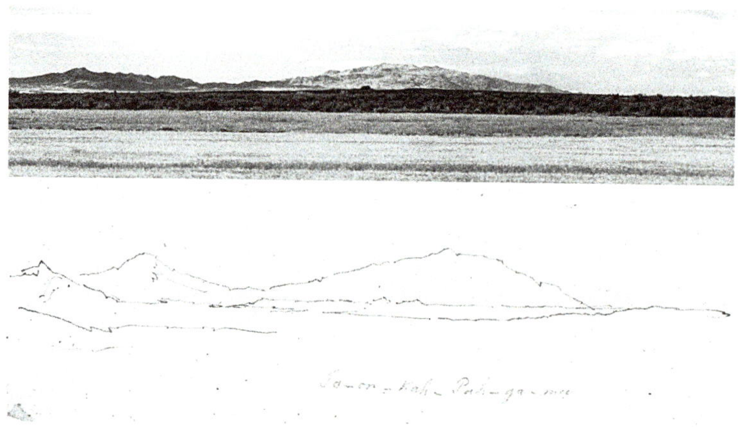

PLATE 362. Composite

region might well have forestalled the disaster that finally overtook the expedition.

> Captain Gunnison had encamped early in the afternoon, while the wind and storm were yet fresh, and doubtless feeling the security which men come to indulge after passing long periods of time surrounded by savages without actually encountering them. The abundant grass and fuel of a little nook in the river bottom, sheltered by the high second bank of the river on one side, and thick willows, distant scarcely

> thirty yards, on two of the others, with the river in front, offered a tempting place of comfort and utility, which was perhaps accepted without even a thought of danger (G-B, 73).

There is an undated drawing (Plate 360) captioned "Jo-on-Kah-Pa-ga-mu," a transliteration that strongly implies the subject is in Utah. After searches elsewhere failed I went to the massacre site, and found the subject several miles north of that fatal spot. "Jo-on-Kah-Pa-ga-mu" (I read the first letter as "J") is probably an Indian name for the mountain in the drawing, and in all likelihood came from William Potter, the guide. It would have to have been completed in the late afternoon of October 25, while the small group of men with Captain Gunnison were making their ill-defended camp at Sevier Lake. This simple sketch is the last that Kern ever drew.

# 8

# Scenes Unseen

THESE ARE THE DRAWINGS that I have failed to locate and photograph. First are those that have already appeared in the text, because I have a fairly good idea of where in the sequence they belong.

PLATE 4. Camp No. 1, June 20, 1853, near Westport

PLATE 9. Kansas River [June 29?]

PLATE 10. Uniontown, Kaw River [June 29]

PLATE 14. Crossing Saline Creek, July 7, 1853

PLATE 15. Crossing Saline, July 7, 1853

PLATE 17. Arkansas Plains

PLATE 16. Elk Island, Arkansas, July 20

PLATE 108. Peaks of the Sierra Blanca

PLATE 206. Western slopes of Sawatch Mountains

PLATE 189. Bottom. Sawatch Mountains [September 5]

PLATE 239. From 10:20 a.m. September 8, affluent of Grand River

PLATE 261. Grand River Canyon (leaving the river), September 10

PLATE 262. Canyon on Grand River

PLATE 263. Grand River Canyons

PLATE 264. Grand River

PLATE 298. Desert between Grand and Green rivers

PLATE 265. Grand River

PLATE 338. [Bluff and Pictograph]

The remaining unlocated drawings are included so that none of Kern's work from the expedition is omitted. The drawings fall into five broad categories: 1. Detailed representations with adequate titles that should, in principal, have been located; 2. Detailed views with absent or very general titles that, if found, would have been recognized without difficulty; 3. Partial or incomplete views with or without captions that even if encountered might well not have been recognized; 4. Landscape details with or without captions that could only by the most extreme good fortune have been located; 5. Drawings of botanical or incidental subjects, with or without titles.

These sketches for which the subjects have not been located are sequenced according to their position within the Newberry album. I would be very interested in hearing from anyone who manages to find one of these. The number in parentheses is that found next to each drawing, on the page where it is attached in the album.

PLATE 363. Untitled (#31).22.4 x 14.6 cm

PLATE 364. Rocky Mountains formation (#34)12.2 x 6.8 cm

PLATE 365. Wasatch Mountains (#46) 12.2 x 6.8 cm

PLATE 367. Sierra Blanca (#88) 12.9 x 6.3 cm

The original of plate 366 was attached face down in the album as it appears on the left; on the right is the same drawing that has been re-reversed to its correct orientation.

PLATE 366. Rocky Mountains (#86) 4.4 x 9.0 cm

PLATE 368. Plains (#89) 9.3 x 6.5 cm

PLATE 369. Untitled (#93)

PLATE 370. Untitled [child in cradle board] (#95), 3.1 x 7.5 cm

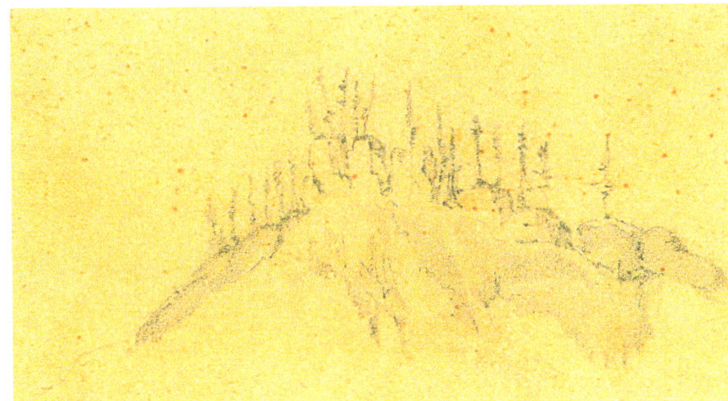

PLATE 371. Untitled (#97), 11.8 x 6.7 cm

PLATE 372. Untitled (#100), 11.7 x 8.2 cm

PLATE 373. Wasatch Mountains (#111), 14.6 x 4.6 cm

PLATE 374. Wasatch Mountains (#112), 14.6 x 5.2 cm

PLATE 375. Rocky Mountains (#120) 11.3 x.8.7 cm

MADELIN PLAINS
PLAINS

# 9

# *Postlude*

## FRIEDRICH VON EGLOFFSTEIN'S DRAWINGS IN THE NEWBERRY ALBUM

*Eleven Views of Mount Shasta by Friedrich von Egloffstein, and Their Relation to Schumann's Illustrations Accompanying Beckwith's Report on the Second Half of the Expedition, from Utah to California, in 1854*

ONE SHEET AMONG THE MANY in Ayer MS 794a stands apart from the others; it is covered with unsigned sketches of Mount Shasta as it appears from various points of view "Mount Shasta (1.) or (l.)" (Plate 376). The only person to whom such skillfully drawn sketches can logically be attributed is Friedrich von Egloffstein. The letter "(l.)" in the title probably acknowledges a now-obsolete version of the name of the mountain. "Shastl" is the spelling used in the text as well as for a caption on an illustration in Frémont's *Memoirs* (1886). As with any transliteration there are yet other variants, an example of which is "Mt. Tsashtl," on Frémont's map that accompanies his *Geographical Memoir upon Upper California* (1848), although "Shastl" is used in its text. An entry in Lippencott's Pronouncing Gazetteer of 1856 adds some more possibilities.

PLATE 376. F. W. von Egloffstein, Mount Shasta(l.) 21.1 x 15.9 cm

> SHASTE, SHASTA OR SHASTY, shăs'te, sometimes written Chaste, a mountain peak of the Cascade Range, in the N. part of California, in lat. about 41° 20' N., lon. 122° W. Height, about 14,000 feet (Thomas & Baldwin, 1856, 1764).

An alternative reading of (l.) is as the number "1," indicating that there was once at least one more sheet from the 1854 expedition devoted to the subject of Mount Shasta (Rowan, 69).

The style of drawing here is clearly not Kern's, who in any case never reached northern California. By contrast, Egloffstein was there for several months with Beckwith, who was not simply attempting to cross the Sierra Nevada range, but was evaluating several alternative paths through it. As a result, the route the expedition followed could fairly be described as convoluted. While the men moved back and forth through the mountains, Mount Shasta was almost constantly in view as the highest and most prominent landmark. The drawings may have been made directly by observation, or they may have been copied from other sketches that encompassed larger views, or perhaps there are some of each. My first thought was to treat the Shasta set much like the Kern sketches by going to northern California to find the vantage points, and to photograph the view of Shasta from each of them. The earliest of the set is in the upper left and labeled "from Mt. Observation" (Plate 377). Now called Observation Peak, it is twelve miles from the Nevada border and accessible from US 395 just east of Eagle Lake. The atmosphere is so hazy that from it I could see nothing of Shasta, which is 100 miles away. This was not the case in 1854, when Egloffstein and other members of Beckwith's party climbed Mount Observation, and perhaps were responsible for its name as well.

PLATE 377. F. W. von Egloffstein, View of Shasta "from Mt. Observation"

> *June* 22.—... The most remarkable feature in this part of the Sierra Nevada, and a conspicuous landmark, is an elevated conical peak, standing immediately on the eastern limit of this plain, and directly in the line of the Madelin Pass in ascending it from the east. The pass winds immediately around its northern base. Some of the gentlemen of the party ascended it, and were gratified with the magnificent view it afforded; of which the snowy Mount Shasta, to the west of the Sacramento, was the striking feature (Beckwith, 40).

Other limitations besides hazy air defeated my project in northern California, among which were impassable roads, inaccessible places, and off-limits private property. What I did accomplish on this trip was to make infrared photographs of Shasta wherever it was possible, all the while remaining reasonably within the bounds of the territory over which

PLATE 378. C. Schumann, Madelin Pass, June 19, at 2 p.m. View taken from Mount Observation

Beckwith traveled with his expedition; from this limited variety of viewpoints there are some fair approximations to the Shasta of the drawings, but nothing as satisfactory as could be achieved with Richard Kern's work from the year before.

Since the attempt to make photographs for direct comparison with the drawings was a failure, I turned instead to relating the individual views of Shasta to the appearance of the peak in the engraved illustrations by Schumann that were published in conjunction with the Beckwith *Report*. All of the engravings include the date and, with one exception, the time of day, all bear the notation "C. Schumann from F.W. Egloffstein," and all carry detailed captions; four of them depict Shasta. The first is a panorama "Madelin Pass from Mount Observation" (Plate 378). Shasta is a tiny presence just visible on the horizon at the far left. The upper left drawing "from Mt. Observation" (Plate 377) can then be placed within a segment of the panorama for comparison (Plate 379).

PLATE 379. Segment of the engraving "Madelin Pass" with the drawing inserted

A second sketch is dated June 19 and so would have been made nearby (Plate 380), and although not from Mount Observation, it is also a fairly good match to the appearance of Shasta in the engraving titled "Madelin Pass" (Plate 381).

PLATE 380. F. W. von Egloffstein, View of Shasta, "12/19 June"

PLATE 381. C. Schumann, Composite segment of the engraving with "12/19 June" drawing inserted

> *June* 30.—... we therefore followed the old wagon road, near which we had encamped, in a general direction for several miles to the south. It led from camp immediately over a high ridge, affording an extensive view of the mountain country around us, and of a few peaks of the Coast range, seen through low openings in the western ridge of the Sierra Nevada. But the smoky state of the atmosphere was such that no distinctive features or outlines could be traced in the distant scenery (Beckwith, 45).

Despite Beckwith's description of the obfuscating quality of the air on June 30, there is a gorgeous panoramic engraving from 9:00 a.m. that day. Mount Shasta is a dominant presence in "Northern Slopes of the Sierra Nevada, June 30th at 9 A. M. View towards the West" (Plate 382).

The table of observations indicates that it was cloudy that morning, but changed to just light clouds during the day.

PLATE 382. C. Schumann, Northern slopes of the Sierra Nevada, June 30 at 9 a.m., View towards the west, 1854

PLATE 383. F. W. von Egloffstein, View of Shasta "From 1st cañon"

PLATE 384. Composite of engraving, drawing, and photograph

At 8:15 a.m. the expedition was at the "Summit, returning to eastern base of Sierra Nevada," and it must be from that summit that Egloffstein drew the panorama (Beckwith, 92). The expedition was now much closer to Shasta than before, and correspondingly its representation on the horizon is larger. Its appearance is most similar to that seen in the

PLATE 385. C. Schumann, "West End of Madelin Pass. June 26 at 8 A.M. from a Peak Overlooking Madelin Creek. Sacramento River descending through Round Valley in the Distance"

undated sketch "View of Shasta" (Plate 383) and in the composite in Plate 384.

For once, I was able to make a photograph of Shasta from near the spot where Egloffstein had been working. Although its viewpoint is lower down and somewhat off to one side, the photograph (Plate 384, here juxtaposed with both the engraving and the drawing) is still a reasonable match, though it does not show the distinctive palisades that are to the right in the engraving; it is also hard to discern the contours of the land in the mid-distance because of the density of the forest.

PLATE 386. F. W. von Egloffstein, "3/26 June"

PLATE 387. Composite drawing and segment of the engraving

None of the sketches match very well this distant and indistinct view of Shasta in "West End of Madelin Pass. June 26 at 8 A.M. from a Peak Overlooking Madelin Creek." (Plate 385), but the drawing in the top center of the sheet titled "3/26 June" ("July" was overwritten to read "June") is of the same

PLATE 388. C. Schumann, “Portion of the Main Mountain Passage. Of the Upper Sacramento or Pitt River. July 20 at 1 P.M. 25 Miles South of Mt. Shasta”

date and from a position that the expedition occupied just seven hours later (Plate 386). Visually its correspondence with the engraving is adequate but not entirely satisfactory (Plate 387).

Mount Shasta dominates the horizon in the handsome engraving “Portion of the Main Mountain Passage of the Upper Sacramento or Pitt River. July 20 at 1 P.M. 25 Miles South of Mt. Shasta” (Plate 388), but I have my doubts about its identifying title. From the south the appearance of Shasta includes a distinctive interruption on its left slope by a secondary peak, Shastina. On July 20 the expedition was actually southeast of Shasta near the Big Bend of the Pitt River, a position from which Shastina is more hidden, but still presents as a small, clearly visible protuberance on the left slope. The only one of the multiple drawings that by its specificity of outline is a clear candidate to match that silhouette is the large drawing toward the upper right of the sheet, and titled “Camp 27-28.” To make the connection this identification must be interpreted not as the camp numbers, but rather as the dates for the camp, July 27-28. It would then have been drawn from somewhere southeast of Shasta and close to the source of my photograph, which was along Moose Camp Road (Plate 389). Both the sketch and the photograph show the correct irregularities on Shasta’s left slope, but none of this is much help with the engraving, which does not.

It remains unclear just what the relationship of the set of multiple drawings of “Mount Shasta(l.)” is to the illustrations printed for the Beckwith *Report*. My tentative conclusion is that Egloffstein drew this sheet of views simply as a sequential document of Shasta's appearance from various positions. Their occasional similarity to details in Schumann's engravings probably results from the fact that the large-scale landscape drawings for the engravings and these small sketches were created by the same person and from the same places. The sheet of drawings are an intriguing but secondary presence within Ayer MS 794a, the lost, then found, lost again, and finally found again album of Richard Kern's drawings in the Newberry Library of Chicago.

PLATE 389. Composite drawing and photograph of Shasta from the southeast

# *Bibliography*

Because many of the historical works that I cite are available in reprint editions, I have provided direct reference to what I believe to be the most useful the most accessible of those.

The maps I have found to be the most useful and functional for this project are the detailed atlases published for the individual states of Kansas, Colorado, Utah, and California by DeLorme Mapping. I recommend them to anyone attempting to follow the route of Gunnison's expedition, either by armchair or upon the ground. In every case where reference is made to modern geographic details, locations, road designations, or place names I have taken them from these DeLorme publications, unless otherwise indicated.


Albright, George Leslie. *Official Explorations for Pacific Railroads 1853-1855*. Berkeley, California: University of California Press, 1921.

Beckwith, E. G. *Report of Explorations for a Route for the Pacific Railroad, of the Line of the Forty-First Parallel of North Latitude.* 33rd Cong., 2nd sess., House Exec. Doc. 91. Vol. 2. Washington, DC: A. O. P. Nicholson, Printer, 1855, 1-132. (Beckwith's *Report* immediately follows the Gunnison-Beckwith *Report* in Vol. 2; its page numbers restart from 1 instead of continuing at 129.)

Beckwith, E. G. *Journal*. Beckwith Archive, the Huntington Library, San Marino, California.

Briggs, Walter, with oil paintings by Wilson Hurley. *Without Noise of Arms: The 1776 Domínguez-Escalante Search for a Route from Santa Fe to Monterey.* Flagstaff: Northland Press, 1976.

Call, Anson. *The Journal of Anson Call.* Salt Lake City: E. L. Call and C. S. Call, 1986.

Creutzfeldt, Frederick. *Memorandum-book*. Smithsonian Institution Archives, Record Unit 7157, Frederick Kreutzfeldt Journal, 1853.

DeVoto, Bernard. *Across the Wide Missouri*. Boston: Houghton Mifflin Company, 1947.

Dingus, Rick. *The Photographic Artifacts of Timothy O'Sullivan.* Albuquerque: University of New Mexico Press, 1982

Fielding, Robert Kent, ed. *Trails, Narratives and Campsites of the Gunnison Expedition in Utah Territory September 21-November 30, 1853, Preliminary Student Edition*. Typescript, Orem, Utah, 1994. Paradigm Publications, 44 Linden St., Brookline, MA. Distributed by Gunnison Memorial Associates, P. O. Box 377, Higganum, CT 06441-0377 (also may be available from the Utah Humanities Council, Salt Lake City).

Frémont, John Charles. *Memoirs of My Life*. Chicago: Belford, Clarke & Co., 1886.

Frémont, John Charles. "Prospectus" for *Memoirs of My Life*. Chicago: Belford, Clarke & Co., 1886.

Frémont, John Charles. *Geographical Memoir upon Upper California, in Illustration of His Map of Oregon and California*. 30th Cong., 1st sess., S. Misc. Doc. 148. Washington, D. C.: Wendell and Van Benthuysen, Printers, 1848. Reprinted in Mary Lee Spence, ed. *The Expeditions of John Charles Frémont*. Vol. 3. Urbana and Chicago: University of Illinois Press, 1984, 495-570, and Jackson and Spence, 1970, 1: Map Portfolio.

Goetzmann, William H. *Exploration and Empire: The Explorer and the Scientist in the Winning of the American West*. New York: Alfred A. Knopf, 1966. Reprint. New York: Monticello Editions, 1993.

Goetzmann, William H. *Army Exploration in the American West, 1803-1863*. New Haven: Yale University Press, 1959. Reprint. Austin: Texas State Historical Association, 1991.

Goodman, George J., and Cheryl A. Lawson. *Retracing Major Stephen H. Long's 1820 Expedition*. Norman and London: University of Oklahoma Press, 1995.

Gunnison, John Williams. *Letters*. Gunnison Archive, the Huntington Library, San Marino, California.

Gunnison, John W., and E. G. Beckwith. *Report of Explorations for a Route for the Pacific Railroad*. 33rd Cong., 2nd sess., House Exec. Doc. 91. Vol. 2. Washington, DC: A. O. P. Nicholson, Printer, 1855, 1-128. Retrieved from:
http://books.google.com/
books?id=ynFyL-SHDpYC&printsec=frontcover
The four maps from the Gunnison-Beckwith *Report* are also available on the Internet at a site maintained by
David Rumsey: http://www.davidrumsey.com/

Hafen, LeRoy R., and Ann W. Hafen, eds. *Central Route to the Pacific by Gwinn Harris Heap*. Glendale, Calif.: Arthur H. Clark Company, 1957.

Hawks, Francis L. *Narrative of the Expedition of an American Squadron to the China Seas and Japan, Performed in the Years 1852, 1853, and 1854, Under the Command of Commodore M. C. Perry, United States Navy, by Order of the Government of the United States*. 33rd Cong., 2d sess., House Exec. Doc. 97. 3 Vols. Washington, DC: A. O. P. Nicholson, 1856; New York and London: D. Appleton & Company, 1857.

Heap, Gwinn Harris. *Central Route to the Pacific, from the Valley of the Mississippi to California: Journal of the Expedition of E. F. Beale, Superintendent of Indian Affairs in California, and Gwinn Harris Heap, from Missouri to California, in 1853*. Philadelphia: Lippincott, Grambo, and Co., 1854. Reprint, edited with an introduction and notes by LeRoy R. Hafen and Ann W. Hafen. Glendale, Calif.: Arthur H. Clark Company, 1957.

Hendricks, Gordon. *Albert Bierstadt: Painter of the American West*. New York: Harrison House/Harry N. Abrams, Inc., 1988.

Hine, Robert V. *In the Shadow of Frémont: Edward Kern and the Art of Exploration, 1845-1860*. 2d ed. Norman: University of Oklahoma Press, 1982.

Hockney, David. *Secret Knowledge: Rediscovering the Lost Techniques of the Old Masters*. New York: Viking Studio, 2001.

Humboldt, Alexander von. *Cosmos: A Sketch of a Physical Description of the Universe.* Vol 2. Translated by E. C. Otté. London: Henry G. Bohn, 1849(b).

Huseman, Ben W. *Wild River, Timeless Canyons: Balduin Möllhausen's Watercolors of the Colorado.* Ft. Worth, Texas: Amon Carter Museum, 1995.

Ives, Joseph C. *Report upon the Colorado River of the West.* 36th Cong., 1st Session, Exec. Doc. No. 90. Washington: Government Printing Office, 1861.

Kane, Elisha Kent. *Arctic Explorations: The Second Grinnell Expedition in Search of Sir John Franklin, 1853, '54, '55.* 2 Vols. Philadelphia: Childs & Peterson, 1857.

Klett, Mark, Ellen Manchester, JoAnn Verburge, Gordon Bushaw, and Rick Dingus. *Second View: The Rephotographic Survey Project.* Albuquerque: University of New Mexico Press, 1984.

Klett, Mark, Kyle Bajakian, William L. Fox, Michael Marshall, Toshi Ueshina, and Byron Wolfe. *Third Views, Second Sights: A Rephotographic Survey of the American West.* Santa Fe: Museum of New Mexico Press, 2004.

Lander, Frederick W. *Maps and Reports of the Fort Kearney, South Pass, and Honey Lake Wagon Road.* 36th Congress, 2nd Session, House Exec. Doc. No. 64. Washington, Dc: Department of the Interior, 1861.

Lavender, David. *Bent's Fort.* New York: Doubleday & Company, Inc. 1954. Reprint. Lincoln and London: University of Nebraska Press, 1972.

Lynes, Barbara B., Lesley Poling-Kempes, and Fredrick W. Turner. *Georgia O'Keeffe and New Mexico: A Sense of Place.* Princeton: Princeton University Press; Santa Fe: Georgia O'Keeffe Museum, 2004.

Naef, Weston J., and James N. Wood. *Era of Exploration: The Rise of Landscape Photography in the American West, 1860-1885.* Albright-Knox Art Gallery and the Metropolitan Museum of Art. Boston: New York Graphic Society, 1975.

Parke, Lt. John G., and Richard H. Kern. *Map of the Territory of New Mexico.* Santa Fe, New Mexico: 1851. Printed by J. & D. Major, New York.

Preuss, Charles. *Map of Oregon and Upper California from the Surveys of John Charles Frémont and Other Authorities.* Washington City: Printed by E. Weber & Co., Baltimore, 1848. Reproduced in Jackson, Donald, and Mary Lee Spence, eds. *The Expeditions of John Charles Frémont.* Vol. 1. Urbana, Chicago, and London: University of Illinois Press, 1970, 1: Map Portfolio.

*Reports of Explorations and Surveys, to Ascertain the Most Practicable and Economical Route for a Railroad from the Mississippi River to the Pacific Ocean, Made under the Direction of the Secretary of War, in 1853-4.* Volumes I-XII. Washington, Government Printing Office, 1855-61.

Reps, John W. *Views and Viewmakers of Urban America: Lithographs of Towns and Cities in the United States and Canada, Notes on the Artists and Publishers, and a Union Catalog of Their Work, 1825-1925.* Columbia, MO: University of Missouri Press, 1984.

Richmond, Patricia Joy. *Trail to Disaster.* Niwot: University Press of Colorado, 1990.

Rowan, Steven. *The Baron in the Grand Canyon: Friedrich Wilhelm von Egloffstein in the West.* Columbia and London: University of Missouri Press, 2012.

Rudisill, Richard. *Mirror Image: The Influence of the Daguerreotype on American Society.* Albuquerque: University of New Mexico Press, 1971.

Sandweiss, Martha A. "Undecisive Moments: The Narrative Tradition in Western Photography." In *Photography in Nineteenth-century America,* edited by Martha A. Sandweiss. Fort Worth: Amon Carter Museum, and New York: Harry N. Abrams, Inc., 1991, 99-129.

Schiel, Jacob H. *Journey through the Rocky Mountains and the Humboldt Mountains to the Pacific Ocean*, edited and translated by Thomas N. Bonner. Norman: University of Oklahoma Press, 1959.

Schiel, James. *The Land Between,* edited and translated by Frederick W. Bachmann and William Swilling Wallace. Los Angeles: Westernlore Press, 1957.

Senefelder, Alois. *A Complete Course of Lithography.* R. Ackermann, London, 1819. Reprint edition: *Senefelder on Lithography.* Minneola: Dover Publications, 2005.

Shlaer, Robert. *Sights Once Seen: Daguerreotyping Frémont's Last Expedition through the Rockies.* Santa Fe: Museum of New Mexico Press, 2000.

Simpson, Captain J. H. *Report of Explorations across the Great Basin of the Territory of Utah for a Direct Wagon-Route from Camp Floyd to Genoa, in Carson Valley, in 1859.* Washington: Government Printing Office, 1876.

Stanley, John Mix. *Papers.* Smithsonian Archives of American Art, Microfilm reel 687.

Stevens, Isaac I. *Narrative and Final Report of Explorations for a Route for a Pacific Railroad.* 36th Cong., 1st sess., S. Exec. Doc., Vol. 12, Bk. 1. Washington, DC: Thomas H. Ford, Printer, 1855.

Taft, Robert. *Photography and the American Scene.* New York: The Macmillan Company, 1938. Reprint. New York: Dover Publications, 1964.

Taft, Robert. *Artists and Illustrators of the Old West, 1850-1900.* New York: Bonanza Books, 1953.

Thomas, J., M.D. and T. Baldwin. *Lippincott's Complete Pronouncing Gazetteer.* Philadelphia: J. B. Lippencott & Co., 1856.

Trenton, Patricia, and Peter H. Hassrick. *The Rocky Mountains: A Vision for Artists in the Nineteenth Century.* Norman: University of Oklahoma Press, 1983.

Weber, David J. *Richard H. Kern: Expeditionary Artist in the Far Southwest, 1848-1853.* Albuquerque: University of New Mexico Press, 1985.